REFERENCE PRESS
4831/24, Ansari Road,
Darya Ganj,
New Delhi-110 002.

Tel.: 23260807, 41563444
Fax: 41563334
E-mail: info@essessreference.com
www.essessreference.com

Rs.650/-

First Published - 2008

ISBN: 81-8405-040-2 (10 Digit)
978-81-8405-040-0 (13 Digit)

Published By Reference Press and printed at Salasar Imaging Systems

PRINTED IN INDIA

Dedicated

To

SHRI. LAM SITA RAMAIAH

University Librarian (Retd.)

Ramesh Mohan Library, Central Institute of English and Foreign Languages, Hyderabad, who is my good friend, guide and philosopher in all my academic efforts

Preface

In his book , *principles of Islam,* Maulana Wahiduddin Khan wrote that, Islam is a religion which teaches non-voilence. According to the Koran "God does not love violence. One is a good muslim, and that is a quintessential message – without wielding a gun and striking at the enemy targets."

Legally terrorism is defined as the sustained and clandestine use of murder. bombings and hostage taking to achieve a political purpose. Terrorism is more monstrous and reprehensible than war because it targets innocent civilians much more than a war does. Terrorism is not a modern invention. Instinctive terrorism existed throughout the history and State Terrorism is as old as State itself. Most of the States today practice, "reign of terror" secretly to liquidate all of those opposed to the establishment. In the seventies of last century, the rise of international terrorism was characterized by hijacking of planes and attack on diplomats.

Walter Lacques the authority on terrorism and a prolific writer on the subject said that there are as many as one hundred and nine definitions of terrorism. The aim of the terrorist, wrote Lacquer, is to induce a state of fear in the victim. The terrorist is ruthless and does not conform to humanitarian norms. A Chinese Philosopher explained the terrorist tactic. "Kill one, frighten ten thousand". An IRA terrorist issued frightening warning to the then British Prime Minister, "you need to escape a thousand times a day, I need to succeed only once". Such a single act brought a tragic end to the lives of Indira Gandhi and her son Rajiv Gandhi in the last century.

Terrorism, caused by groups both national and international, has become a great menace and threat to human rights as terrorism is not selective but purposefully strikes the innocents taking out their lives.

Terrorism broadly falls into three categories.

1. Terrorism going by the name of "freedom struggle" without outside interference. Palestinians, cause for their homeland falls under this category..
2. Terrorism sponsored from across the border by foreign nation like Pakistan in Jammu and Kashmir is the best example of cross-border terrorism.
3. State terrorism a military response by the nations affected by terrorism of the first and second category.

It is quite unfortunate that the U.N General Assembly failed to adopt even after a five days debate in the month of October 2001, a resolution over definition of terrorism and distinction between the scourge and the freedom struggle. Therefore, in many countries where the terrorism became a menace, it is feared that if with the U.N we might fail then, without the U.N we are bound to fail.

In view of the above *Jihad* (freedom struggle) in Kashmir is being fought stupidly in the name of so called *Jihad* which do not fall in any of the above three interpretations. To be more specific Kashmir is not an occupied land and as a matter of fact, it is a part of the culture, civilization and political unity of India for over the centuries. There is neither religious intolerance nor social oppression. The Kashmir Muslims are not discriminated in law or in its practice and, as a matter of fact, since independence the State is ruled by the Chief Ministers who belonged to the Muslim community. Since because majority of the population in the State consists of Muslims, it does not acquire the right to break from India.

After the terrorist attacks on the United States of

America on 11/9/01 the whole world has felt the travails and traumas of treacherous acts of terrorism what India had been suffering from a long time in Jammu and Kashmir and in other places. It is a well known fact, that Pakistan is the breeding ground for terrorists for many years for carrying sabotage and subversive activities in India. The western world turned a Nelson's eye towards the *Madrassas* and terrorist training camps in Pakistan.. The U.S.A and its allies are reaping now what they sowed earlier. Terrorism may be a new thing for the U.S.A and the West but India has been feeling its heat for the last sixty years. The world is now treating terrorism as the number one problem as it is not acceptable to global community. The bomb blasts in London and other places undoubtedly lead to a tighter anti-terrorism legislation. There is no agreed definition for terrorism which is acceptable to all the heads of governments. The definitional difficulty springs from the worry that legitimate struggle against colonial rule or foreign occupation may be branded as terrorist activity. Mr. Kofi Annan's simple definition is that "regardless of your cause you cannot kill or maim innocent civilians and non-combatants. That is terrorism pure and simple." The justification for terrorist acts under the slogan of freedom struggle has been effectively repelled by Senator Jackson. "The idea that one person's "terrorist" is another's freedom fighter' cannot be sanctioned. Freedom fighters or revolutionaries don't blow up buses containing non-combatants; as the terrorist murderers do. Freedom fighters don't set out to capture and slaughter school children; .terrorists murderers do.......It is a disgrace and democracies would allow the treasured word 'freedom' to be associated with acts of terrorists."

In Jammu and Kashmir and in several holy places in India hundreds of innocent tourists and pilgrims were killed The U.N. Security Council Resolutions have unequivocally condemned all acts of terrorism regardless of their motivation. When ever heads of different countries meeting they are condemning terrorism in all its forms. In the recently held G-8 conference at St. Petersburg and at the meeting of the Non-alignment movement at Havana the joint statements signed by the leaders backed India's war on foreign-aided terrorism and emphasized the urgency of enhancing co-operation to end terrorism.

In spite of the grave concern expressed by the world leaders the terrorists are still perpetrating the attacks killing several innocent people. Threatening calls are given now and then by the al-Qaeda leaders to attack the important places in the U.S and the U.K and other countries supporting them.

The specter of violence is still haunting Kashmir and militants are attacking the sacred places of Hindus and Trade Centers. We have spent more than Rs.150,000,00,00,000 in the last 55 years on keeping Kashmir in India and the problem is still unresolved.

From 11/9/2001 the insurgent acts of al-Qaeda, Taliban and other militants are in the increase in spite of taking several strict security measures all over the world. The militants are lurking for every opportunity to strike at any place causing considerable damage.

Attacks on the World Trade Center and other places in the U.S brought over to surface the evil designs of the Muslim fundamentalists like bin-Laden, Omar and others who vowed to obliterate the western domination over the rich oil Arab countries

Basetty Narsing Rao

Acknowledgment

In this book I gathered the terrorist acts that took place on the U.S on 11/9/2001 and in other foreign countries and particularly in India. After the attacks on World Trade Center I briefly narrated the attack on the Assembly building of Jammu and Kashmir and Indian Parliament House that took place in that year. Since then, the tentacles of terrorism spread like a wild fire in London, Bangladesh and in Temples, Trains and Trade Centers in India

In my attempts to bring forth the facts, .in the shape of this book I do not forget the encouragement and help rendered by Shri L.S. Ramaiah who is always a guiding star in my every such efforts.

I will be failing in my duty if I do not mention the names of Shri P.Ashwin Kumar, Managing Director. Infologic Systems, Hyderabad and his staff members particularly Smt. K. Kameswari and Miss M. Arundathi who were very helpful in all my endeavors in completing the book.

I am also grateful to Shri Sumit Sethi, Managing Director, Reference Press who showed lot of zeal and zest for publishing this work with high standards of printing.

Basetty Narsing Rao

Contents

1

Terrorist Attacks on World Trade Center, Indian Parliament and Other Places

The first recorded sighting of the area, which is now known, as *New York* was in the year 1524 by *Giovanni da Verrazano,* an Italian explorer in the employ of the king of France. It was after another eighty-five years that is in 1609, an Englishman exploring on behalf of the Dutch Government landed on Manhattan and claimed it for Holland.

As the time passed, the Englishmen acquired stronghold throughout the American colonies and established settlements in 1607 in James town, Virginia and in Plymouth and Massachusetts in 1620. In between 1652 and 1664 the Dutch settlers and the Englishmen engaged in slew of small skirmishes. Finally in 1664 English warships cruised into the harbor and forced the Dutch to surrender *New Amsterdam* to the realm of English. The Dutch, however, regained the colony, but in a treaty of peace relinquished it to the English, where upon the town was renamed as New York.

Fascinated by the fast development of *New York* there were floods of immigrants in the 19th century from Germany, Ireland, China, Italy, Russia and other Eastern European countries creating ethnic enclaves that still exists. By the end of 20th century there was mass exodus of population from Israel, India, Japan and from number of other countries of the world. Whether one is a native of *New York*, an immigrant or a casual visitor it is not only the city of light but the city of life, which normally never sleeps, bustling late into the night on any day of the week, traffic normally busy at all hours. .In this famous city of light where traffic normally busy at all hours the *World Trade Center* has been constructed.

The *World Trade Center* often called simply the WTC was housed in the twin sky scrapers built in 1973 in *New York City* by the Port Authority of *New York* and *New Jersey* and designed by the architects *Minoru Yamasaki* and *Emery Roth*. Every characteristic of these immense towers were placed in a unique category: They were 110 stories of 411 m (1,350 ft) high making them second in height only to the *SEARS TOWERS* in Chicago. They comprised 1.2 million m2 (13 million ft 2) of office space and the total building cost amounted to 750 million dollars before it collapsed.

When the *World Trade Center* with its 1,350 foot Twin Towers opened in 1974 it changed the scene of skyline and, in a certain sense, the heart of Manhattan. The 110 story monolithic towers were the tallest buildings in Manhattan. They also occupied the eminence of the world's fastest elevators housing one of the New York's most spectacularly sited restaurants, real estates agents, customs brokers and all other interests related to international trade before it was attacked. Added to all these adjectives the establishment of World Trade Center gave a new birth of Lower Manhattan.

The material scooped for the basements of the two massive and majestic towers created a twenty-three acre landfill along the *Hudson River*. The World Trade Center after its completion was leased by its owner, the Port Authority of New York and New Jersey for 99 years. The grand and sublime 110 story structures became a symbol of glory of the United

States with cream of nationals of eighty countries once engaging themselves in international trade and giving boast to American's economy.

On the fateful day of Tuesday the eleventh of September 2001 at 8.42 a.m. in one of the most audacious attack ever against the United States, the hijackers *Marwan Al Shehi, Fayez Rasheed Ahmed Hussain Al Qadi Bamihammad, Mohald Alshehri, Hamza Alghamdi* and *Ahmed Alghamdi* seized the control of United Airlines Flight 175 and slammed into the Northern Tower of *World Trade Center* in *New York.* Before anybody could recover from the shock another batch consisting of *Waleed Alshehri, Wali Al Shehri, Mohammad Atta, Abdul Aziz Aloman* and *Satam Al Suqami* hijacked a second American Airlines Flight 11 and destroyed the two towers of the World Trade Center completely at 9.00 a.m. with an interval of just 18 minutes. It was beyond the imagination of anybody, more so of the citizens of the U.S that the massive and majestic 110 story twin towers of World Trade Center will one day collapse like a pack of cards.

The 110 story World Trade Center has gone. About 50,000 people from eighty countries worked at the Trade Center and the two hijack planes that slammed World Trade Center were carrying a total of 156 people. It is feared that about 3000 have either died or missing in the above havoc. The complexity of this kind of attack claimed the lives of 300 US fire fighters too. It has taken three months for the US to extinguish the fire caused by the terrorist attacks on the World Trade Center. The glory of twin massive spires of New York departed leaving the hearts of every American with a great deal of poignancy and profound sorrow. As if the above havoc was not enough the terrorists attacked *Pentagon* the impregnable military headquarters of the U.S.

Pentagon is the headquarters and nerve center of the United States. On the 11th September *Khalid Al-Midhar, Majed Moqued, Nawaz Alhamzi, Salem Alhamzi* and *Hanjour* have hijacked the American, Airlines Flight 77 and gouged a hole in the *Pentagon* building at 9.30 a.m. resulting a portion of one side of the five sided structure collapsed.

As if, all the misdeeds done at *World Trade Center* and *Pentagon* were not enough, the terrorists consisting of *Ahmed Alhaznir*, *Ahmed Alnami*, *Ziad Samir Jarrah* and *Saeed Alghamdi* took control of the United Airlines Flight 93 en-route from *New York*, New Jersey to San Francisco on the black Tuesday and got crashed about 130 km South East of Pittsburgh killing all the 45 people aboard. It was really surprised to see how the world's mightiest fighting force with advanced technology succumbed to the stratagem of few scamps in the name of religion. The series of tragedies that took place on the fateful day of 11th September reminisced the *Nostradamus* prediction. As the time passes the predictions made of great-men go unnoticed or completely forgotten and recollected after experiencing the tragedies. This has what happened in the case of the U.S, a super power in the world with mighty establishment.

Sometimes fictions are turned into facts and the predictions go unnoticed. The Super Power of the world with advanced Science and Technology could not escape from the prediction of *Nostradamus* and the fortified like *Pentagon* was attacked not with any military powers of other country but by their own planes hijacked by some unscrupulous elements.

The terrorist attacks quickly spread fear and chaos in the United States and *President Bush* was taken to a secret location in *Nebraska* and the White House and the State Departments were also evacuated. The blow by blow attack forced the U.S to shut down all of its airports and all the U.S bound flights diverted to Canada.

President Bush said in Sarasota Florida "today we have had a National tragedy" and ordered a full-scale investigation "to hunt down the folks who committed this act". After consulting his top Security Advisors, President *Bush* asserted that "the hidden enemy would not be allowed to hide for ever". While leading the Memorial Service in Washington President *Bush* emphasized his tough stand saying the enemy has chosen the timing of the first shots of the war but the US would dictate when and how it ended and declared a State Emergency.

After an hour long meeting with the US Defense Secretary *Donald Rumsfeld* with regard to the military plans for mobilizing reservists to beef up domestic defenses against terrorism, *President Bush* at times raising his voice in anger told reporters, "I want justice" and want *Osama* dead or alive". He further declared that "we are going to find those evil doers those barbaric people who attacked our country people and we are going to hold the people who housed them accountable" and made clear that the Taliban should take his statement seriously. At the joint session of Congress on the 20th of September President Bush asked his country to prepare for a long "war on terrorism" and reiterated again that the *Taliban* should turn over Laden and his leading followers or share their fate. President Bush said all evidence gathered so far pointed to *Laden* and *al-Qaeda* organization and responsible for the 11th of September attack.

The above attitude and awareness of America needed long back when India times without number called upon it to condemn terrorist attack unleashed by Pakistan in Jammu & Kashmir State.

President *Bush* declared that the Saudi dissident *Osama Bin Laden* is the prime suspect in the unprecedented and horrific attack on the United States for its support of Israel. Three weeks before the attack *Laden* warned that he and his followers would carry out an unprecedented attack on the U.S interests for its support of Israel. Experts in the U.S who studied the *Laden's* track record of deadly attacks on the U.S targets combined with the unparalleled networks and deep war chest made Laden the prime suspect in the strikes on *New York* and Washington. He was already alleged for master minding the 1998 twin bombings of the U.S Embassies in East Africa that killed more than 200 people.

Laden the Saudi born lives in Afghanistan as a "guest" of the Taliban militia since 1996 and leads al-Qaeda terrorist organization. He is surrounded himself with a tight circle of mostly Saudi and Egyptian lieutenants who run a complicated worldwide network.

The U.S. has released the much awaited videotape of *Laden* on the 13th December, 2001 apparently recounting plans for the September,11 attacks on the U.S. and said his comments in *Afghanistan* were proof that the Saudi born fugitive masterminded the devastating strikes on the U.S. According to the translation released with the tape Laden said "we calculated in advance the number of casualties from the enemy who would be killed based on the position of the tower. We calculated that the floors that would be hit would be three or four floors. I was the most optimistic of them all."

Mullah Mohd.Omar was born in 1959 in the small village of Nodah near *Kandhar* to a poor peasant and lost his father when he was young and the responsibility of running the family fell on his young shoulders. He is the most secretive leader and not even a photograph of Mullah exists. He is believed to have been seen by two non-Muslims and indeed by few of his own 20 million Afghan people.

He has brought trouble for his movement and his Government. He defied the U.S, the United Nations and earlier hurt millions by ordering the destruction of the *Bamiyan Buddhas*. *Laden* cultivated him by first buying over a mosque at Binnori, outside *Kandhar* that *Omar* headed and then building a house for him. In addition, Laden gifted him a house in *Kandhar's* upmarket Shahr-I-Na (New Town) where he lives with three wives and five children.

Apprehensive of American attacks the *Taliban* Supreme leader whose words once were the law of land placed the

Afghans to live in lurch.. The horrendous and horrible attacks on the *World Trade Center* and *Pentagon* by the terrorists brought the whole world once on the tenterhooks of world war. Several world leaders condemned the attacks as brutal and barbaric.

When India was crying to condemn terrorist attack on its soil no big power of the world was able to appreciate and took notice of the menace. It should have been nipped in the bud itself instead of taking neutral stand appeasing the aggressor. Taking advantage of the insouciant attitude of the super powers the terrorists grown into leviathans and spread their tentacles as long as to strike America and issue threats to others. After the terrorist attacks on America now the world has felt the trauma what India was suffering from a long time and unanimously called upon the nations to end terrorism in any part of the globe.

For the first time, *Laden* has admitted on 11th November that *al-Qaeda* group carried out the attacks on the twin towers of the *World Trade* Center and the *Pentagon* on September, 11 and further threatened the lives of *President Bush* and British Prime Minister *Tony Blair* and warned Australia, Germany and Japan to stay out of the conflict. "The twin towers were legitimate targets, they were supporting US, economic power" and the pilots who hijacked the planes were blessed by Allah" said *Laden.* He said, further that "history should be a witness that we are terrorists. Yes we kill their innocents". In the video footage which was shot in the Afghan Mountains at the end of October, '01 a smiling Laden goes on to say that the killing of at-least 2800 people was justified because they were" not civilians" but were working for the American system. The video which was circulated for fourteen days among his supporters in the network formed a center piece of America's and Britain's new evidence against *Laden.*

Anticipating the U.S. attack *Laden* sneaked out of *Afghan* town of *Kandahar* to a safer place in the countryside with his four wives and several children. After admitting once he denied again that he had any hand in Tuesday's terror attacks in the U.S. Afghanistan ruling *Taliban* said they felt responsible for the security of *Laden*. One of the leading papers of Pakistan reported that *Laden* took oath of allegiance from 500 of his Arab supporters in *Kabul* and shifted to an unknown place. Knowing the impending danger of military action by the U.S. in Afghanistan, the *Taliban* ruling party after about a week of the terrorist attacks said that *Laden* was missing. The claim was received with absolute disbelief by the U.S. and they increased the reward from five million dollars to twenty five million dollars for information leading to *Laden's* arrest.

The *Taliban* regime continued to keep the world in suspense over the fate of *Laden* and the *Taliban* supreme leader *Mullah Mohammad Omar* and said that allegations against *Laden* by the United States were a pretext to wage a war against Islam and at the same time offered to talk with the U.S. Appealing to the U.S. to show patience *Omar* maintained that *Laden* was incapable of carrying out such strikes and has denied his involvement. The Taliban supreme leader *Mullah Mohammad Omar* accusing the U.S. committing "atrocities" against the Muslims world said that the event in America was the result of cruel policies and was meant to avenge their cruelty". He further added that "you must think of where attack took place and who was behind it, but *Afghanistan* is being made, the target and preparations are being made to attack Afghanistan." He reiterated that *Laden* was incapable of planning the sort of sophisticated suicide hijacking, which leveled the *World Trade Center* and part of the *Pentagon* on September 11,2001.

As the clouds of war looming large crucial and intense diplomacy took place between Pakaistan and the *Taliban* regime in Afghanistan. Though the *Laden* issue was unresolved during the discussions the *Taliban* was hopeful of defusing the crisis with the U.S. They however, geared up for war and deployed

Soviet-era Sued missiles and an estimated 10,000 troops along its border with Pakistan. They also took measures to hide *Laden.* Pakistan had given the *Taliban* seventy two-hour deadline to accede to the request for handing over *Laden* to the U.S. Efforts at finding solution to the tangle of handing over Laden was in confusion as the *Taliban* was apparently buying time. Having spent twenty-four hours the Pakistan negotiators stayed for another day in *Afghanistan.* Indications of the Ulemas who attended the council were on the lines that they would not agree to handing over *Laden* without concrete proof of his involvement in terrorism even if the whole *Afghanistan* is devastated. America after giving sufficient time to hand over *Laden* thought no other alternative save to declare war on *Afghanistan* to ferret out *Laden* from his hiding place.

The search for the world's most wanted man six foot five inches tall *Laden* was started by CIA in 1998 itself. They sent teams of U.S. officers to Northern Afghanistan in an attempt to persuade the leader of the Anti-Taliban Afghanistan opposition to capture and perhaps kill *Laden.* The CIA clandestine deal with *Ahmed Shah Masood,* the then military leader of the most sensitive and highly classified elements of broader long-term campaign was continuing unsuccessfully through the end of *Clinton* administration and into the Bush administration to destroy the network of *Laden.* After innumerable checks and counter-checks through satellite and human intelligence the American and allied forces in *Afghanistan* were convinced that Laden was hiding in Pamir mountain range

According to U.S. officials the administration of the President *Bill Clinton* has secretly spoken with the Sudanese Government on a plan to seize the Saudi born extremist, but it could not be fructified. *Laden* had been living in Sudan at that time after being expelled from Saudi Arabia. "Had we been able to roll up *Laden* then, there would not have been September 11 tragedy" they said.

In view of the belligerent attitude of the *Taliban* regime not to surrender *bin Laden* and *Omer* the U.S declared war on the *7th October, 2001.* After the thirty-eight days fierce battle *Kabul* was taken over by the *Northern Alliance* forces aided by the American pounding from the sky. After driving out *Taliban, Hamid Karzai* was sworn in on 23rd December, 2001 as leader of *Afghanistan* with 29 other members of the cabinet including two women. The U.N. delegates, diplomats and a top U.S. General gathered to witness the ceremony.

Attack on J&K Assembly Building

While America and its allied forces were preparing to attack *Laden* and his followers in *Afghanistan* the militants with a suicide bomber on 1st October,'01 rammed a Tata Sumo packed with explosives right into the main gate of the heavily fortified Assembly building of *Jammu and Kashmir* State killing 42 people. The *Jaish-e-Mohammad*, the group floated by Pakistan based *Moulana Masood Azhar* said it was behind the attack and even identified the bomber as *Wajahat Hussain* of Pakistan's North-West Frontier province.

The attacks on the *World Trade Center, Pentagon* and in *Pennsylvania* lasted for half-an-hour to forty-five minutes. The Americans have suffered the agony and emotional shock of terrorism for forty-five minutes. To avenge these attacks President Bush invaded and devastated every part of Afghanistan killing hundreds of people to ferret out *bin-Laden* and his militant group.

On the other hand terrorism is causing serious concern in India for the last fifteen to twenty years. Thousands of innocent people are being killed in *Jammu and Kashmir* and in other parts of India by the terrorists. The Government of India is spending crores of rupees on defense to guard the line of control and to stop infiltration of militants from the neighboring country like Pakistan.

Does it show that Indians are pusillanimous not to declare

war against the country where from acts of terrorism are penetrating? Or as ardent supporters of peace following the path of non-violence shown by *Mahatma Gandhi*, our Father of our Nation, irrespective of suffering of many unfortunate persons.

ATTACK ON INDIAN PARLIAMENT HOUSE

While the attention of the whole world was concentrated on the developments of war in Afghanistan five terrorists carrying deadly explosives and weapons in a camera bag drove in a stolen white Ambassador car with the Home Ministry car label and flashing a red beacon stormed the *Parliament House* of India on the forenoon of 13th December, 2001. On this fateful day both Houses adjourned at 11.05 a.m. and around two hundred Members of Parliament started to leave the Parliament House. The terrorists who hoodwinked the security guards entered into the Parliament House at 11-40 a.m. and started firing indiscriminately at Gate No.2 and few minutes later at Gate Numbers 12 and 8. The then Vice-President *Krishna Kant* had providential escape as his departure for home was delayed by few minutes. The drama lasted for fifty minutes leading to fourteen causalities - nine security personnel and five terrorists (including a suicide bomber "fidayee" of terrorist group who blowed himself up).

Fortunately *Shri Atal Behari* Vajpayee, the then Prime Minister of India, *Shri L.K.Advani*, ex-Home Minister and Mrs. *Sonia Gandhi*, the present U.P.A Chairperson were not present in the House at the time of the incident. Unable to bear the menace of terrorism in India, the then Prime Minister declared war against terrorism on the 13th December,'01 terming terrorism has entered the last phase and should be fought in a decisive manner. Then Prime Minister addressing a meeting of Confederation of Indian Industries in Kolkata termed the attack on *Parliament* as an attempt to wipe out the political leadership and bring turmoil in the country. He said that the terrorist acts on Indian soil have transgressed the limits of patience of the Indian people and assured the nation that such attacks will be repulsed.

The Delhi Police after thorough investigation confirmed that the five militants killed while trying to storm the *Parliament House* were all Pakistanis and active *J-e-m* members. They were *Mohammad*, the group leader, *Hamza Haider alias Tufial*, *Rana* and *Raja*. The arrest of the Delhi University lecturer *Syed Abdul Rahman Geelani* and his subsequent interrogation revealed that he along with *Mohd. Afzal* and *Shaukat Hussain Guru*, both residents of Sopore in Baremullah district of *Jammu and Kashmir* had been in constant touch with the five militants of *Jaish-e-Mohammad* and planned to storm the *Parliament House* on 13th September with the active support of *Laskar-e-Toiba* and at the instigation of Pakistan ISI.

The trail court had awarded death penalty to *Shaukat*, *Afzal* and *Geelani* while sentencing *Afsan* to five years imprisonment for their role in the 13th December,'01 terrorist attack on *Parliament*. The Delhi High Court upheld the death penalty to *Afzal* and *Shaukat* but had acquitted both *Geelani* and *Afsan*. On cross appeals filed by the Delhi Police, *Afzal* and *Shaukat* the Supreme Court on 4th August,'05 upheld the death penalty of *J-e-M* militant *Mohd.Afzal* but reduced it in the case of his cousin *Shaukat Hussain Guru* to ten years imprisonment The Bench further said that there was a needle of suspicion on *Geelani* regarding his role in the "diabolical act" of attacking the supreme seat of democracy but there was no direct evidence to convict him in the case. Terming the attack on Parliament as an unparallel the bench passed judgment stating that there was clinching evidence against *Afzal* regarding his nexus with the slain terrorists who carried out the "terrorist act of most diabolical nature".

When *Afzal* was fleeing in a truck along with his cousin *Shaukat*, a co-accused in the case the police arrested them and recovered the laptop used by the *J-e-M*, terrorists to plan the 13th December,'01 attack on *Parliament*. The laptop became a tool for Delhi police to unravel the conspiracy and also proved to be a clinching evidence on *Mohd.Afzal's* involvement resulting in confirmation of his death penalty by the Supreme Court. The Supreme Court held that "the recovery of laptop from the truck in which *Afzal* and *Shaukat* traveled on being pointed out by them is a highly incriminating circumstance against them."

A Sessions Court on 26th September,'06 ordered that *Mohammad Afzal*, convicted in the December, 2001 *Parliament* attack case, be executed on October,2006.The order stated that Afzal "hang by neck till death at 6.00 a.m. on 20th October,'06 On 18th December,2002 the court had sentenced Afzal to death, along with Delhi University lecturer *S.A.R. Geelani and Shaukat Hussain Guru* for the terrorist strike on Parliament. The court had also sentenced *Shaukat's wife Afsan Guru* to five years rigorous imprisonment for concealing knowledge of the conspiracy. The Delhi High Court acquitted Geelani and Afsan Guru.

Afzal's death sentence was confirmed by the Supreme Court on 4th August, 2005, while *Shaukat Guru's* sentence was to ten years rigorous imprisonment

In 1987, *Afzal* and his cousin, *Shaukat Guru*. were studying in the Muslim Educational Trust (MET) – an English-medium higher secondary school in Sopore. *Afzal* was the class's best student who would surprise teachers with his wit and intelligence. Born in a well-to-do business family of Doabagh in North Kashmir, *Afzal* was raised by his elder brother after he lost his father.

Afzal's uncle, *Abdul Ahad Guru*, was one of Kashmiri's most prominent cardiologist, who later became an ideologue of the pro-independence JKLF and was later killed by a rival group in an internal militant feud. Inspired by his doctor uncle, Afzal too, chose medicine and joined the Jhelum Valley Medical College in Srinagar. When in the autumn of 1989, militancy erupted in the valley spearheaded by the JKLF,Kashmir changed and so did *Afzal's* life. He suddenly said goodbye to his medical college, joined the JKLF,crossed the line of Control to take arms training. *Afzal* returned home and kept a low profile even as he was associated with JKLF. He was arrested by the Border Security Force and after spending several months in jail, was released

After his release, Afzal tried to return to study medicine but failed. He then headed for New Delhi, planning to continue his studies at the Jawaharlal Nehru University. This, too didn't work and he returned to start a health-care appliances business after he shifted his base to Srinagar where he lived in a rented accommodation in Rajbagh. His business was doing well.

His cousin *Shaukat Guru*, however, had left for New-Delhi for further studies. In the capital, Shaukat , while studying to become a journalist met a Sikh girl, who later married him and took a new name *Afsan Guru*. Soon, Afzal too got married. He has a child. Then suddenly *Afzal's* name, along with that of his cousin *Shaukat*, propped in the Parliament attack investigation. How *Afzal* joined the JeM and helped to facilitate the suicide attack on Parliament is a mystery.

The execution of *Afzal Guru* which was to take place on the 20th October,06 postponed as his family filed a mercy petition with President *A.P.J.Kalam* in the midst of the raging controversy over a reprieve for the Parliament terror attack convict. While the matter stood thus, the families of the security personnel killed in the 2001 attack on Parliament approached the President *A.P.J.Kalam* on 3rd October,'06 requesting him not to grant any pardon to Afzal Guru, who has been sentenced to death by the Supreme Court.

After about 27 months of attack on the Indian Parliament, *Javed Ashraf Gazi* who was the ISI Chief from 1993-1995 during *Benazir Bhutto's* second government made a very significant statement in the Pakistan Parliament on 5th March,'04 admitting that JeM was behind the Parliament attack of 13th December,2001, as well as the death of "thousands of Kashmiris." *Afzal Guru* is still not executed. His family's appeal for mercy is pending with the President of India.

SPRAYNG OF BULLETS ON AMERICAN CENTRE , KOLKOTA

A day after top American officials arrived in Delhi to work out ways to fight terrorism with their counterparts and hours before the FBI Chief began his official engagements in New-Delhi the *American Center* in Kolkata's Chowringee area as sprayed by as many as fifty-four bullets on the early morning of 22nd January,2002 killing four policemen. Four gunmen on two motorcycles fired AK-47 and injured fourteen people including twelve policemen in front of the high walled building that houses the U.S consulate's public affair section and the library. After spraying the bullets the gunmen fled.

The U.S center attackers at Kolkata *Mohammad Idris alias Wajid Alias Zahid* a resident of Sakin Khannewal in Pakistan and *Mohd. Salim* a resident of Punjab were killed in a police encounter in Hazaribagh in Jharkhand on 28th January,'02 Both of them confessed the crime to the police before they breathed last.

Aftab Ansari alias Farhan Malik who was caught in Dubai and transported to New-Delhi had admitted on 10th February,'02 to having carried out the American Center attack at Kolkata in order to revenge the killing of *Arif Raza Khan* in a police encounter. He had further admitted to the kidnapping of *Khadim's Partha Roy Burman*, the coal merchant, *Anand Agarwal* in Benaras and *Niranjan Shah* in Mumbai. *Farhan Malik* and his accomplice were taken to Gujarat for further investigations.

STRIKE ON AKSHRADHAM TEMPLE

Nearly four years after the terrorist strike on the Aksharadam temple in Gujarat a local court on 1st July, '06 convicted six persons for the attack and awarded them the death sentence. The POTA Court, which held its proceedings in camera and delivered the judgment in the high security Sabarmathi jail awarded life imprisonment to *Mohammad Salim Mohammad Anif Sheik* while *Mufti Abdul Miya Yasim Miya Kadhri* and *Altaf Hussain Asghar Hussain Malik* were awarded prison terms of ten and five years respectively. Thirtythree people, including two national Security commandos and two State Police commandos, were killed and 81 injured in the terrorist attack on 24th September,2002. The three sentenced to death were *Chand Khan*, one of the prime accused from Jammu and Kashmir, *Adam Suleman Ajmeri* and *Abdul Kayum Mohammad Mansuri*. While pronouncing the judgment the judge held the three persons given the death sentence were directly responsible for the killing of people in the temple.

There were thirty-four accused in the case, and the police had arrested the six men who were sentenced on the 1st of July, 06 while 26 were absconding and two were shot dead during the attack The police had told the court that four of the absconders had fled to Pakistan and Saudi Arabia and nothing could be done to bring them back as the authorities did not have their photographs or passport details.

ATTACK ON HYDERABAD TASK FORCE OFFICE

The 12th October, 2005 suicide bomb attack on the Hyderabad Task Force Police Office, the first in the history of Hyderabad, Andhra Pradesh, has confirmed that fundamentalist modules are surely busy. If one could study the background of *Mohd. Abdul Kaleem* he will know how the local youth are being lured into *Jihad* developments..

Mohd. Abdul *Kaleem*, was a welder by profession, and led a life of poverty in the Old City of Hyderabad,Andhra Pradesh. *Kaleem's* encounter with a member of fundamentalist group changed his life. He changed his name to *Arshad Khan* and played a role in the first suicide bombings. The youth traveled to Bangladesh around July,'05 to learn the use of explosives and weapons. By the time he returned in Sept.'05, he was a *Jehadi* (holy warrior) willing to die for the cause. During his two month stay at Rajashahi, a border town in *Bangladesh*, Kaleem met several youth from Hyderabad who were undergoing, similar training. He slipped back into the country accompanying *Motasim Bilal* alias *Dalin* (the suicide bomber of Bangladesh origin) and the bomber struck on 12th.October,'05. Dalin died, as did a home guard.

The terror network attained a concrete shape over the years and not surprisingly, Pakistan ISI figured whenever a terror group carried out suicide operations. It was on 29th November,1992 the terror groups came to the fore for the first time in Hyderabad when *Hizbul Mujahideen* operatives killed Additional Superintendent of Police *Krishna Prasad* and his gunman, in a shoot out in Golkonda Police Station limits. Since then, terror groups struck at different places in the State by killing politicians, blasting places of worship and triggering explosions in public places.

The striking feature of terror modules is that they work in tandem with the group of *LeT*. In 1993 three modules blasted four places in Hyderabad. The most feared and deadly module was that of Azam Ghori, which carried out blasts and killing in several places in the State in 1999 and 2000. This was followed by the bombing of Churches by the *Deendar Anjuman* group. Over fifty persons were convicted.

L-e-T made its presence felt in the State of Andhra Pradesh in the form of *Abdul Aziz* module and the conspiracy was to cause explosions during Ganesh immersion procession in the city of Hyderabad in 2001. In 2001, the LeT succeeded in its plans by triggering a scooter bomb at *Saibaba Temple* in Dilsukhnagar, Hyderabad and made a futile attempt to eliminate BJP State Unit President in 2004.

The *Jaish-e-Mohammad* terror module which carried out the suicide bomb attack on the *Hyderabad City Task Force* Office in October, 2005 had its crosshairs: Hitech City, the

Office of the Director-General of Police and the City Police Commissioner. Their modus operandi was to trigger the blasts with the help of a mobile phone or alternatively through a suicide bomber. What could have been a major disaster was, however, averted with the City Police arresting two members of the module – *Shakeel Ahmed* and *Haji.* Shakeel and Haji assembled an improvised explosive device with a pressure activated switch – the 14 kg. ammonium nitrate base stuffed in a bag was powerful enough to down a five-storied building. Luckily, the module could not find a *"jihadi"* who could plant it. *Shakeel* and *Haji* were arrested based on the confession of *Zahed* and *Kaleem* who were in police custody. Zahed confessed that his brother *Shahad* gave one bag containing two bombs to *Shakeel and Haji.* The same was in turn handed over to *Sajju*, a tailor, who was unaware that he was keeping a bomb. After the blast at the Task Force Office and *Zahed's* arrest *Sajju* got anxious and he took the bag and kept in Chalki village near Zaheerabad which was later recovered by the police. All the above incidents confirm the fact that fundamentalists modules are surely busy in the State of Andhra Pradesh.

The view at the Old City of Hyderabad is hospitable to terrorists may have a quite a few takers. However, some interesting facts that have tumbled out of the confessional statement made by LeT operative *Abdul Rehman* alias Sami *Ahmed* arrested in Gulbarga might warrant a rethink. The confessional statement of *Abdul Rehman* revealed that when he was staying in the Old City of Hyderabad he printed and distributed some pamphlets among the people. It was titled "*Ramzan-e-Mubarak*" which contained provocative remarks pertaining to *jihad.* But the people there got enraged with it and told him to leave. They threatened that if he remained there and would inform the police. Scared, he left the place for Zaheerabad. He further confessed that he often wondered if *Nagarjunasagar* a big dam in Andhra Pradesh irrigating thousands of acres of land and other power grids could be destroyed. His chief in Pakistan, *Abdul Aziz*, also e-mailed him saying that he would provide material to blast the dam. He was till then asked to lob grenades at crowded places. Another task given to him by *Aziz* was to blast electrical transmission towers in and around Hyderabad for which *Aziz* sent him $2,300. The primary task assigned to *Rehman* was to recruit people and send them for training but he did not succeed. He procured the explosives kept in the eye ward of Magani Civil Hospital. Rehman, who was born in Goa completed 12th standard in Mumbai and traveled to Oman and in 2002 went to Saudi Arabia where he involved in "*Jehadi* activities."

One of the two LeT militants arrested in Delhi on 16th Oct. 06 *Mohammad Alamgir Hussain alias Roni*, is an accused in the Task Force Office blast in Hyderabad on 12th October, '05. Roni was one of the key conspirators in the Task Force Office blast. Roni, a native of Bangladesh, is a member of the LeT module active in Rajashahi in Bangladesh.

Lashkar-e-Toiba popularly known as LeT is the buzz word of Andhra Pradesh and Karnataka during '05. *Hafeez Mohammad Saeed* referred as *'Tayaji'* by his strong committed followers founded the most feared terrorist group in 1989. The LeT whose true translation is 'Army of Pure' is a militant outfit of the *Harkez-e-Tawatul Irshad*, a religious seminary at Murdke in the Punjab province of Pakistan. During the last 16 years the LeT left a trail of destruction in *Jammu and Kashmir* and nine other States. Ten years after it took birth, the LeT made its presence felt in Hyderabad through *Saleem Junaid* module in 1998. In 2002 and 2004, the LeT had sent its modules to blast temples

In Bangalore, the LeT operations came to the notice of Intelligence agency for the first time in the last quarters of the year 2000 when it had sent a two-member module to blast the house of *Wipro Chief Ajim Premji*. The module could not execute the plan for logistical reasons. Soon after 9/11, the LeT came under the scanner of the U.S.A and the Pakistani government had kept Hafiz Mohammad Saeed under house arrest before releasing him on court order. *Tayaji*, the super boss considered to be ruthless and dangerous. He decided on the number of *'jihadis'* to be sent to Kashmir and other parts of India.

The LeT's supreme commander in Kashmir was *Zia-ur-Rehman Lakhvi* alias '*Chachaji*'. Next in the hierarchy was deputy supreme commander *Abrahman-ur-Dakhil*. The chief operation commander in Kashmir valley was *Abdullah Shehzad alias Abu Anas alias Shamas.*

KILLING OF PROF. M.C.PURI

Of late the districts of Telengana of Andhra Pradesh have become breeding ground for fundamentalists. On the night of 28th December, 2005 a terrorist has opened fire at the delegates participating in an International Conference at J.N.Tata auditorium in the IISc campus,Bangalore. Prof. M.C.Puri was killed in the attack. The LeT links were established by the Bangalore police and Razi-ur-Rehman, a native of Miryalguda in Nalgonda district was arrested for his alleged role in the IISc attack..

Attempt to blow off RSS, Mahal

A major attempt to attack the *Rashtriya Swayamsevak Sangh* (RSS) headquarters at Mahal Mumbai was foiled when three heavily-armed militants were shot dead in an encounter with the Maharashtra police while trying to enter the heavily-guarded sprawling premises in the wee hours of 1st June,'06. The militants dressed in police uniform and traveling in a white Ambassador car with a red beacon light tried to pass through the barricade but were challenged by the policemen deployed there. Both the police and the RSS had prior information about the terrorists' plan to carry out attack on the headquarters in the first week of June,'06. The police team, therefore, gave chase to the vehicle after they broke the first barrier about 100 meters from the headquarters. When challenged by the police the militants opened fire from their AK-56 rifles and when the police retaliated the trio were killed in firing. Two police officers were also injured. The militants were believed to have come to Nagpur from Patna and the police suspected the hand of the Pakistan-based *Lashkar-e-Toiba.* Three AK-56 rifles, a large quantity of RDX and 12 hand grenades were recovered from the slain militants after the encounter that took place around 4.00 a.m. about 100 meters away from the R.S.S headquarters. The terrorist attacks have been taking place on and off killing innocent people in some State or the other in India. The terrorist bomb blasts in the famous Mecca Masjid in Hyderabad killing fourteen and injuring forty on Friday the 18th of May '2007 is a recent episode. While a majority of the victims died in the blast, at-least four of them fell to bullets as police resorted to firing to quell the violence that followed the explosion. By killing the praying Muslims, the militants wanted to create a communal trouble in the State of Andhra Pradesh. Investigations are still on and the culprits are at large.

2
Appointment of September 11 Commission

It was beyond the imagination of anybody, more so, of the U.S. that the massive majestic 110 story twin towers of the World Trade Center will one day collapse like a pack of cards. The Americans were stunned into disbelief. They thought what hit them was no more terrorism. It was a war declared against the U.S. For all the technological prowess and military might the U.S. did not visualize the attacks on the *W.T.C. Pentagon* and *Pennsylvania* and proved beyond doubt that this was stunning the American Security Intelligence failure. As there was total intelligence lapse it took measures to reassess the intelligence operations of the country and appointed a Commission. The 10 member September 11 Commission made of five Republicans and five Democrats was asked to determine and present a unanimous report on the September 11 attacks in 2001 which killed almost 3000 people.

After a thorough investigation the Commission issued a report saying that *Khalid Shaikh Mohammad*, believed to be the main planner of the September 11 attacks which killed nearly 3000 people, had originally drawn up a more-extensive scheme in which he would also pilot a hijacked airplane. The report revealed that *al-Qaeda* had originally planned to crash hijacked planes into 10 targets in the United States and carry out simultaneous attacks in Southeast Asia. The panel investigating authorities, further revealed that *al-Qaeda* had drawn up a list of targets including the sites hit on September 11 – *the World Trade Center*, twin CIA towers and the *Pentagon* – plus the White House, the U.S. capital and FBI headquarters, nuclear power plants and the tallest buildings in California and Washington State. The Commission gathered its information in part from written reports of probe of *al-Qaeda* captives, including *Mohammad* and *Ramzi bin al-Shaibah*, another suspected September 11 plotter. According to the Commission report, that the plot was launched in 1999 when *al-Qaeda* leader *Osama bin Laden* approved a proposal by *Mohammad* – who is referred to in the report as KSM – to use aircraft as weapons.

Mohammad had originally hoped to pilot one of the ten airplanes to be involved in the attacks. But instead of crashing the plane, he would have killed all adult male on board then landed at a U.S. airport to make a speech denouncing the U.S. policies in the West Asia. *The al-Qaeda* leadership rejected the proposal as too ambitious. When *bin Laden* approved the plan it was split into two parts – one in which hijackers would command flights and crash them into the U.S. targets, and another in which operatives would hijack the U.S. airplanes in Southeast Asia and explode them in mid-air. By mid-2000, *bin Laden* decided to cancel the Southeast Asia part of the hijack plot because he believed it would be too difficult to synchronize operations on opposite sides of the globe. *Al-Qaeda* had also intended to use up to 28 hijackers for the September 11 plot, as opposed to the 19 who actually participated in hijacking the four commercial aircrafts. The report further revealed that even as late as the summer of 2001, KSM wanted to send as many operatives as possible to the United States in order to increase for successful attacks. It gave details of 10 candidate hijackers who were slated to be part of the attacks but were pulled out because they failed to get the U.S. visas, faced pressure from their family or had trouble with immigration officials. The actual date of the attacks was not chosen until about three weeks before September 11, the report said. *Bin Laden* had reportedly pressurized *Mohammad* for an earlier date but the hijackers were not ready. The report also said, accused in September 11 conspirator *Zacarias Moussaoui*, who was facing a possible death sentence on charges of conspiracy in attacks might have been earmarked to replace one of the pilot hijackers.

The Commission further revealed "deep institutional failings within our Government" and details missed opportunities by both the *Bush* and *Clinton* administrations to thwart the hijackings. A U.S. Official who has reviewed the Commission's final report said it would confirm there was no "collaboration" between Iraq and *al-Qaeda*, but lists contacts with Iran and Pakistan. The Commission found that *al-Qaeda* had active ties with Iran than with Iraq. The report, however, not blamed either the Republican President *G. W.Bush* or former Democratic President *Bill Clinton* for failing to prevent the attacks. "Rather than finding that there was failure at the Presidential level, what they find... Is that there are failings, deep institutional failings within our Government" the official said, quoting from the report.

The commission investigating the September 11 attacks rejected, the claims that Saudi Arabia provided money and assistance to the hijackers, challenging one of the most contentious allegations raised by a joint congressional inquiry that concluded in 2003. The report concluded that there is no evidence that the Saudi Government or Saudi Officials know of or supported the plot to attack the United States. In particular, the 500-plus page report dismisses long standing suspicions that two hijackers who resided in *San Diego* obtained money and logistical support through a Saudi intelligence network in the United States that had agents in southern California who were funded in part by a member of the Saudi royal family. The commission's report "exonerates the Saudi to a large degree". The commission, thus, has concluded that contacts between *San Diego*-based hijackers and two Saudi men "can be explained away as innocent and incidental".

After one week of the terrorist attacks in the U.S.A., the counter terrorism Director *Paul Kurtz* wrote in a memo to the National Security Advisor, *Condoleezza* Rice that no "compelling case" existed for Iraq's involvement in the attacks and that links between *al-Qaeda* and *Saddam Hussain's* Government were weak. Kurtz's classified memo further stated that not only did *Osama bin Laden* resent the Iraq regime's secularism, but there was no confirmed information about collaboration between them on weapons of mass destruction. The September 11 Commission which had thorough investigation into the matter supported *Kurtz's* view. Although the polls have shown that more than 40 percent of the American public convinced that Iraq collaboration with *al-Qaeda* had a role in the terrorist attacks, the commission reported findings had no evidence of a "c llaborative operational relationship" between the two or an Iraqi role in attacking the United States. It stated that representatives of the two may have been in contact in 1994 or 1996,1998 and possibly 1999, largely because of what the commission described as a shared hatred of the United States.

British Prime Minister *Tony Blair* admitted on the 26th of September, 2004 that intelligence on Iraq's weapons programme was wrong but said withdrawal of troops from the war-torn country would mean a "surrender" to the terrorists. "Some of the intelligence used to justify the war had been unreliable but it had still been right to topple Saddam Hussain" Blair said. Denying any lapses in planning for the post war situation in Iraq, *Blair* said the degree to which terrorists from outside the country had moved in had surprised everybody. *Blair* also sought to dismiss suggestions that he had focused more on foreign affairs, particularly Iraq, than on the domestic front.

Immediately, after a week of terrorist attacks in the U.S.A., the counter-terrorism director Paul Kurtz wrote a memo to the National Security Adviser, Condoleeza Rice that no "compelling case existed for Iraq's involvement in the attacks and that links between *al-Qaeda* and *Saddam Hussain's* government were weak. As the U.S.A. did not visualize the attacks on the *World Trade Center*, *Pentagon* and *Pennsylvania*, it showed their total failure of intelligence. President *Bush* who had to be taken to a secret *Nebraska* location on the fateful day has got the bitter experience of the lapse of his country's intelligence. With all these, inglorious happenings, President *Bush* still believed the intelligence of the U.S.A. alleging that Iraq possessed dangerous and forbidden weapons. He even turned blind eye on the report of the *U.N.O.* official, who, after inspecting the suspected places in Iraq cleared the charge that it did not have weapons of mass destruction. Since, President *Bush* bent upon invading Iraq and dethrone *Saddam Hussain*, he took shelter under the hypothetical intelligence report of the U.S.A. Even after making mayhem of Iraq, ousting *Saddam Hussain* and his subsequent execution, the U.S.A. could not producc any evidence of mass destruction in Iraq. This was another failure of intelligence which forced the U.S.A. to invade Iraq, resulting in the loss of several human lives. The U.S.A., however, installed a new government of their choice which is deemed to be puppet government and remote controlled by them. Obviously, restlessness prevailed in the country. They are revolting against the government and are being crushed mercilessly in the name of terrorism by the U.S. forces.

During the course of Presidential elections of the U.S.A the war of words between President *Bush* and his Democratic rival Senator *John F.Kerry* have increased enormously. In the nationally televised debate at the University of Maimi in Coral Gables, Florida on 30th September 2004, President *Bush* and *John F.Kerry* sparred on a range of issues including Iraqi war on "terror" and the attack of *bin Laden* on the U.S.A. Accusing, President Bush of diverting the resources from the hunt for terror mastermind *Osama bin Laden* to the war in Iraq, *Kerry* said, "this President has made, I regret to say, a colossal error of judgment. And judgment is what we look for in the President, adding "I can do better job in Iraq. Bush countered Kerry, saying that the world is better off without *Saddam Hussain* and insisted he had to act quickly on Iraq. Kerry reminded him that the U.S. and Britain were enforcing a no-fly zone over Iraq before the war and there was no way *Saddam* could have become stronger. In the 90 minute debate *Kerry* said *Bush* had erred by defending Iraq invasion with the claim that "the enemy attacked us." "*Saddam Hussain* did not attack us, *Osama bin Laden* attacked us. *al-Qaeda* attacked us". *Kerry* reaffirmed that he would not have gone to war against Iraq without U.N. sanction and without a broad alliance, with the result that America is bearing 90 per cent of the causalities and 90 per cent of the cost and the *al-Qaeda* are still active in Afghanistan. *Kerry* said pessimistically that whatever has been accomplished in Iraq is not worth the thousand body bags and two billion dollars expended till 1st week of October, 2004.

From the above debate two issues are emerging; one is that President *Bush* has made a *Himalayan* blunder in attacking Iraq without provocation and without the sanction of U.N.O. If, *John F.Kerry* won the election there would have been substantial change in the policies of the U.S. in regard to Iraq. The second issue, that makes it very clear is that, if, *John F.Kerry* ascended the Presidential post, he would have still pursued the policy of chasing *bin Laden* and his aides and crushed the deviant *al-Qaeda* organization as he affirmed that *bin Laden* and his militant organization attacked the U.S.

After annihilating *Saddam Hussain*, his regime and installing a puppet government, the U.S. Defense Minister, *Donald Rumsfled* admitted on the 4th October, 2004 that he had seen no strong, hard evidence linking former Iraqi President *Saddam Hussain* with *al-Qaeda*, backing away from his pre-war assertions that contacts between the two went back over a decade. He further added that" I have seen answer to that question migrate in the intelligence community over a period of a year in the most amazing way". *Rumsfled* said that there were differences in the intelligence community as to what the relationship was. "To my knowledge I have not seen any strong hard evidence that links the two" he said. It appears that the suspicion of the nexus between terrorism and the Iraq's regime was key point in the U.S. effort to persuade the world, that *Saddam Hussain* had to be dealt with after the September 2001 attacks on the United States.

Charles Duelfer, Chief U.S. Weapons Inspector issued a report on the 6th of October, 2004 saying Iraq did not have weapons of mass destruction at the time of U.S. – led invasion in March, 2003. The inspector told the Senate Armed Services Committee that some small finds had been made of chemical and nerve agents dating from before 1991. Despite these reports and finds, I still do not expect that military significant weapons of mass destruction stocks are cached in Iraq", *Duelfer* said. *Saddam Hussain's* weapons development programme was in such disrepair that little work was ever done on warheads. After weapons inspections began in 1991, *Saddam Hussain* sidelined chemical and biological weapons programmes with an eye to future development, he said. "As in the other weapons of mass destruction areas, *Saddam* sought to sustain the requisite knowledge base to restart the programme eventually and, to the extent it did not threaten the Iraqi effort to get out from sanctions, to sustain the inherent capability to produce such weapons as circumstances permitted in the future" he told the panel.

At the time of Presidential elections, *G.W.Bush* and *Kerry* challenged each other's capability to lead the U.S and the world during the 90-minute town-hall debate on the night of 8th

October, 2004 at the Washington University in St.Louis. *Kerry* charged again that *Bush* rushed to war against Iraq while the *al-Qaeda* threat remained in *Afghanistan*. The President was challenged over his decision to invade Iraq in the wake of the *Duelfer* report that *Saddam Hussain's* regime had no weapons of mass destruction. Kerry disputed over Iraq with the Republican *Bush* describing *Saddam* as a "unique threat" and *Bush* accusing *Kerry* of making wrong decisions and turning his campaign into a "weapon of mass deception".

After getting it cleared that the deposed President *Saddam Hussain* was not having any weapons of mass destruction and also had no links with *bin Laden* the question arises as how far there was failure of the U.S. aviation officials. The report of the Commission said that the U.S. aviation officials ignored dozens of Intelligence reports that warned of *al-Qaeda* plots, some of which specifically discussed airline hijacking and suicide operations, just months before the September 11 strikes. Aviation officials received and reviewed warnings from the federal Aviation Administration about *Osama bin Laden and al-Qaeda*. But they were "lulled into a false sense of security and intelligence that indicated a real and growing threat leading up to 9/11 did not stimulate significant increases in security procedures" the commission report said. The commission report disclosed that the FAA despite being focused on risks of hijackings overseas, warned airports in the spring of 2001 that if the intent of the hijacker is not to exchange hostages for prisoners, but to commit suicide in a spectacular explosion, a domestic hijacking would probably be preferable". The report also takes the FAA to task for failing to pursue domestic security measures that could conceivably have altered the events of September, 11 like toughening airport screening procedures for weapons or expanding the use of on-flight air marshals. Officials appeared more concerned with reducing airline congestion, lessening delays, and easing airlines' financial woes than deterring a terrorist attack, the report concluded.

The declassified version provides the firmest evidence to date about the warnings that aviation officials received concerning the threat of an attack on airlines and the failure to take steps to deter it. Among other things, the report said that FAA received fifty two intelligence reports from their security branch that mentioned *bin Laden* or *al-Qaeda* from April to Sept. 10, 2001.

3
Desecration of Holy Koran

After the U.S. led troops drove the *Taliban* from power in late 2001 *Hamid Karzai*, the President of Afghanistan is trying to restore peace and took many development activities with the assistance of America and other countries. Muslims consider the *Koran* the literal word of God and treat the book with deep reverence. The U.S was holding more than 500 prisoners from its war on terrorism at the naval base in Cuba. Many of them were detained in *Afghanistan* after the Taliban were driven out. The investigators probing abuses at the U.S military prison in *Guantanamo Bay* had found interrogators "had placed *Korans* on toilets and in at least one case flushed a holy book down the toilet'. Protests over the report began in the eastern city of Jalalabad on the 10th of May, 2005. The following day police opened fire on crowds after government offices were set on fire, shops looted and the United Nations buildings and diplomatic missions attacked. On 12th May angry villagers, some armed, confronted police in a district southwest of Jalalabad. Protesters in Logar province, just South of Kabul, threw stones and damaged police vehicles. Demonstration spread in *Afghanistan* on 12th May, 2005 over desecration of the *Koran*. Three protesters died on the day, in a blast. Several hundred students shouting 'death to America' held a peaceful protest outside the Kabul University but in other areas of the country demonstrations turned violent and a day after four people were killed and seventy wounded in riots in Jalalabad. Protesters attacked police posts and government offices in a district of Wardak province, southwest of *Kabul*, and an ammunition store was torched. A depot of ammunition was set on fire and exploded. One protester was killed and four were injured.

The United States has sought to defuse the anger over the *Koran* report by emphasizing its own outrage and promising that the allegation would be investigated. *Richard Boucher* a spokesman of the State Department told reporters in Washington that "a desecration of religious texts and objects is repugnant to common values and anathema to the American people". The United States commanded a foreign force in Afghanistan of about 18,300 most of them American, fighting the *Taliban* insurgents and hunting the *Taliban* and the *al-Qaeda* leaders, including *bin Laden*, architect of the September 11 attacks on the U.S cities. Over the report that the U.S interrogators desecrated the *Koran*, students in the capital of *Afghanistan* burnt an American flag and shouted slogans against the United States and the U.S backed government of President Hamid Karzai

The publication of an article in the May 9 issue of the *Newsweek* Magazine provoked protests and left at least seventeen people dead in violence in *Afghanistan*. After occurrence of the tragedy, the *Newsweek Magazine* has apologized for a report in its edition on the desecration of Koran by American interrogators at *Guantanamo* bay detention center saying it might have erred in reporting the incident that triggered protests across the Muslim world. "We regret that we got any part of our story wrong and extend our sympathies to victims of violence and to the U.S. soldiers caught in its midst, "*Newsweek* Editor *Mark Whitaker* said in a note to readers. Another article in the magazine said "the spark was apparently lit at a press conference held on the 6th of May by *Imran Khan*, a Pakistani Cricket legend and strident critic of Pakistan

President *Pervez Musharraf.* "Brandishing a copy of that week's *Newsweek*, May 9, Khan read a report that the U.S. interrogators at *Guantanamo* prison had placed the Koran on toilet seats and even flushed one". "This is what the U.S is doing" *Khan* was quoted as saying, "desecrating the Koran".

The United States' image abroad has suffered lasting damage due to the news story which claimed that the U.S interrogators at the *Guantanamo Bay* detention center desecrated the *Koran.* A day after *Newsweek* magazine retracted its story on the alleged desecration, the White House said the administration would encourage the magazine to go beyond retraction and apology to assuage ruffled feathers in the Muslim World. *Scott McClellan*, the White House Press Secretary said that "all we are saying is that we would encourage them to help undo the damage that has been done. Some of it's not going to be able to be undone some of it is lasting". So many people lost their lives due to that story based on a single anonymous source, *McClellan* said. Launching a damage control exercise, the *Pentagon* issued detailed rules on 17th May, 2005 for respecting the *Koran* at the detention center in Cuba.

Though the *Newsweek* Editor *Mark Whitaker* apologized for wrong reporting of desecration of Koran by the U.S interrogators, a confidential U.S army report contained graphic details of the widespread abuse of detainees in Afghanistan in 2002 carried out by "young and poorly trained soldiers". *The New York Times* reported that the abuse, described along with the details of the deaths of two inmates at the Bagram detention center, emerged from a nearly 2000 – page file of the army's criminal investigation into the case. The report centers on the death of a 22 year-old taxi driver known as Dilawar and that of another detainee, *Habibullah*, who died earlier in December 2002. According to the report, *Dilawar* was chained by his wrists to the top of his cell for several days before he died and his legs had been pummeled by guards.

"The file depicts young, poorly trained soldiers repeated incidents of abuse. The harsh treatment, which has resulted in criminal charges against seven soldiers, went well beyond the two deaths". According to the newspaper, in sworn statements to army investigators, soldiers described mistreatment, ranging from a female interrogator stepping on a detainee's neck and kicking another in the genitals to a shackled prisoner being made to kiss the boots of interrogators as he rolled back and forth on the floor of a cell. Another prisoner was made to pick plastic bottle caps out of a drum filled with a mixture of excrement and water to soften him up for interrogation. The newspaper said that the U.S. officials have characterized incidents of prisoner abuse at Bagram in 2002 as isolated problems that were thoroughly investigated. Pentagon spokesman *Larry di Rita* told the paper that "what we have learned through the course of all these investigations is that there were people who clearly violated anyone's standard for human treatment". "We are finding some case that were not close calls". The army's criminal investigation command concluded in October 2004 that there was probable cause to charge twenty-seven officers and enlisted personnel with criminal offenses in the *Dilawar* case and fifteen of them were cited in the *Habibullah* case. It is further said that the two army interrogators have been reprimanded and seven soldiers have been charged. It also said most of those who could still face legal action have been denied wrong doing.

Karzai, the President of *Afghanistan* a staunch ally in the U.S. – led war against terrorism wanted to forge a broad long-term partnership with his most important ally like the U.S.A. was shocked by a U.S army report on abuse of detainees in *Afghanistan* saying his Government wanted custody of all *Afghan* prisoners and control over the U.S. military operations. He said that "no operations inside Afghanistan should take place without the consultation of the *Afghan* Government."

President *Hamid Karzai* who met President *Bush* on 23-

05-05 in Washington announced strategic partnership between the United States and *Afghanistan* and pledged close and extensive co-operation in a wide range of areas. Both agreed to foster co-operation between *Afghanistan* and its neighbors and deter meddling in its internal affairs. The United States and *Afghanistan* have also pledged they would consult with respect to taking appropriate measures in the event that *Afghanistan* perceives that its territorial integrity, independence or security is threatened or at risk. The joint declaration also envisaged strengthened ties between *Afghanistan* and NATO and enable long term American involvement in *Afghanistan's* security and reconstruction. Issues addressed by the two Presidents at the joint appearance before the media included alleged abuse of *Afghan* prisoners by American military personnel. *Bush* said, "our policy has been to work out way through those who are being held in *Guantanamo* and send them back to the host countries, and we will do so over time, with the *Afghan* Government". In the security area, the U.S. military forces operating in *Afghanistan* will "continue to have access to Bagram air base and its facilities. The U.S. and coalition forces are to continue to have the freedom of action required to conduct appropriate military operations".

Denying the U.S.State Department predictions that *Afghanistan* was on the verge of becoming a 'narco-state', Afghan President *Hamid Karzai* said his country could be free of opium poppies in five or six years. With the President *Bush* at his side, *Karzai* said that he was hopeful that poppy production would be down 20 per cent to 30 percent during 2005. He added that the elimination of the poppy could be achieved only if Afghan farmers can cultivate other corps as alternative. Opium / poppy is the raw-material for heroin. The *Afghan* narcotics situation represents an enormous threat to world stability. In the month of March, 2005 the U.S State Department reported that the area in *Afghanistan* devoted to poppy cultivation in 2004 set a record of more than 5,10,000 acres, more than triple the figure for 2003.

Anti-demonstration rocked *Jammu and Kashmir* also against the alleged desecration of the *Koran* by the U.S. troops at *Guantanamo Bay* prison.. About a dozen demonstrators were taken into preventive custody by the police from different parts of the city while more than ten others were wounded in stone pelting. Police fired several rounds in the air and burst tear gas shells to disperse the anti-U.S demonstrators. Thousands of people took to streets near the historic Jama Masjid immediately after the Friday prayers. Shops, business establishments and educational institutions remained closed and traffic was off the roads. Work in government offices, banks, ration depots and other public sector undertakings was affected due to low attendance. The strike was called by the *Hurriyat Conference* (Geelani) *Dukhtaran-e-Milat* and Kashmir Bar Association and supported by other organizations.

Violent protests erupted in some other Muslim countries and at least sixteen people died in rioting in Afghanistan. Southern Command launched the inquiry after a May 9, 2005 *'Newsweek'* article, later retracted by the magazine, that stated United States 'interrogators at *Guantanamo* had flushed a *Koran* down a toilet to try to make detainees talk. The U.S military for the first time detailed how jailers at *Guanranamo* mishandled the *Koran*, including a case in which a guard's urine splashed through a vent onto the Islamic holy book and others in which it was kicked, stepped on and soaked in water.

The U.S. Southern Command responsible for the prison for foreign terrorism suspects at the U.S. naval base at *Guantanamo Bay*, Cuba described five cases of 'mishandling' of Koran by the U.S. personnel confirmed by a newly completed military inquiry officials said in a statement on the 3rd of June, 2005. In the incident involving urine, which took place in March, the Southern Command said that "a guard left his observation post, went outside and urinated near an air vent, and the wind blew his urine through the vent and into a cell block".

It said a detainee told guards the urine 'slashed on him and his *Koran*'. The statement said that the detainee was given a new prison uniform and Koran, and that the guard was reprimanded and given duty in which he had no contact with prisoners. Army Capt. *John Adams*, a spokesman at Guantanamo, said the inquiry deemed the incident 'accidental.' the Southern Command said a civilian contractor interrogator apologized in July, 2003 to a detainee for stepping on his Koran. The interrogator "was later terminated for a pattern of unacceptable behavior, an inability to follow direct guidance and poor leadership." the statement said.

In August, 2003 prisoners complained that "Koran became wet when night-shift guards threw water balloons in a cell block". In February, 2002 guards kicked a prisoner's Koran, it added. In the fifth confirmed incident of mishandling a Koran, the Southern Command said that a prisoner in August, 2003 complained that 'a two-word' obscenity had been written in English in his Koran. The Southern Command said "it was possible a guard had written the words but' equally possible' the prisoner himself had done it." It did not offer an explanation of the detainee's possible motive. Brig.Gen.Jay Hood,Commander of the Guantanamo prison who headed the inquiry said that "mishandling a *Koran* at *Guantanamo Bay* is a rare occurrence. Mishandling of a *Koran* here was never condoned". *Hood* disclosed on May, 2005 that the inquiry announced on May 11,2005 had turned up five cases of 'mishandling of a Koran' by U.S personnel at *Guantanamo*, but declined at the time to describe the incidents other than saying they did not involve flushing one down a toilet. In the statement *Hood* reiterated that the inquiry found 'no credible evidence' that a member of the military joint task force at *Guantanamo* ever flushed a Koran down a toilet. The matter is considered closed.

4
Laden – Invisible Object

Osama Bin Laden and some of his top aides are hoodwinking, the Pakistani and the U.S. forces for the last several years.. A Senior U.S. Official claimed that "everything is in place and a little bit is needed to localize these people and catch them". The U.S. department's co-ordinator on counter-terrorism *J. Cofer Black* said on 3rd September, 2004 "in counter-terrorism, the programmes are in place. We are after these guys globally. Success against people you know about, *Osama* could happen tomorrow, could happen the day after, a week from now, or month from now." He further said, "I tell the people and the media in the U.S. that I would be surprised but not shocked that *Osama* and all his lieutenants have been caught and that these guys were in jail. It will be a good for the people".

Describing Bin Laden as an "invisible moving objective", Pakistan President *Musharaff* had dismissed suggestions that he knew where the world's most wanted terrorist was and that he would be captured before the U.S. presidential poll to ensure the reelection of *G.W. Bush*. "I think that is quite hilarious. I know this is a feeling. There are some in Pakistan who ask me this," said President *Musharaff*. "During the interviews to NBC news and CNN a questioner asked the President that there was a suspicion in the Democratic Party of the U.S. that he knew where *Laden* was and that he would be captured before the American Presidential election. The President replied that he wondered how anyone could even imagine that he knew where *Laden* was. "Here in the world, where you can't hide anything. The media, you people are so active. Everyone is everywhere "he added. Stating that he was "reasonably sure" that Laden was alive, Gen. *Musharaff* said he could not say whether the fugitive would be captured alive or dead. Asked why *Osama* was so elusive, he said "well because of the terrain. He has supporters, and also the terrain is very inhospitable, very high mountains, easy to hide, easy to move unnoticed".

August Hanning, head of Germany's Federal Intelligence Service told a news conference on 7th October, 2004 that he believed that *Osama bin Laden* was alive and continued to exert influence in his *al-Qaeda* terror network. "German intelligence officials believe, as they have for some time, that bin Laden is living in the Afghan-Pakistani border area" Hanning said. He did not specify which side of the border. "We continue to see traces of his activity. He tries to organize, to motivate," his followers, *Hanning* said.

Ahmad Muaffaq Zaidan, al-Jazeera's bureau chief in Pakistan said on 30th October, 2004 that they have received the latest videotaped message from *al-Qaeda* leader *Osama bin Laden* at his office in the Pakistan capital. The tape was dropped off at the gate of the station's office in an envelop on 29th October, 2004. *Zaidan* said that the guard brought it to him along with other mail. In his video message *Laden* threatened the United States with attacks similar to September 11,2001 and accused President *Bush* of "misleading" his people. In the video, broadcast by Qatar-based *al-Jazeera* television, *bin Laden* also accused Bush of negligence during the September 11 attacks, further inflaming the already intense final struggle between *Bush* and his rival *John Kerry* to win the White House. *Bin Laden* told the American people that their security is not in the hands of *either Bush or Kerry* but depends on the United States policy. "Despite the fact that we are into the fourth year after September 11, Bush is still misleading you and hiding the real reason from you, which means that the reasons to repeat what happened remain" said *bin Laden*. He further added that "your security is not in the hands of *Kerry*, *Bush* or *al-Qaeda*. Your security is in your own hands. Any (presidential) mandate which does not play havoc with our security would automatically ensure its own security." The tape, deemed authentic by the United States Intelligence agencies, showed *bin Laden* standing at a pulpit against a plain brown background, reading from a prepared statement and dressed in a white turban and beige cloak.

A White House spokesman said the tape appeared to have been recorded recently, while an U.S. official added that a reference to the United States casualties in Iraq reaching 1,000 dead meant it could have been filmed in September, 2004. *Bin Laden* also accused *Bush* of negligence during the September 11 attacks in 2001, that killed nearly 3,000 people. He further accused Bush saying he was slow to react to the first attack on the *World Trade Center* after he was passed on the information.

On the eve of the U.S. Presidential election, *bin Laden* tried to demoralize the Americans through the video posted on websites often used by the Islamists. Within a period of fortnight two videos had come out from *Laden* denouncing President *Bush* on the invasion of *Afghanistan* and Iraq. His sole intention appeared to defame President *Bush* and get defeated in the election. His videos had also given lie to the poplar belief that he was already arrested and under the custody of President *Musharaff* of Pakistan and news of his arrest would be announced by Pakistan at the time of the U.S. election to boost the prospects of President *Bush*. The rumours had not become true, but the fact remains, that *bin Laden* is still active in his network and planning sabotage activities to again strike the U.S. and its allies.

On the 3rd of November, 2004 *bin Laden* said in a full internet broadcast of a video partly aired by *al-Jazeera* in the last of week of October, 2004 that President *Bush* has dragged America into a quagmire in Iraq and warned of retaliation for Iraqi deaths. *Laden* said President *Bush* had ignored advice against waging "an justified war on Iraq for which there would be no end". The black gold blinded him and he put his personal interests above the general interests of America so the war took place, many died, American money squandered and *Bush* was dragged into a quagmire in Iraq which threatens his future, "said the al-Qaeda leader.

"More than 15,000 of our people were killed and tens of thousands wounded and more than 1,000 of your people (Americans) were killed and tens of thousands wounded. Bush's hands are sullied with the blood of those on both sides just for oil and to employ his private companies, bin Laden said. "Remember that for every action, there is reaction", he said. The complete 18-minute tape was posted on the Internet after *al-Jazeera* aired excerpts in the last week of October, 2004 in which bin Laden warned of possible attacks.

President *Musharraf* met President *Bush* on 5-12-2004 and congratulated him on his re-election to lead the U.S.A for four more years and praised his commitment to establish a Palestanian State. During their meeting, President *Bush* emphasized Middle East peace and praised President *Musharraf* in his efforts in the war on terrorism and the search for *bin Laden*. One of the most sensitive issues between the two countries was the unsuccessful hunt along the Afghan-Pakistan border for the *al-Qaeda* Chief blamed in the September 11 attacks on America. "The President of Pakistan has been a determined leader to bring to justice not only people like *bin Laden*, but to bring to justice those who would inflict harm and pain on his own people" Bush said after their meeting in the Oval Office.

For several months there was no intelligence of Pakistan

indicating where Laden and his top lieutenants were hiding. During the course of interview with *The Washington Post*, President *Musharraf* said "his country's army is hunting for Laden and the search for the *al-Qaeda* leader has gone cold. He, however, maintained that the Pakistani forces are still aggressively pursuing the world's most notorious terrorist" President *Musharraf* acknowledged that recent security force operations have been able to determine only one fact – that bin Laden is alive. "He is alive, but more than that, where he is, no, it'll be just a guess and it won't have much basis "Musharraf said.

A newspaper in Pakistan had published photos and sermons of *al-Qaeda* chief bin Laden and elusive *Mullah Omar*. The Sindh province government issued a notice to "*Ummat*" a daily Urdu-language paper to stop them and issued a notice asking them to explain from where they were getting these statements and sayings of *bin Laden* and *Omar* who were declared as international terrorists. The newspaper said it had already ceased publishing them and denied of having received any funds from any group. In order to capture *bin Laden* and his deputy *Zawahiri* and *Taliban* supremo *Mullah Mohammad Omar* the U.S. increased their forces to flush out the *al-Qaeda* militants who had reportedly taken refuge in the mountains of Gilgit and Baltistan.

The whereabouts of *bin-Laden* are not yet known and an audiotape broadcast on 27th December, 2004 by *Al-Jazeera* Satellite television, a man purported to be *Laden* endorsed *Abu Musab al-Zarqawi* as his deputy in Iraq and called for a boycott elections to be held in the month of January, 2005. The voice on the tape described *al-Zarqawi* as the '*emir*' of *al-Qaeda* in Iraq and called upon Muslims there "to listen to him". *Al-Zarqawi* declared allegiance to *bin Laden* and changed his group's name to *Al-qaeda* in Iraq. The voice on the tape called it "a great step on the path of unifying all the *mujahideen* in establishing the state of righteousness and ending the state of injustice". The voice sounded like that of *bin Laden* and the statement and language used appeared to conform with previous announcements condemning the 30th January, 2005 elections to elect a national assembly that will draft a new constitution. The speaker said that "in the balance of Islam, this constitution is infidel and, therefore, everyone who participates in this election will be considered infidels." The voice further said that "beware of henchmen who speak in the name of Islamic parties and groups who urge people to participate" in the election, The speaker said *al-Zarqawi* and those within are fighting "for God's sake".

Neither the U.S. intelligence nor the Pakistani forces were able to trace *bin Laden* and his top aides though, his warning to attack the U.S. continued to flow. The U.S. was not taking them in a superficial or casual way as, they once experienced the monstrous acts of *bin Laden* on the *World Trade Center* and the building of *Pentagon.* The U.S. Justice department, therefore, advertised huge rewards in a top Pakistani daily on 7th January for information leading to the capturc of *Osama bin Laden* and 13 other 'most wanted people'. *bin Laden* and his deputy *Ayman al-Zawahiri* each carried a reward of $ 25 million while *Taliban* supreme *Mullah Muhammad Omar* had a $ 10 million price on his head. "All the information would be kept secret" the advertisement issued by the U.S. Justice Department said. About *Laden,* the advertisement said, "he is accused of September 11 attacks on the *WTC* and *Pentagon* and attacks on U.S. embassies in Kenya and Tanzania". *Ayman al-Zawahiri* was indicted in attacks on the U.S. embassies in Kenya and Tanzania.

With the trial of *Laden* having gone cold, the *Bush* administration expected to double the sum on the terror mastermind's head to $ 50 million, besides chalking out a new publicity blitz to help to trace him. As part of the publicity blitz, the U.S. State Department reminded Afghans and Pakistanis of the existing $ 25 million bounty. In the second term of President Bush the White House expected to double the sum on bin Laden's head, to $ 50 million, *bin Laden* was thought to be hiding somewhere along the 2,500 k.m. mountainous *Afghanistan*-Pakistan border, but the Intelligence officials in *Kabul* and Islamabad believe there had been no trace of him for the past several months. State Department advertisements began appearing in January, 05 in a widely circulated Pakistani newspaper, offering rewards for *bin Laden*, his lieutenant *Ayman al-Zawahiri*, *Taliban* leader *Mullah Mohammad Omar* and eleven other suspected terrorists.

Though *Osama bin Laden* no longer exercised centralized control and direction in Saudi Arabia, a top U.S. Intelligence Official said, that "the primary threat for the foreseeable future is a network of Islamic extremists hostile to the United States and its interests". He said that "we expect continued assassinations, infrastructure attacks and operations directed to discredit the regime and discourage individuals and businesses, especially those affiliated with the Saudi military, from remaining in the kingdom". He further said that "we now face an '*al-Qaeda*' associated movement of like minded groups who interact, share resources and work to achieve shared goals". Adding the network is a transnational and has a broad range of capabilities, to include mass causality attacks. Some of the groups include *Jemah Islamiyya*, responsible for the 9th September bombing of the Australian embassy in Jakarta and Hezb-e-Islami-Gulbuddin. Some of the groups in the movement provide safe haven and logistical support to *al-Qaeda* members, other operate directly with *al-Qaeda* and still others fight with *al-Qaeda* in the Afghanistan / Pakistan". Remnants of the senior leadership presented a threat as could be seen that 15 significant attacks occurred in Saudi Arabia against the regime, America and other western targets in 2004 and that the Al-Saud rule in the Kingdom is under pressure. It is clear from the public statements of *bin Laden* and Zawahiri that their strategic objectives include another major casualty-producing attack against the U.S. homeland.

The Congressional Research service which advises the U.S.Congress and writes policy briefs for the Country's law makers believed both *bin Laden* and *Zawahiri* escaped the December 2001 U.S. war in Afghanistan and fled into Pakistan where they have continued to elude capture by Pakistani forces and agents. A Pakistan forces' offensive against suspected terrorist hideouts in the South-Waziristan region in March 2004 also failed to find these two or other major *al-Qaeda* leaders. After September 11, 2001 attacks on the *World Trade Center* and *Pentagon*, the U.S. agencies have identified thirty-seven top *al-Qaeda* operatives and since then, fifteen have been either killed or captured. Prominent among them was number three leader *Mohammad Altef*, September 11 planner *Khalid Sheik Mohammad* and key recruiter and planner *Abu Zubaydah*. To hunt and Capture, *al-Qaeda* chief *Osama bin Laden* and his deputy Ayman Al-Zawahiri, the CIA para-military officer and other U.S. personnel, disguised as "civilian contractors" were based in Pakistan.

According to an Official of the U.S. Counter terrorism there had been communication between *bin Laden* and *Abu Musab al-Zarqawi* with *bin Laden* suggesting to *Zarqawi* to consider the territory of the U.S. as a target of terrorist attack. The U.S. Department of Homeland Security warned the State Officials around the country that the government had received nonspecific information about *al-Qaeda's* plans to attack the United States. They, therefore, sent out a classified intelligence bulletin to state homeland security advisers to give details of "recent credible but nonspecific" threat information. "This nonspecific information reiterates *al-Qaeda's* desire to potentially target the homeland."

According to a confidential U.S. Government report, despite a huge investment in Security the American aviation systems remained vulnerable to attack by *al-Qaeda* and other terrorist groups who are eyeing non-commercial planes and helicopters as particularly tempting targets. Intelligence indicates that *al-Qaeda* might have discussed plans to hijack chartered planes, helicopters and other aircraft for attacks because they are less well guarded than commercial airlines. The report also revealed that the commercial airliners are also "likely to remain a target and a platform for terrorists", and members of *al-Qaeda* appeared determined to study and test new American Security measures to "uncover weakness". The assessment, came as the *Bush* administration, with a new intelligence structure and many new counter-terrorism leaders in place, was taking stock of terrorists' capabilities and of the country's ability to defend itself.

In an interview to BBC in the third week of Mach, 2005 Pakistan President *Musharraf* has claimed his country's forces lost track of *al-Qaeda* chief *Laden* several months ago. He said Pakistani intelligence services had their strongest indication about his whereabouts till July,2004. "We thought we knew roughly the area where he possibly could be. That was, I think... Not very long ago". The President further said that a dragnet had been closing on *bin Laden* along the border between Afghanistan and Pakistan, but he fled." He also said that the Pakistani forces got their clearest trace of *Laden* after the Pakistani army launched a big offensive in 2004, in the tribal belt on the Afghan border. But since then, the military had seen no sign that the *al-Qaeda* leader or his associates were in the area. "They can move and then you lose contact", Musharraf said. Both *bin Laden* and his deputy *Ayman Al-Zawhiri* were widely believed to be hiding in or close to North and South Waziristan the border regions where the Pakistani army has faced its strongest resistance in its operations against the al-Qaeda.

There was speculation about the health of *bin Laden*, who was reported to be suffering from a kidney ailment. *Mullah Akthar Usmani, a Taliban* commander dismissing the above speculation said that *bin Laden* was in good health. He told a Pakistan private television station that *Taliban* leader *Mullah*

Mohammad Omar was also well and in direct command of *Taliban* forces in Afghanistan. *Usmani*, who was on a ten member *Taliban* leadership council was identified by the government as a top rebel commander. In the interview, his face was partly concealed by a black turban and an assault rifle was propped up at his side. Denying the statement of *Usmani* that *Mullah Mohammad Omar*, and *Zalmay Khalilzad*, the Ambassador of the United States said on 16th June 2005 that "*Mullah Mohammad Omar* was not in Afghanistan. I do not believe that *Osama* is also in Afghanistan". He did not say where the two were believed to be hiding but the Officials repeatedly said that the *al-Qaeda* leader was in the rugged mountains between Afghanistan and Pakistan.

Mr. Porter, Director, CIA told on 19th June, 2005 that he had an "excellent" idea where Laden was hiding, but the *al-Qaeda* leader will not be brought to justice until the weak links in counter terrorism efforts were strengthened. *Goss* did not say where bin Laden was hiding, but intelligence experts have said that *al-Qaeda* leader who has evaded an extensive U.S. led manhunt was probably in the border region of *Pakistan* and *Afghanistan*. He cited some of the difficulties as "dealing with sanctuaries in sovereign states, you are dealing with a problem of our sense of international obligation and fair play". He added that "we have to find a way to work in a conventional world in unconventional ways that are acceptable to the international community". *al-Qaeda* could strike the U.S. again he said. "Certainly the intent is very high. And we are trying to stay ahead of their capability. And so far, I think we have done pretty well carrying the war to them, as it were",

While in Australia in the month of June,2005, President *Musharraf* claimed that *al-Qaeda* was "on the run" in Pakistan and his forces chased them out of cities into mountains and then occupied their sanctuaries. This has created a lot of confusion to the U.S. Central Intelligence Agency. According to sources familiar with the intelligence community discussion on the issue there was mounting evidence that the Pakistani military and its intelligence wing Inter Services Intelligence (ISI) was nurturing its deep ties to Islamic extremists including those sheltering the *al-Qaeda* leadership and leaders of the Afghan *Taliban.* Retired CIA *Gary Shoren* was more explicit about *bin Laden.* He said that "he is hiding in Pakistan in the northern tribal area above Peshawar. The U.S. Government and the U.S. military are not authorized by the *Musharraf* Government to enter there unilaterally" and further speculated that some ISI Officers knew exactly where *bin laden* was hiding. The White House and the State Department knew this but were keeping a debate over how to handle the "Pakistan problem" behind closed doors. They argued that too much pressure could topple the relatively moderate *Musharraf* and bring Islamist extremist to power in a nuclear-armed Pakistan.

Time and again, the Officials of the Afghanistan Government claimed that *bin Laden* and his aides were hiding in Pakistan's tribal region. On 5th July, 2005 the Interior Minister of Pakistan denied the claim of Afghanistan and asserted that *al-Qaeda* chief *Osama bin Laden* was hiding in Southern Afghanistan which witnessed a spurt of attacks by Taliban. He said that "the possibility of *Mullah Omar*, *Osama bin Laden* and his close aide *Ayman Al-Zawahiri*, hiding in that area cannot be ruled out since South Afghanistan is not under the effective control of the Afghan Government".

Mourners world-wide marked the fourth anniversary of the September 11 attack on 11-9-05 with memorials and calls for peace, while in *New York*, grieving family members read the names of the victims at ground zero. In Italy, *Pope Benedict* XVI marked the anniversary by calling for global renunciation of hatred and to build a world of justice and peace. "Today, 11 September, we remember the victims of terrorist violence throughout the world", *Benedict* said on the 11th of September, 2005 from the *Papal Summer Palace* at Castle Gandolfo south of Rome. "May God inspire men and women of good will everywhere to renounce hatred and to build a world of justice, solidarity and peace". In Germany, a memorial service was held for the victims of September 11 and hurricane Katrina in Berlin's Kaiser Wilhelm memorial church, "a landmark left only partly restored after suffering bomb damage in World War II – as a reminder of the evils of war. Some 50,000 people took to the streets in the southern Russian city to mark the anniversary, forming a 40-km-long human chain. Marchers chanted "we choose peace" and "no terrorism.

On the eve of the fourth anniversary of the September 11 attacks, the U.S President *George Bush* said the terrorists who killed thousands of innocent people could not defeat the spirit of the nation as the tragedy was overcome by "displays of selflessness, courage and compassion". He said every American has memories of that day that will never leave them. "We remember the images of fire and terror at the *Pentagon*, in *Pennsylvania* and in *New York city*. We remember the ruthless of those who murdered the innocent and took joy in their suffering. We remember the courage of the police, firefighters and rescue personnel who rushed into burning buildings to save lives, knowing they might never emerge. And we remember the victims and the loved ones they left behind". "Four years later, Americans remember the fears and uncertainty and confusion of that terrible morning", Bush said. But above all, we remember the resolve of our nation to defend our freedom and rebuild a wounded city".

While the world was marking the fourth anniversary of the September 11 attacks on the U.S, the where about of the alleged mastermind of the strikes *Osama bin Laden* remained a mystery. The U.S leaders as well as Pakistan had several times claimed cornering Laden and predicted his arrest but none was realized. President *Musharaff* said more than once that *Laden* with a small group of his supporters was on constant move in the mountainous areas along the border between *Pakistan* and *Afghanistan*. The U.S. Afghan and

Pakistani forces have frequently combed the area but the chief suspect of the September 11 attacks was not located. The U.S. persistent failure to spot the two fugitives raised many questions among the *Afghans* about the U.S. seriousness over the arrest of the king of terror and the on going war on terrorism.

Some intellectuals believed that the alleged architect of the September 11 attacks could be hidden in Pakistan's semi-autonomous Pashtun belt tribal area along the porous border with Afghanistan. "*Laden* might have been enjoying the hospitality of extremists in tribal areas as the government of Pakistan has little control over the region. They also observed that little access of Islamabad to tribal areas has facilitated *Osama* to take refuge among the deeply religious and valiant Pashthuns ethnic on the other side of the border. "Tribalism in conjunction with Islamism in the deeply religious people of tribal-belt Pashutuns has enabled Osama and his loyalists to survive as neither Pakistan nor U.S. military has control over the tribal-belt region. The U.S. has launched big manhunt military operations in the region and also announced $ 25 million head price, but failed to capture *Laden*.

As the matter stood thus, an *al-Qaeda* operative threatened on 11-9-05 in a broadcast on *ABC News* new about attacks against the U.S. and Australia. "Yesterday London and Madrid. Tomorrow, Los Angeles and Melbourne, God willing. At this time, don't count on us demonstrating restraint or compassion," The tape warned. "We are Muslims we love peace but peace on our terms, peace as laid down by Islam not the so-called peace of occupiers and dictators.

Osama bin Laden, who hate everything the West stands for, had sought asylum in Britain even as he was planning the September 11 attacks on the U.S. The *al-Qaeda* leader wanted to abandon his base in Sudan at the end of 1995 and asked some of his followers in London to sound out whether he would be able to move to Britain. The then Home Secretary of Britain told "*The Times*', daily how his aides informed him of the asylum request from the Saudi-born militant of whom the world knew little of ten years ago. A number of his brothers and other relatives, all members of the wealthy *bin Laden* Construction Empire, owned properties in London by the mid-1990s.

'*News of the world*' tabloid reported that the *al-Qaeda* leader *Osama bin Laden*, the world's most wanted terrorist, has evaded capture by Pakistani troops just 30 minutes as they zeroed in on him in a remote village close to *Afghanistan* border. Data from a mobile phone used by one of Laden's closest aides helped the Pakistani troops to pinpoint his hideout but by the time they could mount a raid, *the al-Qaeda* Chief had slipped away. The Pakistani embassy in London confirmed in the second week of November 2005 "we think we missed him (*bin Laden*) by thirty minutes. It was the closest we have been since 2001." *Bin Laden* has not been seen in videos, issued by his terror network, for over a year and Western intelligence agencies believed he might be dead. But President *Musharraf* disagreed saying, "it is important we finish terrorism and to do that *bin Laden* must be hunted down," the tabloid reported.

Pakistan President *Pervez Musharaff* said on 8th December 2005 that he did not know whether Osama Bin Laden was alive or dead. "I don't know if he is alive or dead, so I will not guess, Nobody knows, whoever is talking about this does not know. May be I know the most. But I will not conjecture" said *Musharaff* at a press conference on the sidelines of a summit of the Organisation of the Islamic Conference in Mecca.

Al-Qaeda's deputy leader *Ayman al-Zawahiri* said in a video posted on a web site frequently used by militants had urged Mujahideen to attack oil sites in Muslim states and said Laden's battle against the West was only just beginning. "I bring a message of joy to all Muslims and *Mujahideen* that *al-Qaeda*, thanks to God, is spreading and expanding and strengthening. Its prince *Sheik Osama bin Laden*, May God protect him, is still leading its *jihad* (holy war). He further said that "I call on *Mujahideen* to concentrate their attacks on Muslims' stolen oil, most of the revenues of which go to the enemies of Islam while most of what they leave is seized by the thieves who rule our countries". The tape appeared to have been filmed sometime during or after September 2005 with Zawahiri speaking against a white background.

The U.S Defense Secretary *Donald Rumsfeld* said on 21st December'05 that *al-Qaeda* leader *bin Laden* might be no longer be able to run the militant network and has not been heard for nearly a year. *Rumsfeld* said that the *Bush* administration considered it a priority to capture the mastermind of the September,2001 attacks who was believed to be hiding somewhere in the mountains along the Afghanistan-Pakistan border. He further asserted that *Laden* was spending a major fraction of his time trying to avoid being caught. He contradicted the assertion of *al-Qaeda 's* deputy leader, *Ayman al-Zawahiri* in a video interview in the month of December,2005 that *Laden's* battle against the West was only just beginning.

It was believed, that the voice heard on the audio-tape aired over television network *al-Jazeera*, seemed to be that of *al-Qaeda* leader. In the taped message, he threatened more attacks on the United States and offered a truce if Washington pulls out of Afghanistan and Iraq. The White House bluntly rejected the offer saying that "we do not negotiate with terrorists" and maintained that "*al-Qaeda* is not the same organization that it was when it attacked the U.S on September,11 because of the actions that we have taken and because of what we have done to put their leaders out of business or bring them to justice.." The spokesman of the White House further said that "how-ever, the terrorists want to attack again, and they seek to drive the U.S out of the Middle East because they view democracy and peace as a threat to their existence. And they know because that the U.S remaining involved in the Middle East is a threat to their ambitions."

A U.S strategic think-tank had claimed that both Ayman al-Zawahiri and bin Laden were in the rural western areas of the North-West Frontier Province and frequently attend tribal gatherings there, indicating that they feel secure with –and have influence over- the locals whose support they need if they were remain secure. It said the *al-Qaeda* leadership was headquartered in Dir and Swat districts and, possibly, the Malkand area of North-West Frontier Province (NWFP). Observing that global attention had been focused on North and South Waziristan areas of the province due to the ongoing unrest there. Dir bordered the Bajaur agency of Pakistan, which in turn was close to Afghanistan's Kunar province,"a hotbed of *Taliban* and *al-Qaeda* activity". It was suspected that neither bin Laden nor *Al-Zawahiri* would risk staying close to the *Afghan* border "as it would leave them vulnerable to a U.S air-strike from the *Afghan* territory. On the contrary, they would wish to remain as deep within Pakistan territory as possible, where the U.S. might not venture into and described the region as "the best hiding place they can find in all of Pakistan".

Al-qaeda's deputy leader *Ayman al-Zawahiri* criticized the U.S President *Bush* as a "butcher " in a video tape aired on 30th January, 2006 saying that January, 2006 U.S air strike targeting him had killed only innocent people. In the tape aired by *al-Jazeera* television, *Zawahri, Laden's* right-hand man, also mentioned a truce which the *al-Qaeda* leader had offered the U.S in an audio tape aired in the month of January, 2006. "U.S warplanes have launched a raid on a village near Peshawar just after the *Enid al-Adhere* (feast) in which 18 Muslim men, women and children were killed in their (U.S) fight against *Jihad* which they call terrorism". " This was intended to kill myself and four of my brothers but now the whole world has discovered the U.S lies and their failure and brutality", *Zawahiri* added. "I will meet my fate (death) as set by God the Almighty but if my time did not come you (U.S President) *Bush* or all the powers on earth......cannot bring it one second closer." Broad-casting more of *Zawahiri's* remarks, Jazeera later said that he invited Bush to become a Muslim. "Should you accept, you become a brother and God forgives you all that is past".

Reacting to the new tape, the White House spokesman said that "the *al-Qaeda* leadership is clearly on the run and under a lot of pressure. *Al-qaeda* remains a lethal and determined enemy". We continue to take the threat from *al-Qaeda* seriously, and continue to pursue all those who seek to do us harm.". The State Department spokesman said that "whatever the status of *Zawahiri* there continues to be a determined *al-Qaeda* effort to destroy peace and innocent lives."

A dinner invitation to *al-Qaeda's* second-in-command triggered a U.S air strike on Pakistan's tribal region but *Ayman al-Zawahiri* failed to show up. Pakistan condemned the air strike conducted by the U.S on 13th January,'06 which killed at-least 18 people, including women and children and summoned the U.S ambassador to protest.

Ayman al-Zawahiri, al -Quad's deputy leader who escaped from the U.S air strike in an audio tape posted on the internet on 3rd, March,'06 called on Muslims to attack the West as those against *New York*, London and Madrid in recent years. He also urged the Islamism militant group Hams not to recognize the peace deals signed by the Palestinian Authority with Israel. He called on Muslims to boycott countries where satirical cartoons of *Prophet Mohammad* had been published, including Denmark, Norway, France and Germany and said that Muslims should prevent the West from "stealing Muslims' oil." He urged the Muslims to inflict losses on the crusader West, especially to its economic infrastructure with strikes that would make it bleed for years.

Osama bin Laden who avoided arrest promised on 20th Feb.'06 on a militant website that he never to be captured alive and declared the U.S had resorted to the same 'barbaric' tactics used by the deposed *Saddam Hussain*. In the 11 minute 26 seconds tape *Laden* said that "I have sworn to only live free. Even if I find bitter the taste of death, I don't want to die humiliated or deceived." The war against America and its allies has not remained confined to Iraq as *Bush* claims, but rather Iraq has become a point of attraction and recruitment of qualified forces". He accused the U.S forces of 'barbaric' acts in Iraq comparable to those committed by *Saddam Hussain*. He further said in the tape posted with an English-language voice over that "the U.S criminality has gone as far as raping women and holding them hostage before their husbands....As for the torture of men it has now come to the use of burning chemical acids and electric drills in their joints. "Despite all these barbaric methods.... the Mujahideen are strengthening and increasing by the grace of Allah."

In January,'06 the Qatar-based *al-Jazeera* television aired parts of the tape, in which Laden said that the *al-Qaeda* was preparing further attacks in the U.S. It was the first *bin Laden* tape since 2004. In the audio on 20th Feb,'06 *Laden* said "the insurgency in Iraq was gaining strength despite 'barbaric' and oppressive steps taken by the American army and its agents to the extent that there is no longer any mentionable differences between this criminality and the criminality of *Saddam*.

The tape was first broadcast by *al-Jazeera* before new images surfaced of Iraqi prisoner abuse by the U.S forces at Abu Garb prison in a 2004 scandal. The images showed sexual humiliation of prisoners and physical abuse.

The U.S officials had often accused *Saddam* of links to *al-Qaeda*, one of the reasons of the U.S-led war on Iraq which was chiefly. based on allegations Iraq was developing weapons of mass destruction. *Bin Laden's* remarks appeared to disassociate his group from *Saddam's* regime.

The U.S President *George W. Bush* made his first visit

to South Asia on the 1st of March,'06 with a surprise stop over in Afghanistan. President *Bush* had talks with President *Hamid Karzai* and promised to develop Afghanistan into a democracy. He said that he was confident that al-Qaeda chief Osama bin Laden would be brought to justice. At a joint press conference with Afghan President *Hamid Karzai* the President of America said that "we have got U.S forces on the hunt for not only bin Laden but anybody who plots and plans with *bin Laden*." They are making progress of dismantling *al-Qaeda*. Slowly and surely we are bringing the people to justice and the world is better for it as a result of our steady progress."

The whereabouts of *Mullah Omar* were not known even after frenzied search both by the forces of Pakistan and Afghanistan. On the 16th of March,'06 the elusive chief *Mullah Omar* warned the U.S-led forces of "unimaginable" violence in the future. He claimed a large number of Afghan youth were signing up as suicide bombers. *Omar* said that *Taliban* would intensify attacks in the summer of 2006.

The President of Pakistan's hard-line *Jamat-e-Islami* (JI) *Qazi Hussain Ahmed* was quoted to have been said on 18th March,'06 that *al-Qaeda* chief *bin Laden* had visited his party headquarters in Lahore and offered to "buy" Members of Parliament to win majority for former Prime Minister *Nawaz Sharif*. He declined the offer as the *al-Qaeda* chief himself had no firm ground in neighbouring Afghanistan. Further, bin Laden offered to "buy" Pakistan's members of National Assembly to get support for *Sharif*. It was not made clear when the offer was made but *Nawaz Sharif* was out of power when *Benazir Bhutto* was the Prime Minister. It appears that Ahmed's reference pertains to 1990 elections when Pakistan's intelligence agencies were accused of propping up an alliance called IJI headed by *Sharif* to defeat *Bhutto*. *Laden* was a big supporter of IJI.

Both as an act of provocation and as a 'rehearsal' for 9/11 attacks, *al-Qaeda* supreme *Laden* ordered to destroy the giant *Buddha* statues in *Bamiyan*. The two figures were carved into the side of a mountain more than 1,500 years ago. The Taliban chief *Mullah Omar* and the Afghans in *Bamiyan* opposed the demolition.

Khalid Shaik Mohammad, the mastermind behind the September 11 attacks described *al-Qaeda* as an almost mystically efficient corporation that operated in ways American would never understand. The portly Kuwaiti, who had studied engineering in the U.S and was captured in Pakistan in 2003 told his interrogators that "you must study these matters to know the huge difference between the Western mentality in administration and the Eastern mentality, specifically at al-Qaeda." The hallmark of the system, he said, was unquestioned control. Everyone up the chain of command did as they were told, did not ask questions and never bucked authority-all for the common cause, which in this case was killing as many Americans as possible". Yet *Mohammad* described a terrorist outfit fraught with the conflicts and petty animosities which plagued the corporations. *Mohammad* stated that he was usually compelled to do whatever bin Laden wanted with respect to operatives for the September, 11 operations. *Mohammad* noted that he disobeyed bin Laden on several occasions by taking operatives assigned to him and using them how he best saw it. His independence from bin Laden had its limits, however, because it was the *al-Quaed's* money and operatives that enabled the plot to go ahead. *Mohammad* succeeded in rejecting three attempts by bin *Laden* to accelerate the plot. But he said his boss cancelled an entire overseas element of the hijacking scheme that he was orchestrating. The seeds of conflict were planted at the beginning, when *Mohammad* first presented his idea in 1996 to hijack U.S planes and fly them into buildings., He said that he specifically suggested that they send "mujahedin" to study in the flight institutes and use large planes, rather than the smaller military ones that *al-Qaeda* operatives were trained in flying. This was rejected by bin Laden as he viewed unworkable. Three years, later, bin Laden summoned *Mohammad* to Afghanistan and gave the green light. Soon *Shaik Mohammad* moved his family from Pakistan to an *al-Qaeda* base in *Kandahar*, Afghanistan to proceed with the operation.

Pakistan has no information on where bin Laden could be hiding. According to their Interior Minister, Pakistan's efforts to fight terrorism were not focused on just trapping *bin Laden* but to curb terrorism in all its forms and manifestations. Hoodwinking the security forces, *bin Laden* has called for the killing of people who ridiculed the *Prophet Mohammad*, weighing into the furor that erupted after a Danish newspaper ran cartoons lampooning Islam's Holy Messenger. "Heretics and atheists, who denigrate religion and transgress against God and his *Prophet*, will not stop their enmity towards Islam except by being killed".

Moussaoui was sentenced in a U.S Court to life in prison with no chance to release for the September 11 attacks. The speaker who sounded like *Laden* on a website audiotape released said that *Zacarias Moussaoui* had nothing to do with the operations. On 23rd May,'06 *bin Laden* said he had personally assigned tasks to 19 hijackers who staged the attacks on U.S cities which killed about 3,000 people. "The truth is that he has no connection whatsoever with the events of September 11. I am certain of what I say because I was responsible for entrusting the 19 brothers.... with the raids". The U.S officials confirmed that the audio recording was authentic and the voice was indeed of Osama bin Laden.

With a heavy heart, the U.S President George *Bush* joined thousands across the country in observing the fifth anniversary of the September 11 attacks with all faith prayers, wreath laying ceremonies and silent marchers in the areas hit by the terrorists. The two day commemoration ceremonies began with President *Bush* and First *Lady Lara Bush* laying two wreaths of red, white and blue flowers in reflecting pools at the sites where the *WTC's* twin towers once adorned and reflecting as the wreaths drifted. The two also attended a prayer at St..Paul Chapel, visited a fire station overlooking the pit left by fallen towers to show their appreciation for the work that the first responders did and remember hundreds of them who died as the structures collapsed. They walked down the long ramp hand-in-hand but without uttering a word to the site of the pools which were five stories below ground level with police lining both sides and bagpipes striking a solemn tune. After emerging from the firehouse, *Bush* said that "he is approaching the anniversary with a heavy heart" as he recalled those lost their lives. He also called the day one for renewing resolve. I vowed that am never going to forget the lessons of that day."

Al-qaeda warned in a video aired on the fifth anniversary of the September 11 attacks that U.S allies and the Gulf Arab States would be its next target in a campaign that would seal the West's economic doom. Deputy *al-Qaeda* leader *Zawahiri* said in a remarks apparently addressed to the Western leaders; "I tell them do not bother yourselves with defending your forces in Iraq and *Afghanistan.* These forces are doomed to failure. You have to bolster your defenses in two areas – the first is the Gulf, from which you will be evicted, God willing, after your defeat in Iraq and then your economic doom will be achieved", he said in the video broadcast in part on the Arabic *al-Jazeera* television channel." And the next target is Israel. The current of holy war is closing on it and your end there will put an end of the Zionist-crusader supremacy".

Jawahiri's warning of attacks to the Gulf, the world's top oil exporting region, follows previous calls by *al-Qaeda* leader Laden to target oil facilities to cripple the west. *Al-Qaeda* had also in the past branded the U.S-allied governments in the Middle East as infidels and traitors, and has used this collusion with the West to justify their attacks. Gulf Arab leaders all had strong ties with Washington and Saudi-born *bin Laden* has in the past singled out the Saudi Royal family for censure. The Saudi wing of *al-Qaeda* launched in 2003 a campaign of shootings and suicide bombings, many targeting foreigners to topple the house of Saudi.

In the video, *Zawahiri* urged Muslims to step up attacks against the U.S and the West, according to excerpts aired by CNN television network. It quoted *Zawahiri* as saying that 'new events' were on the way. "Your leaders are hiding from you the true extent of the disaster", *Zawahiri* said. The video appeared to be part of *al-Qaeda* commemoration of the September 11 attacks.

President *Bush* said capturing *Laden*, who has eluded a U.S manhunt since the September 11 attacks five years ago (from 11-9-2001 to 11-9-2006) still mattered. "Of course. It matters. He is the head of *al-Qaeda*," The hunt continues for Laden and his deputy *Zawahiri*," *Bush* said. "And we will get him. It's just a matter of time. We've got a unit in the CIA who is spending a lot of time thinking about those high-value targets" he added.

Osama bin Laden is a household name in the U.S and on the FBI's "ten most wanted list" but his name does not officially figures in the 9/11 terrorist attacks. There is a legal reason why the FBI has not formally put bin *Laden's* name to the 9/11 attacks. *David Kelly* a former U.S attorney in *New York* said that "it might seem a little strange from the outside, but it makes sense from a legal point of view. .If I were in government, I'd be troubled if I were asked to put up a wanted picture where no formal charges had been filed. According to the FBI notice bin Laden is a suspected mastermind of the deadly American embassy bombings of 1998, but is not listed which means that the justice department is not seeking criminal charges for the "most notorious": and perhaps spectacular terror hit of 9/11, or at least to the end of31st August,2006. "The absence has also provided fodder for conspiracy theorists who think that U.S government or another power was behind the September 11 hijackings. From this point of view, the lack of a September 11 reference suggests that the connection to *al-Qaeda* is uncertain". There is no mystery here. They could add 9/11 on there, but they have not because they don't need to at this point." FBI spokesman Rex Tomb said.

Osama bin Laden was put on the ten most wanted list in June 1999 after being indicted for murder, conspiracy and other charges in connection with the embassy bombings, and a $5 million reward was put on his head at that time. After 9/11, the reward money was upped to $25 million, but the terrorist attacks were not officially mentioned. "The indictments currently listed on the posters allow them to be arrested and brought to justice," the FBI said. "Future indictments may be handed down as various investigations proceed in connection to other terrorist indictments, for example, the terrorist attacks on 9/11".

In a rare face off, President *Bush* had threatened to send American forces in pursuit of *Laden*, inviting a firm refusal by President *Musharaff* who said his troops were capable of doing the job themselves. Responding to a question if he would order U.S forces to go after bin *Laden* in Pakistan if he received good intelligence on the fugitive *al-Qaeda* leader's location, Bush in an interview in CNN said on 20th September '06 'absolutely'. "We would take action necessary to bring him to justice", said *Bush*, who met Musharaff at the White House in the last week of September '06. Bush, praised the Pakistani President for his efforts to dismantle *al-Qaeda* terror network.

France's Defense Ministry on 23rd September, '06 issued the statement after the French regional newspaper *L,est Republican* said that Saudi Arabia was convinced *bin Laden* had died of typhoid in Pakistan in the month of August, '06 The Information published on 23rd September morning in the *L,est Republican* newspaper relating to the supposed death of *Osama bin Laden* cannot be confirmed." the Defense Ministry said.

Saudi Arabia said on 24th September, 06 it had no evidence that Laden had died shedding further doubt on a secret document leaked in France. Saudi Embassy in Washington, however, issued a statement saying :"the Kingdom of Saudi Arabia has no evidence to support recent media reports that *Laden* is dead. Information that has been reported otherwise is purely speculative and cannot be independently verified." There was skepticism about whether Riyadh was well placed to be the first to pick up on such a development. "If anyone was in the picture, I doubt it would be Saudi intelligence." Even if Saudi Arabia had information, they'd pass it on to the United States, not France, It didn't ring true. .A U.S intelligence source said Washington, which has made capturing Laden a priority in its war on terrorism, had no evidence the report was any more credible than earlier rumours of his demise. "We have heard these things before and have no reason to think this is any different." The British Prime Minister Tony Blair said "No I can't. I have not heard anything that indicates that might be the case." French President *Jacques Chirac* told reporters bin Laden's death "has not been confirmed in any way whatsoever and so I have no comment to make".

Previous 'Dead'rumours

2001 he Pakistan *Observer* newspaper said in December that "*bin Laden* died of lung disease, been buried in Tora Bora, and his grave leveled in line with the beliefs of Wahabi Sect.

2002 " Essam Darez, an Egyptian freelance writer who spent time with Laden in Afghanistan between 1986 and 1990, said in an interview that "ninety-nine percent certain he was killed"

2002 Pakistan in January described as absurd a report that "*Laden* secretly underwent dialysis in a Pakistani hospital a day before the September 11 attacks on U.S.

2003 Pakistan's President *Pervez Musharaff* said in an interview that "intelligence services believed Laden was dead. It is an assessment, not proven proof"

Dubai-based al-Arabiya television on 26th September,'06 quoted a Taliban official as saying *al-Qaeda* leader *Laden* was alive. *Al-Arabiya* channel promised more details in a subsequent bulletin. France, the United States and Britain all said that they were unable to confirm the report in the French regional daily *L'est Republican*, which quoted of a document, from the DGSE foreign intelligence service.

Brushing aside a French intelligence report that stated " bin Laden has died of typhoid," Pakistan President *Musharaff* said that "intelligence input suggested that the *al-Qaeda* leader is hiding in the eastern Afghan province of Kunar, possibly with the help of the warlord *G.Hekmatyr.* "It is not a hunch. Kunar borders on Bajaur agency. We have moved some army elements. We did strike them twice there. We located and killed a number of them". he said on 29th September,'06. The popular belief is that bin Laden is still alive and he is an invisible object with mysterious powers. Therefore, the U.S Senate disturbed over the upsurge in terrorism doubled the price on the head of *bin Laden.* The Senate called for a reward of $50 million for the "capture or information leading to the capture" of the al-qaeda leader.

5

Trail of Terrorists

FATHER OF FARAJ FROM LIBYA

Pakistani security agency sources told the *'News line'*, North African *Abu Faraj-al–libby*, described as more dangerous than the terrorist mastermind bin Laden and his deputy *Al Zawahiri*. According to '*News line*' Libby had taken over the command of *al-Qaeda* operations worldwide, especially in the U.S. and the United Kingdom. According to the Pakistani Security Agency the debriefing of several dozen militants captured in Pakistan had resulted in identifying *Abu Faraj al-Libby*. "Every time we interrogate a militant linked to *al-Qaeda, al Libby's* name comes up". The sources further said not only did *al-Libby* orchestrate major terrorist acts on Pakistan soil, including the suicide attack on Prime Minister *Shaukat Aziz*, he was also the man behind sending coded messages to *al-Qaeda* sleeper cells in the U.S. and the U.K. through computer whiz *Mohammad Naeem Noor Khan*, who was arrested in July, 2004. The coded messages deciphered revealed that not only *al-Libby* co-ordinating pre-election terrorist acts in the United States, but he had also sent messages to several militants in the U.K. in the months from January to March, 2004 sharing notes about future terrorist attacks in Britain. At least two or three U.K. based militants were believed to have traveled to Pakistan and held meeting with *al-Libby* to finalize these attacks. Agency officials said *al-Libby* was believed to have worked under *Khalid Sheikh Mohammad, al-Qaeda's* operational head for the 9/11 attacks, as his deputy, as well as heading al-Qaed's North African operations. *Al-Libby* took over after *Mohammad* was captured from Rawalpindi in March, 2003 "*Al-Libby* was immediately elevated to the terror network's top position because he was *Mohammad's* right hand man and trusted by *bin Laden*" the sources said. Drawing parallels between him and his predecessor, counter-terrorism experts say *al-Libby* is less dangerous than *Khalid Sheikh Mohammad*, but more dangerous than *Laden* or *Zawahiri*. "He is less dangerous than *Mohammad* who had lived in the West and was familiar with the chemistry of these regions, while *al-Libby* had no exposure to the Western World" a Pakistani official said. However, he said al-Libby "is more dangerous than *bin Laden* or *Zawahiri* because both of them are confined to underground concentrating only on ensuring the secrecy of their where about while *al-Libby* is constantly in touch with al-Qaed's sleeper cells, providing them with back-up and financial assistance to carry out their missions." Pakistan announced a reward of Rs.20 million for capture of al-Libby, meaning '*Father of Faraj from Libya*'.

On 14th December, 2003 President *Musharaff* narrowly escaped when a powerful explosion rocked a bridge in a heavily guarded military area in Rawalpindi just seconds after his motorcade had passed. The explosion was delayed by electronic jammers which were of President *Musharaff's* convey. He survived a second attempt by the same area on the 25th of December, 2003. Therefore, the Government of Pakistan had launched a manhunt for Libyan born *al-Qaeda* operative Abu *Faraj Al-Libby*, who allegedly masterminded the attacks and offered a hefty sum of Rs.3.45 lakh for information leading to his arrest. According to Pakistani officials, *Libby* is one of the most-wanted men in Pakistan. Libby's close associate and an activist of the banned Islamic militant group, *Jaish-e-Muhammad, Amjad Hussain Farooqui* was killed on September

26, 2004 in Nawabshaw in Pakistan. *Farooqi* was blamed for his close association with *Libby* in attacks on President *Musharaff*. A military jawan, Islamuddin was sentenced to death while havaldar *Younis* was awarded with 10 years hard labor in prison after the military court found them guilty of attempting to blow up the bridge on which President *Musharaff* convoy passed near Rawalpindi on the 14th of December 2003.

Libya was also in the news when the top nuclear scientist and father of Pakistan's atomic bomb *Abdul Qadeer Khan* has clandestinely sold nuclear gear to Libya worth $ 100 million and blue prints for a 10-kiloton nuclear bomb. The U.S. experts were unsure who else had those designs besides Libya. They were not certain if the designs had also been passed on to Iran, Syria or *al-Qaeda*. The U.S. Intelligence learnt the full details of the transactions in 2004, when the Libyans handed over two large plastic bags with the names of an Islamabad tailor on one side, and a dry cleaner on other, one of the several clues that it had come from *Khan* laboratories. The design inside included drawings of more than 100 parts, all fitting in a sphere about 34 inches in diameter, just the right size for a rocket. According to the report, nearly a year after *Dr. Khan's arrest*, secrets of his nuclear black market continued to uncoil, revealing a vast global enterprise. The report alleged that the Dutch company where *Dr. Khan* worked, as well as the Dutch intelligence, were suspicious of the scientist and viewed him as a potential danger and had wanted to arrest him. Intelligence experts believed that *Dr.Khan* traded his centrifuge technology to the Chinese for their bomb design.

Dr. Khan, the disgraced top nuclear scientist was under house detention since early part of 2004 after his admission that he proliferated nuclear technology to Libya, Iran and North Korea. He was subsequently pardoned by President *Musharaff* and the Pakistan government rejected demands by the International Atomic Energy Agency to question him. Instead the Pakistan government offered to provide the results of its own investigations to the I.A.E.A. They, therefore, barred over a dozen scientists and staff of the Khan Research Laboratories, who were under investigation for proliferating nuclear technology to other countries and from traveling outside Islamabad without permission. The order included not meeting or exchanging any information with any foreigner. The 'suspects' of alleged transfer of nuclear technology had been asked to remain prepared for appearing before the investigation teams.

Abu Libby who was avoiding arrest for the past two to three years had at last been arrested. *Sheik Rashid Ahmed*, Minister for Information, Pakistan said that Pakistan authorities arrested al-Qaeda No.3 commander – a close associate of *Osama bin Laden* with a $10 million bounty on his head on the 2nd of May, 2005 after a fierce gun battle with Pakistani commandos on the outskirts of Mardan, 50 km northeast of Peshawar. *Al-Libby* a Libyan who authorities believe master minded two attempts to assassinate President Pervez Musharaff was most senior operational commander in *al-Qaeda*, behind only *bin Laden* and his top deputy *Ayman al-Zawahiri*. He believed to be responsible for planning attacks abroad, including on the U.S. This arrest gave Pakistan a lot of tips, and their security agencies were on the right track in the hunt for *bin Laden*, as *Al-Libby* knew many people and many hideouts. The American official said that relationship between al-Libby and *bin Laden* predated the 9/11 attacks, and *al-Qaeda's* inception in the 1990s. Pakistani Intelligence officials said that *al-Libby* was one of the two foreigners arrested on 2nd May, 2005 after the Mardan firefight. Along with the above two eleven more terror suspects – three Uzbeks, an Afghan and seven Pakistanis were arrested on the same day in a tribal region. *Al-Libby* reportedly spent time in South Waziristan, a tribal region along the Afghan border that was considered a likely hideout for *bin Laden* and No.2 *al-Zawahiri*.

Abu Farray al-Libbi, the reputed No.3 and closest associate of *Osama Bin Laden* was arrested on 2-5-2005 in a quite dramatic fashion. Auto mechanic *Bakth Munir* was sitting alone in a private guesthouse in thc bustling town in northwestern Pakistan, when a bearded man with a pistol in his hand climbed in through the low roof. "I am a *jihadi* Police are after me" the man gasped in the local Pashto language before locking himself inside a room, not waiting for a reply. *Munir* didn't know it at the time but the, *jihadi* or 'holy warrior', was Pakistan's most wanted man, Abu Farraj al-Libby who was evading arrest for more than two years. Minutes after the Libyan terrorist entered the house, armed police and intelligence *jihadi* agents rushed into the house and asked Munir, a 32 year old local man, whether he had seen anybody come in. "I signaled towards the room". When the police rounded of the guesthouse *Al-Libby* refused to come out, so police fired tear gas shells through a window, forcing him out. With his pistol in one hand and a handkerchief in the other to cover his streaming tears, *al-Libby* emerged, muttering prayers. Then, the Police disarmed him, confiscated his mobile phone and then led away, his head hooded.

The U.S. agents and Pakistan authorities interrogated *al-Faraz Abu Libby* after his arrest. He was kept in the custody of the Pakistan Government and was not handed over to anyone else. *Abu al-Libby's* arrest was very vital in helping several links between the terror network's members and central command. The Pakistan President said on 15th May 2005 "we have broken their back. They cease to exist as a cohesive, homogeneous body under good command. Whatever they are now capable of doing individual and group actions divorced from central command and co-ordinated centrally. They are on the run in the mountains, not in contact with each other". Although the arrest of *Abu Libby* had not led investigators to *bin Laden*, it had led to other key arrests in Saudi Arabia and Abu Dhabi.

ZACARIAS MOUSSAOUI

Zacarias Moussaoui's sentencing trial opened on 6th March,'06 with the selection of a jury that will determine whether he is put to death for conspiring with *al-Qaeda* terrorists to hijack planes and commit other crimes. *Moussaoui*, a thirty-seven- year-old French citizen, has acknowledged his loyalty to the *al-Qaeda* terrorist network and his intent to commit acts of terrorism but denied any prior knowledge of the September, 11 plot. His mother, *Aicha el-Wari*, spoke up for her son in an interview. She said that "all they can have against him is the things that he said, the words that he has used. But actual acts that he committed, there are not any."

Zacarias Moussaoui was only person charged in the United States in connection with the September, 11 attacks. He revealed that he was supposed to fly a fifth plane into the White House as part of the September, 11 plot and he knew that two planes were to fly into the *World Trade Center* in New York Taking the stand at his death penalty trail Moussaoui disclosed that "shoe bomber *Richard Reid* was to join him as part of the crew in the suicide mission. *Reid* failed in attempt to blow up an American Airlines plane from Paris to Miami in December, 2001 after passengers and crew tackled him as he tried to ignite explosives in his shoe. He was sentenced to life imprisonment in January, 2003.

Moussaoui contradicted what he said in 2005 in pleading guilty, that he was not supposed to be part of the September 11 hijackings but was meant to be in a second wave of attacks and fly on airplane into the White House. When he was asked whether he was meant to be part of the September, 11 attacks, *Moussaoui* replied that "I was supposed to pilot a plane to hit the White House." He further revealed that he did not know the precise date of the planned attacks when he was arrested in Minnesota on 16th August, 2001, and had scant details of the overall plan. He said that "I had knowledge that the two towers would be hit but I did not have the detail." He further told that he had not seen any of the other hijackers in the United States.

Moussaoui said he had no regrets for those who died in the hijacked plane attacks and told jurors in his death penalty trail he wished "there would be more pain". He expressed disgust with family members of victims who shared their grief in the courtroom. "In order to get the death of someone else we wanted you to have pain in your country." *Moussaoui* said during two-and-a half hours of testimony at his sentencing trail, "I just wish it would have happened September, 12, September, 13, September, 14. There is no remorse for justice." Asked by the prosecutor if he had any regrets about the attacks in which nearly 3,000 people died, *Moussaoui* replied, "no regret, no remorse." He also said he had enjoyed images in Court showing the *Pentagon* after it was attacked on September 11 and said reports of all the deaths 'make may day', His comments prompted tears from a distraught family member of one victim who eventually got up and left the courtroom. *Moussaoui*, 37 who pleaded guilty to six counts of conspiracy in connection with the September,11 attacks, also pulled back from statements made after he was indicted in late 2001 that indicated he would welcome a death sentence. His lawyer showed him a filing he made to the court in August 2002 in which he said the greatest *jihad* in Islam is to speak the truth in front of the tyrant and be executed for it." *Moussaoui* said he no longer wanted to include 'and be executed' part of that statement, because he had consulted Islamic books and decided that violated Muslim religion beliefs. When *Moussoui* pleaded in '05 he vowed to fight the death penalty.

Taking the stand for the second time at his sentencing trail against the advice of his lawyers, *Moussaoui* criticized his court-appointed defense team. He said their strategy should have included the argument that life in prison was a better punishment since execution would reward him with martyrdom. Defense Lawyers were trying to persuade the jury that *Moussaoui* was mentally unstable with delusions of importance in *al-Qaeda* and should not be sentenced to death. *Moussaoui* said in the Court in the month of March,2006 that he was supposed to fly a fifth plane into the White House as part of the *al-Qaeda* hijacking plot. This testimony contradicted his previous claims that not part meant to be part of the September 11 hijacking but was supposed to be in a second wave of attacks.

For is role in the September 11, 2001 terrorist attacks in the U.S.A the District Judge sent *Zacarias Moussaoui* to prison for life. *Moussaoui* is a French citizen of Morroccon origin and obtained Master's degree in International Business from the South Bank University in London. He attended Khalden training camp in Afghanistan in 1998 and attended flight training courses in the U.S from 26th February to 29th May,2001. On 16th August, 2001, *Moussaoui* was arrested by *Harry Samit* of the FBI in Minnesota and charged with an immigration violation. When he was sentenced to prison for life on 2nd May '06 to "die with a whimper for his role in September 11, attacks *Moussaoui* declared "God save *Osama bin Laden*, you will never forget him." He was sentenced to six life terms without the chance of parole. Moussaoui walked into the courtroom flashing a victory sign. He said that "God save *Osama bin Laden*, you will never forget him. You have branded me as a terrorist or criminal or whatever. Look at yourselves, I fight for my belief."

Kuwaiti Mehmood *Ahmed Mohammad*, alias *Omar Faruq* was one of the four *al-Qaeda* members who escaped from the Bagram airbase in July,2005. In his first comments on the escape, posted on-line on 28th Feb.'06 , he said that the stupidity of his guards enabled the escape. "God blinded our captors and aided our escape. Our enemies the Americans, kept us totally isolated from the *Afghan* prisoners and the prison guards were too busy playing computer games to prevent their escape, describing how the four men changed their clothes, left fake bodies under their bed clothes then left the cell said Omar Faruq.. He derided the stupidity and inattention of their jailer. *Al-Faruq* continued that he and his companions, Libyan *Mohammad Hassan*, Syrian *Abdullah Hashmi* and *Saudi Mohammad al-Qahtani* had hidden under parked cars outside the prison to evade prison guards and then in haystacks as the U.S soldiers sought to recapture them. He ended his comments with a warning to the United States. He warned that "you will never be able to stop the march of the Mujahadeen. We will fight you here, in Afghanistan, in Iraq and throughout the world. .We will pursue you into your own homes.."

Hamid Hayat, charged with lying to the FBI and providing material support to terrorists by attending terrorist training camps in Pakistan. Hayat's father, *Umer*, 48 was also charged with lying to the FBI about his son's suspected attendance at the camps. The federal grand jury indictment in the case said that "*Hamid Hayat* intended to wage violent *Jihad* against persons and personal property in the United States."

The U.S and Iraqi forces had arrested *Hamed Juma Faris* al-Saudi, also known as *Abu Hummam* or *Abu Rana*, the second most senior figure in *al-Qaeda* in Iraq. He was the deputy to *Abu Ayyub al-Masri*, who took over the insurgent group after *Abu Musab al-Zarqawi* was killed in a U.S air strike in June, 2006. He was captured in the first week of September, 2006 when he was hiding in a building used by families. He wanted to use children and women as human shields as the U.S and Iraqi forces attempted to capture him.

6
Attack on Ayodhya

The *Temple of Sri Rama* at *Ayodhya* is a place of high reverence for Hindus. Any disturbance to the temple or the idols would lead mass and serious retaliatieon from all corners of the country. Islamic terrorists never concealed their irreverence for holy places of Hindu worship. The places of Hindu temples became their easy targets. This may perhaps, due to the fact, that the militants are seething with vengeance on the demolition of three domes of *Babri Masjid* on the 6th of December, 1992 by the Kar Sevaks. The Kar Sevaks not only demolished the three domes of the Masjid but also brought back and put the idols exactly where they stood for four decades. In retaliation of the above, the *Ragunath temple* in Jammu was attacked by the Islamic terrorists twice in 2002 in which seventeen people died. The same year *Aksharadam Temple* in Gujarat was attacked claiming the lives of thirty people. Year after year, the terrorists threatened to attack Hindu devotees trekking to *Amarnath* and *Vaishnovadevi* temples. Fortunately every time the brave and ever vigilant Indian Security forces foiled the ill-conceived plans of the terrorists.

On the morning of 5th July, 2005 also the bravery of CRPF men saved the day from a big calamity. At 8.00 a.m. on the 5th of July, o5 five men in the guise of pilgrims hired a Tata-Sumo at Akbarpur near Kichaucha. At Faizabad they abandoned the Tata Sumo and hired a jeep driven by *Rehan*

Alam who drove according to the directions given by them to drive them up to a point after which he was asked to move aside from the driving seat by the militants at gun point after which one of the terrorists drove the jeep to the site of incident. According to *Rehan*, when the vehicle reached Digamber Jain temple facing the Northern side of the iron railings the militants asked him to leave and triggered a blast in the jeep after getting down. He further told the police that the militants had thrown away the SIM card of his cell phone and threatened that they had a silence pistol and no one would hear if they opened fire at him. The driver further disclosed that he was nabbed by the police while he was trying to flee from the scene of the blast. *Rehan* Alarm passport indicated he once worked in Dammam, an oil rich region of Saudi Arabia.

Investigations revealed that they were not checked or frisked at the first security check. Once inside the first zone the vehicle drove up to second barrier and ran into the CRPF. Five of the terrorists then burst out with the guns. The fifth driving the vehicle blew himself up with the vehicle. He was acting as human bomb and explosives strapped on him. The terrorists had AK 47 and AK 56 assault weapons, twenty-five unexploded hand grenades plus a rocket launcher. The jeep which was blown into smithereens slammed into the first ring of the security wall near *Sita ki Rasoi*. From the breached portion three terrorists crossed the first security cordon and one terrorist threw a grenade while the others opened fire from AK 47 and AK 56. The *Sita ki Rasoi* is around 100 meters from the 2.77 acre disputed site. A Quick Response Team of CRPF took position behind *Sita ke Rasoi* and killed all the four terrorists. The operation took place for about ninety minutes. The swift operation by the Security force not only prevented the desecration of the make-shift *Ram Temple* at *Ramajanmabhoomi* Complex and the idol of *Ram Lala* but also saved a huge crowd of devotees congregated at the nearby *Hanuman Garhi Temple*. In order to save the make-shift temple and *Ram Lala* from the mad desire of the five terrorists three CRPF personnel sustained serious injuries.

The Congress President and the United Progressive Alliance Chairperson *Sonia Gandhi* condemning the terrorist attack said that the strike on the *Ayodhya temple* was an attack on the secular fabric of the country. She complemented the CRPF force which blunted the attack and averted a major incident.

Immediately after knowing the attack Prime Minister *Manmohan Singh* consulted the cabinet colleagues and reiterated his Government's resolve to deal firmly with all such acts of terrorism. He said that "it is fortunate that the attack was foiled. It is also fortunate that no damage occurred. The Government views the incident as serious one". Condemning the abortive bid by the terrorists to attack the make-shift *Ram Temple* Pakistan voiced its opposition to all forms of terrorism and asserted that the incident would not have any impact on the Indo-Pak peace process.

Among the six killed on the 5th of July, 2005 in the terrorist attack one was recognized as *Ramesh Pandey*, a local guide who was living adjacent to the temple. His family claimed the body and his nephew *Venkatesh Pandey* told that he recognized the dead body of Ramesh Pandey from the watch, chappals and clothes on his mutilated body. His family operated as guides and approached visitors coming to the temple town. *Ramesh Pandey* did the same on the fateful day when he saw the jeep and must have been killed when the militants blew it up.

Preliminary probe revealed that the militants who carried out the attack on the make-shift temple complex at the disputed site in *Ayodhya* had undertaken a recce of the area before they struck. This came to light during the interrogation of the two arrested drivers, *Rehan* and *Raj Kumar*, who drove the vehicles carrying the militants from Akbarpur in Uttar Pradesh to Faizabad, near *Ayodhya*, and then to the temple complex. According to them the militants guided them to the complex, indicating they knew the route to their destination. The two drivers told that the militants spoke in some unknown language. The probe also divulged that the militants visited the state capital Lucknow on 3rd July, 2005 to buy bags for carrying arms and explosives. From the two visiting cards found in the pockets of the slain militants in was disclosed that the three militants had bought some bags for carrying arms, ammunition and explosives to the complex for launching the attack on 5th July. The shopkeeper has identified the photographs of the militants and confirmed that they had bought bags from his shop.

The investigators' job became difficult as no group has claimed responsibility for the attack and the other belongings recovered from the slain militants did not throw much light on their identity. Even as the detained jeep driver Rehan was subjected to intense interrogation by security agencies for leads in the terrorist attack his family pleaded his innocence. "My husband is innocent. In fact no Muslim living in *Ayodhya* has anything to do with terrorists" Rehan's wife *Uzma* said in a hysterical tone. However, she added that "it would not pain me even if my husband is shot dead after being found guilty". *Rehan's* uncle said that the only fault of his nephew was that he did not enquire much about the terrorists when they hired his jeep at the taxi stand on 5th July before the attack.

Security agencies have raised questions over the security within Ayodhya. They pointed that the terrorists roamed the town with a huge armoury without being detected and reached within twenty-five yards of *Lord Ram's idol.* It was suspected that the driver *Raj Kumar* who brought the five militants from Akbarpur to *Ayodhya* and attacked the make shift temple in Ayodhya might have entered India possibly via Nepal. The investigators suspected that there must have been some more bags which could have been contained something to identity the terrorists which were not found. They, however, recovered a pocket-sized *Holy Koran* published in Delhi from the slain terrorists and caps which show that these had been purchased in Nepal which indicated that they had come via the Himalayan kingdom. The two AK rifles recovered from the terrorists bore the initials "T A K". A T-shirt worn by a terrorist had 'Khushaab'.

I In a major break through in the terror strike at the make-shift temple in *Ayodhya*, police burst a *Lashkar-e-Toiba* module behind the attack and arrested five of its cadres from Mendhar in *Jammu and Kashmir*. These persons have provided logistical support for the *L-e-T* militants who carried out the attack at the temple. The police seized two Tata Sumos used for transporting them and the weapons from Poonch to Uttar Pradesh. The Police officials revealed that "a total of eight militants, all hailing from Mendhar Tehsil in Poonch district had helped five Lakshar Fidayeens in the attack. Out of eight, five were arrested on 15th of July, 2005 while three others were absconding. The arrested were identified as *Farooq Ahmed* of Patta Kar village working at a popular Shahdara Sharief shrine (Rajouri), *Mohd.Naseem* of Dera Jattan village, Adbul Aziz of Patti Dara village, *Shakeel Ahmed* and *Musthaq Ahmed* of Derrain Village. The three absconding militants were *Mohd.Akbar* of Sakhi Maidan, *Abu Usman* and *Abu Salam*. A couple of women were also said to be involved in the conspiracy. The two vehicles used for transporting the militants and the weapons were seized, of which, one was driven by Farooq Ahmed for carrying the weapons. Police sources further disclosed that the militants who attempted to attack the temple were speaking Sindhi or Baloch dialects.

The Uttar Pradesh police confirmed the fact that the plot to blow up the makeshift *Ram Temple* in *Ayodhya* was hatched by *Lashkar-e-Toiba* in Pakistan, and the entire operation was masterminded by the Pakistan terror group's Jammu area commander *Mohammad Kari*. Planning for the attack began in August, 2004 when the terrorists snuck into

Delhi. At the beginning of third week of July, 2005 the U.P. Police Special Task Force (STF) had identified two *fidayeen* out of the five assailants killed in the attack in *Ayodhya* on 5th July, 2005 and they were Pakistani nationals. *Yunus*, one of the militants killed in the attack reached Delhi on 25-06-2005 and took a house on rent near *Vasant Kunj* and subsequently took another house on rent in the neighborhood and made several recess of *Ayodhya* and its vicinity. The second slained militant stayed in Akbarpur and Faizabad for fifteen days in May, 2005.

In the first week of June, 2005 arms for operation were carted from an *L-e-T* base in *Jammu and Kashmir* to Panipat, Harayana from where the Delhi-based cell picked it up. *Dawood* and *Omar* two lieutenants of L-e-T area Commander *Mohammad Kari*, gave one lakh rupees to *Farooq* and *Nadeem* to deliver weapons and ammunition. *Farooq* tucked five AK 47 rifles and explosives into a secret compartment in a Tata Sumo and drove to Panipet, where the Delhi-based terrorists received it. In the last week of June, 2005 members of the *fidayeen* squad left Delhi and assembled at Akbarpur. From Akbarpur they reached Lucknow and bought bags to carry their arsenal. They reached Faizabad on 4th July, 2005 and tried to attack the make-shift temple of *Ramajanmabhoomi* on the morning of 5th July, 2005 where they were killed by the alert Police force.

In connection with terror attack in *Ayodhya*, the Police picked up on 22nd July, '05 *Dr.Irfan Khan*, a Unani Doctor, practicing in Sangam Vihar area of Delhi. *Khan* had been in touch with the terrorists and they had also made seven calls to him from Akbarpur. The terrorist identified as *Amin alias Zuber* had visited Nakud on 20th March, 2005 to attend the wedding of his cousin. *Khan* and *Zuber* then visited Deoband. On their way back the duo had stayed in Muzaffarnagar with one *Abdul Rehman*, and also at Nakud. According to him the doctor was aware of the terrorists' plans. The terrorists had made seven calls to.Khan during their stay in Akbarpur in May, 2005. The police also located a hideout of the terrorists in Akbarur from where they were suspected to have traveled to Faizabad-Ayodhya to carry out the attack on 5th July, 2005.

The Uttar Pradesh police identified on 24th July, 2005 the mastermind behind the attack on *Ramjanmabhoomi* in *Ayodhya.* He is a twentyeight year old six-feet tall Pakistani National named *Mahmood.* Mahmood spent some time with the five terrorists, who were gunned down in the Ayodhya attack on 5th July, 2005. He, in fact, was *Younus* roommate. *Mehmood* is the only surviving member of the gang. He is most educated among the five terrorists who were killed. He orchestrated the attack and organized the weapons. *Mahmood* came to India in September, 2004 and got himself admitted as an English / speaking course in Munirka. He attended the classes for nearly three months, although he was quite fluent in the language. The police on 24th July, 2005 released sketches of Mahmood to apprehend him.

The Utter Pradesh Police had quietly buried the bodies of the five Pakistani terrorists at the small Tad ki Takia gravehard in Faizabad within 18 hours of the attack on *Ramajanambhoomi* on 5th July, 2005. "According to Hindu tradition in Ayodhya, the 14 km. 'parikrama (boundary) from the *Ram lalla* is the most holy area this includes the Ayodhya and Faizabad towns. Burying the terrorists inside this boundary area amounts to hurting Hindu sentiments" said senior Viswa Hindu Parishad leader. "We want immediate removal of these graves from Faizabad. Ask Pakistan to claim the bodies or bury them elsewhere after....... all the terrorists have been identified now as Pakistanis' he added.

The Muslims too did not want their dead to be buried anywhere near these graves for they said their loved one would not rest in peace.

Khan, Unani doctor from Saharnur who runs a clinic in Delhi's Sangam Vihar knew about the plans of the *Lashkar-*

e-Toiba terrorists to storm the make-shift temple in *Ayodhya*. The interrogation of *Ifran Khan*, revealed that he was the only person to whom the terrorists disclosed their plans. They told him: "*Unhone masjid giarai thi hum mandir girayange. Aap bhi hamare saath ho lijiye*". *Khan* reportedly admitted that the terrorists had repeatedly told him about the *Babri Masjid* demolition and the injustice meted out to Muslims and that they wanted to take "revenge" I advised them not to go ahead and told them that I was not with them in this. But they were highly motivated and seething with anger, especially after they returned to Delhi in June, 2005 after seeing the *Babri Masjid* ruins." According to the investigating authorities Khan knew the mind of the attackers all this while. The terrorists, in fact, used to sit at his house each evening talking about *Jihad* and *Babri Masjid*. It was surprising that why a *fidayeen* group trusted him so much and divulged their attack plan to him. Had he informed the police, they could have nabbed the terrorists alive". In the interrogation report *Khan* said that "they were all young and hot-blooded. I regret that I never told the police about their plans which I saw it on TV, I knew it had to be them." *Khan's* clinic was opposite to the house where the terrorists stayed in Delhi"s Deoli since August, 2004. *Khan* knew of the movements of the terrorists. There were phone calls from the terrorists to the doctor till the end of June, 2005. The doctor even took one of the terrorists Zuber on his motorcycle to his cousin's wedding at his native place Nakud in Saharanpur, on 20th March,2005. On one occasion, they also stayed together in Muzaffarnagar.

During a detailed interrogation by central security agency on the five persons arrested, it was found that it was J-e-M and not *L-e-T* behind the failed attack on the Ram Janambhoomi temple at *Ayodhya*. Though the concerned police authorities were trying hard to piece together their stories of Lashkar being involved in the attack, several leads clearly indicated involvement of *J-e-M* in the attack which included evidences gathered by central agencies that *Mohammad Kari*, the absconding mastermind was the local commander of *J-e-M* and not of Lashkar.

During investigation, it was found that one of the five militants killed during the attack on 5th July, 2005 had visited Deoband and had stayed there. *J-e-M* is headed by *Masood Azhar*, who was released in 1999 in exchange of hijacked passengers of IC-814. He had mentioned attack on the Ram Temple in his diary when he was arrested in the mid-90's. The arrested militants stated that it was one of the unfulfilled dreams of *Azhar* to attack the sanctum sanctorum of the *Ram temple* at *Ayodhya* and one of the important tasks of J-e-M formed after breaking away from *Harkat-ul-Mujahideen*.

Aasif Iqbal alias *Farooq* who was arrested along with *Shakil* in the month of June, 2006 revealed that he carried four AKs-47 an AK-56, Chinese hand-grenades and a rocket launcher o Ayodhya in a Sumo. He told the police that *Adnaan*, a Sindh-based terrorist handed him the weapons and explosives at Srinagar's Lal Chowk in the early hours of 2nd June 2005. *Farooq*, who worked as a teacher in a government school in Mendhar village told the police that on *Mohammad Qari's* order, he bought the Sumo from *Shakil* for Rs. 2.2 lakhs. *Adnaan* was the second-in-command of *Mohammad Qari* the L-e-t commander who masterminded the attack. *Farooq* further disclosed that he met the terrorists in Panipat but did not deliver them the weapons. A call from *Qari* made him to drive to Aligarh where he handed the weapons to a girl in a house behind the Aligarh Muslim University. He reached Aligarh on the evening of 5th June 2005 and visited the house through a narrow road. He parked the vehicle at a distance. He further disclosed that a girl received him at the door. When it was dark he fetched the weapons from the Sumo in a bag given to him by the girl and kept it in one of the rooms and left for Srinagar after dinner at the House. Police were in search of the girl and *Musthaq* a Pak National who used to stay with her. It was *Musthaq* who delivered weapons to the terrorists in Aligarh, which came from across the Line of Control.

Investigations into the 5th July attack in *Ayodhya* showed that *Arshad Ali* and *Asif* (the two militants involved in the attack) had hired a house in Shejadpur locality of Akbarpur town in Ambedkhar Nagar District and later purchased a cycle and sold pan-masala and match boxes on the roads leading to Faislabad. This was done only to cover up their recce exercise at the *Ramjanambhoomi Temple*. Some of the people, who had purchased *pan-masala* from the slain militants, had identified the pictures of the bodies of the ultras after the *Ayodhya* attack.

Ali had purchased a Hutch SIM card from Sultanpur where he described himself as a retail seller of *pan-masala*. The same SIM card proved essential during the investigations into the case. The Central Security Agencies had also found that the sixth militant could be *Jaish-e-mohammad* local commander *Mohammad Kari*, whose description was made with the help of computer sketches. Kari had infiltrated into the country through Surankote sector and had stayed in Jammu region before moving to Delhi. Kari was believed to have visited Ayodhya and Akbarpur and also gave necessary instructions to the militants who were to carry out the attack on the sanctum sanctorium.

7
Heinous Acts of Terror in Delhi

Over the years, Delhi has been the historical site of great violence. It was the natural target of those who wished to attack the democracy of India. After the serial blasts in Mumbai in 1993 the Pakistan-based Let militants headed by *Arif alias Ashfaq* waged a war against Government of India in December 2000. A Delhi Court awarded death sentence to L-e-t militant *Mohammad Arif*, alias *Ashfaq* on 31st October 2005 for the December 2000 attack on Red Fort. Ashfaq was fined Rs.4.35 lakhs under various sections of the Indian Penal Code for waging a war against the Government of India. Two Rajputana Rifles jawans and a civilian were killed in the attack. *Nazir Ahmed Qasid* and his son *Farooq Ahmed Qasid* were sentenced to life imprisonment and fined Rs.1,00,000/- (Rupees one Lakh). The father-son duo was found guilty of criminal conspiracy.

Ashfaq's wife, *Rehmana Yousuf Farooqi*, was sentenced to seven years rigorous imprisonment for sheltering her husband "before and after the incident". The court said "the offences were committed on account of her non-disclosure of the designs of *Mohammad Arif*" and directed *Farooqi* to pay Rs.20,000/- fine. The judge also sentenced *Babar Mohsin Baghwala*, *Sadaqat Ali* and *Mahboob Alam* to seven years" imprisonment for their complicity in the attack.

While the attention of the whole world was concentrated on the developments of war in *Afghanistan* after attacks on *World Trade Center* and *Pentagon* in the United States, five terrorists carrying deadly explosives and weapons in a camera bag drove in a stolen white Ambassador car with the Home Ministry car label and flashing a red beckon stormed the Parliament House in India on the 13th December 2001 leading to fourteen casualties, nine security personnel and five terrorists.

The terrorists with a view to disturb the successful government running on democratic process in *Jammu and Kashmir* rammed a Tata Sumo with a suicide bomber with explosives right into the main gate of the heavily fortified Assembly building of Jammu and Kashmir on 1st October 2001 killing 38 people.

With a view to take revenge on the United States who drove out *Talibans* from *Afghanistan*, the *American Center* at Kolkata's Chowrangee areas was sprayed by as many as fifty four bullets on the morning of 22nd January 2002 killing four policemen. In order to incite the Hindus, the militants attacked Swamy *Narayan Askharadam Temple* in Gujarat killing several pilgrims who came to offer prayers in the temple.

After the demolition of *Babri Masjid* some section of Muslims developed a revengeful attitude to attack *Sri Ram Temple at Ayodhya.* The temple is fortified by hundreds of security personnel all around the temple. For several months the militant's secretly worked out plans to attack on *Ayodhya* temple. On 5th July 2005 they ultimately tried to attack the temple, which was foiled by the alert security personnel killing on the spot all the terrorists involved in the misadventure.

The hearts of the militants are made of mud. When there was a devastating earth-quake on 8th October 2005 thousands of people were killed in Pakistan occupied Kashmir.. When the whole world was consoling the survivors and sending money, medicines and other essential articles, the militants killed many innocent people in *Jammu and Kashmir* just after the devastating earthquake.

On 29th October 2005, as if the history of Bombay bomb blasts 1993, has been repeated the terrorists again unleashed the unmerciful acts of terrorism in Delhi. Three powerful blasts timed to strike within minutes of each other killed at least 59 people while injuring 210. At around 5.40 p.m. on the fateful day the bombers ripped through the busy Pahadganj market near the New Delhi Railway Station. The market always frequented by backpack foreign tourists and was thronged with *Deepavali* and *Ramzan Id* shoppers. Eleven were killed. After five minutes the next explosion took place in South Delhi where a bomb placed in a bag in a chat and juice shop went off at around 5.45 p.m. killing instantaneously more than 37 people. Seven minutes later another explosion rocked Govindpuri injuring ten persons including the driver and conductor of a Delhi Transport Corporation. The bus was packed when the blast took place. The driver had saved innumerable lives on the bus as he threw the explosives device out of the vehicle hurting himself grievously.

Brazenly, the "*Inquilab*" group has claimed responsibility for the explosions and the group was connected to Pakistan-based *Lashkar-e-Toiba (L-eT)*. The "*Inquilab*" groups was formed in 1996 and was not active. It was no ordinary Kashmiri militant outfit. When IC-814 was hijacked to *Kandhahar* in 1999, the terrorists demanded that India release 36 jailed men and one of them was *Zulfikar Ali Shah*, head of the *Inquilab-e-Mahaz*. Shah, a Pakistani national from Hyderabad Sind, was arrested by security forces on 7th February 1993 after an encounter with the Army in Poonch sector and imprisoned in Jammu. A veteran of the Mujahideen's war against the Soviets in Afghanistan, *Shah* landed in India in 1992. Security forces picked up Inquilabi supporters in *Jammu and Kashmir* for questioning as the RDX-based device used in the serial blasts, had a mechanical timer and not an electronic device, which Laskar-e-Toiba men normally use.

A Paharganj *paanwallah* who saw and overheard a bomber was with the Delhi police in finding out the bomber in Paharganj. He revealed to the police that he heard the terrorist tell 35-years-old rickshaw puller to take the rickshaw till the chat stall. The bomber then got off from the rickshaw, leaving his bag behind. Barely ten meters from the *paan* stall and five minutes later, the bomb, went off killing the rickshaw puller and fifteen others. The second major lead the investigators got was from an eyewitness who had talked to second bomber wearing a red T-short on the Delhi Transport Corporation bus in Govindapuri. The passenger, in fact, had a brief altercation with the bomber who boarded the bus at *Kalikaji Mandir* stop and placed the black bag under the seat of a passenger which was hitting the passenger's feet. When the passenger asked the bomber to remove it, the bomber got of the bus and disappeared after which the conductor asked all the passengers to alight. The driver of the bus, however, threw the device out of the bus and saved the lives of number of people.

Ghulam Mohiddin Lone, aged 22 years was arrested by the police suspected to be involved in the Delhi blasts of 29th October 2005. As per the interrogation his job was confined of a carrier" of explosives used in the blasts. Lone did not meet any of the terrorists in the Sarojini Nagar and Govindapuri blasts. According to Lone the intended targets of the terrorists were first New Delhi Railway station and Jamai Nagar instead of Paharganj and the DTC Bus in which he carried explosives in an apple cart from Banihal to Delhi,. He then met three terrorists in Delhi's *Sanjay Gandhi* Transport Nagar on the morning of 28th October 2005 a day before the serial blasts. It seemed that he just supplied the explosives for the Paharganj blast and was paid Rs.20,000/- in return. He was specifically told not to return to Srinagar and even his head and beard were shaved off. He said the man whose portrait had been put out by the police was co-ordinating the entire plan sitting in Delhi. After the interrogation Lone had been sent back to *Jammu and Kashmir* and the Delhi Police picked up another man called Tariq from the Kashmir valley, a suspected Lashkar-e-Toiba operative, whom security agencies call a "crucial link" to information on the perpetrators of the blasts and the method used.

Tariq Ahmed Dar (33) of L-e-T operative unrivaled the execution of the worst-ever terrorist attack in the capital which left 71 dead and 210 injured. On 29th October the blasts carried out by *Dar* and his accomplices, *Abu Alqama and Abu Huzefa*, both Pakistani nationals and was indeed the handiwork of L-e-T. Dar was working as sales representatives with the *Johnson and Johnson*, and was the choreographer of the 29th October mayhem. *Alqama*, who operates from Pakistan, was the chief of *L-e-T* operations in the valley, while *Huzefa* was his subordinate. *Dar* familiar with the topography of Delhi, conducted a recce of the city in the first week of October, 2005 to select the sites at which to lace the RDX-laced timer devices. After the blasts, *Dar* quickly retreated to Srinagar and overwhelmed by the success of his mission committed the blunder of calling his bosses in Srinagar to brag. The indiscretion roved costly and the security agencies, already tracking the network communication, quickly zeroed in on *Dar*. *Dar* told the police that it was he who called up the Kashmir New Agency two days after the blasts to say that it was not the *L-e-T* but Islami *Inquilab Mehaz*, a non-descript outfit, that was responsible for the serial blasts in Delhi. *Dar* said he spread the lie to protect *L-e-T* from any opprobrium after it had done a lot of good work for the earthquake victims in Kashmir. The evidence against *Dar* included the transfer of Rs. 4.86 Lakhs to his Bank account in Srinagar from a West Asian country a week before the blasts.

The Gujarat police said that *Abu Huzefa* to be the mastermind of the Delhi blasts, was also involved in the

September 24, 2002 terrorist attack on Akshardham temple in Gandhinagar. *Abu Huzefa's* name figured in the charge sheet filed by the Detection of Crime Branch in the *Aksharadham case.* The conspiracy had been master-mined by *Huzefa and three other Lashkar and Jaish commanders. Huzefa* said that he was in charge of L-e-T's Srinagar operation. Another Lashkar commander, *Abu Alkama,* was in overall charge of the outfit's operations in Jammu and Kashmir. These two were involved in planning most of the attacks taken place in *Jammu and Kashmir.*

8

Twin Blasts Rock Varanasi (Kasi)

It was another Black Tuesday at *Varanasi* on 7th March,'06 after the attacks on *World Trade Center* on 11th September, 2001. This time, they had used pressure cookers to claim twenty lives and injuring another fifty. Terrorists especially attack the Hindu community and their temples. The Hindus are feeling completely unsafe. On 29th October, 2005, three blasts hit Delhi on the eve of *Diwali* where over sixty people were killed. Again on the eve of "*Holi*" twin blasts rocked Sankatmochan temple and railway station in Varanasi on 7th March,2006. At least 20 people were killed and another fifty injured when two bombs exploded in quick succession at Varanasis's *Sankatmochan Temple* and the city cantonment railway station. *Sankatmochan Temple*, at *Varanasis's Durga* Kund Road, is considered one of the three major temples of the city. The *temple of Hanuman*, built in early 1900s by *Pandit Madan Mohan Malviya*, is also known as a center of learning, especially in the field of cultural studies.

The first blast took place inside the famous *Sankatmochan Temple* adjacent to the *Kashi Vishwanath* temple when it was teeming with devotees for the evening "*aarti*". Minutes later another blast took place in the holding area of Platform Number 1 of the cantonment railway station where the Delhi-bound Shivaganga Express was waiting. In the railway station blast fourteen were killed and 30 injured. The blast at the railway station was so powerful that it created a deep crater on the platform. The area was splattered with blood and body parts. The blast at the temple set off panic and led to a near stampede as people scrambled for cover.

Within hours of the terror strike in *Varanasi*, two top ranking *Lashkar-e-Toiba* militants were killed by the police in Lucknow and Delhi. *While Salar*, 46, the first Indian militant commander from outside the Valley, was shot near Lucknow, *LeT's Bangladesh* chief, *Gulam Yezdani*, 28, was killed in Delhi. The encounters did not have direct links with the attacks on 7th March,2006 in Varanasi. It was suspected Salar masterminded the attack on *Aksharadam Temple* in 2002 and the *Ayodhya* attack and the Nalgonda-born *Yezdani* was the man behind the assassination of dissident BJP leader *Haren Pandya* and the Shramajeevi Express blast. On the early morning of 8th March, 2006 Yezdani and his accomplice *Ahsanallah Hasan alias Kajal* were killed in Delhi.

Though it was thought first that the killing of Salar at Lucknow did not have any direct links with the attacks on 7th March,'06 in *Varanasi* further investigations, by the Uttar Pradesh Police revealed that the slain LeT operative was certainly involved in the blasts in *Vasranasi*. The two railway engineers who were injured in the blasts at the Varansai Railway station told the Uttar Pradesh Special Task Force that they spotted Salar before 7th March, '06.

The evil designs of the Terrorists at *Varanasi* was to make the Hindus and Mulims to fight and destroy the properties of each other. Contrary to their expectations hours after the initial shock, the city was back on its feet, its traditional Hindu and Muslim amity intact. Massive processions were taken out following the blasts, but not against any community. In the fifty and odd inter-religious rallies taken out jointly by Hindus and Muslims, Varansai spoke in one voice against terrorism. The economic set-up of the city is such that it weaves both communities together so strongly that you have Hindus and Muslims working together to produce the famous Benaras silk saris. The communal harmony here is remarkable.

The main market of the city near the Dasashvamedh and Godalia Ghats reopened at 9.00 a.m. and remained open late into the evening of 7th March,'06. Another instance of the Hindu-Muslim bond came at the Indian Medical Association where refrigerators were full because people lined up in scores to donate blood after the blasts. Muslims and women were the main donors and the Association got 150 units in two days after the blast. *Ahmed Khan,* Secretary to the Shenai legend late Shri Bismillah Khan inspired scores from his community to donate blood for the injured. That was the best way to send the message that Hindus and Muslims are one. India needs many more such Ahmed Khans from both the communities of Hindus and Muslims to teach lessons to the terrorists. Everyone knows that late *Shri Ustad Bismillah Khan* played the Shehnai all his life at the *Sankatmochan temple.*

The main aim of the Pakistan-based militant organizations appeared to create commotion in India and implant ill-feelings in the minds of Hindus and Muslims. A major terrorist strike was averted on 11th March,'06 with the timely detection of two kg. of ammonium nitrate from the Byculla Railway Station in Central Mumbai. Apart from the explosives filled in a plastic water bottle, police recovered a pocket-sized transformer, that could provide the power of a detonator to the explosive device. The recovery came in the backdrop of twin blasts in *Varanasi* on 7th March'06. The ammonium nitrate was detected after the ATS swooped on a tip-off. It was stored on the loft inside the gents' toilet block at the Byculla Railway Station in Central Mumbai.

Possible strike at tourist locations in Goa, Kollur Mookambika and *Udipi Krishna Temple* were prevented with the arrest of a militant with RDX and firearms from Marmagoa railway station. The militant was identified as *Tarique Jalal* alias *Tarique Batto.* He revealed that he was a member of Pakistan-based militant *Tehrique-ul-Mujahiddin* which works under the LeT. He had been trained for two years in Pakistan and had also traveled to Bangladesh and Nepal.

After the twin bomb blasts rocked Varanasi at *Sankatmochan Temple* and Cantonment Railway Station on 7th March,'06 another crude bomb exploded on 16th March,'06 near a medical shop under cantonment area of *Varanasi.* One person was injured who was procuring medicines from the drug store when the incident occurred. A case was registered and investigations were on.

The Special Task Force of Uttar Pradesh arrested six persons including *Waliullah,* the Imam of a mosque in Phoolpur near Allahabad. Three other Bangladeshis who planted the bombs at Varanasi on 7th March were still at large. *Waliullah* was the area commander of eastern Uttar Pradesh. Paraded before reporters, *Waliullah* revealed one of the three Bangaladeshis was also involved in the Delhi blasts in October,'05. *Waliullah,* a product of a *madrasa* in Deoband, was jailed in 2001 by the Allahabad police on the charge of links with terrorists. The plan for the *Varanasi* blasts was given final shape on the night of 23rd/24th February,'o6 at Mau Ayaman near Allahabad. *Waliullah* had gone to attend a religious gathering at Tabligh *Jamaat Ijtima* at *Mau Ayaman.* He received a message there from Huji Bangladesh chief *Asadullah* that three persons were being sent to carry out strikes in the east. *Waliullah* too communicated that he would remain in his house. Around 9.00 p.m. on 3rd March the three Bangladeshi youths reached where *Waliullah* had made arrangements for their stay in a house he had rented opposite the *Madrasa. Waliullah* brought the trio to Allahabad on the 4th morning. He dropped two militants at a *madrasa* near the railway station and then left for *Varanasi* with the another militant to choose the targets. By evening they were in

Allahabad. All four returned to Phoolpur.

On 5th and 6th March,'06 the three youths were in Allahabad the entire day, scouting markets only to return to Phoolpur at night. On the 6th of March,'06 they returned with three pressure cookers. They kept the explosive materials separately inside the cookers. They did not connect the fuse wire as they did not want to carry live bombs and that was why used the timer device in *Varanasi*. On the morning of 7th March,'06 the three youths boarded the Bundelkhand Express for *Varanasi* from Phoolpur to execute their plan with the involvement of local modules.

Six Harkat-ul-Jehad Al Islami (HUJI) militants, including the mastermind behind the Varnasi blasts, had hatched a conspiracy to blow up the two Hanuman temples in the city on *Ramanavami*. A map of the city had been recovered from the possession of the militants who were arrested on 5th April;06 marking the spots which they had planned to strike. The militants had also planned to blow up the old Hanuman temples at Aliganj and the one near Lucknow University in the city on 6th April,06 (*Ramanavami Day*) as a large number of devotees pay obeisance there on that day. From the six arrested persons including Waliullah the STF has also recovered Pakistani passports.

Further investigation is in progress....

9
Mayhem in Mumbai

The Western Railway line in Mumbai carries a world record of 225 million passengers per km of the route every year. The busiest segment on the line between Church gate Terminus and Dahanu Road is Church gate and Virar, which carries 900 million passengers a year. The daily traffic on the line is 2.6 million passengers, which is 43 per cent of the total rail traffic on the Mumbai suburban system, the lifeline of the city. In another BLACK TUESDAY it became the target of terrorists on the 11th of July'06. On this fateful day about 200 people mainly train commuters were killed and over 700 injured in a series of bomb blasts on the western suburban rail network. The blasts took place in the evening peak hours, catching commuters and the police off guard. .

The panic-stricken financial capital immediately shut down, sending waves of fear even as hospitals were flooded with bodies and people around tried to help out the victims of Tuesday's mayhem. The powerful blasts threw out mangled bodies and commuters in adjoining compartments jumped out. The blasts were so powerful that the compartments were ripped apart. Bleeding and injured passengers were seen running helter-skelter.

The blasts occurred between 6.00 p.m. and 6-30 p.m. at Mahim, Bandra, Matunga, Borivili, Mira Road, Jogeshwari, Khar and Bhayander. It was the peak hour and the trains were packed with commuters. Even a bomb of small magnitude can do a lot of damage as compared to one on a half empty train. In the absence of the official machinery at the bomb sites, fellow commuters and other people have rushed victims to V.N.Desai, KEM, Cooper and Hinduja hospitals nearby.

The Anti-Terrorist Squad has said forensic reports have revealed the use of RDX, ammonium nitrate and fuel oil in the seven blasts that rocked the trains in Mumbai on 11th July,'06. The traces of explosives found at the sites were very small in quantity and forensic experts had taken time to analyze them. The assistance of the NSG and the Forensic Science Lab in Hyderabad was taken to come to a conclusion.

Three suspected SIMI activities including two from Bihar, held as prime suspects in the serial blasts in suburban trains and they have been remanded to ten days custody. The two arrested by Maharashtra Anti-Terrorists Squad on information from their police were identified as *Kamal Ahmed Mohd. Vakil Ansari*,32, and *Khalid Aziz Raunaq Aziz Sheik*, 24, both residents of Basopatti village in Madhubani district and the third – *Mumtaz Ahmed Maqbul Ahmed Chowdury*, 38, a resident of Turbhe in Navi Mumbai. The police also seized 1.5 kg. of gunpowder from one of them. The Bihar police had detained another suspect *Mohammad Akram* from Dangra village in Gaya district.

The Anti-Terrorist Squad conducted combing and search operation at all the locations where the three suspects were staying and had seized gunpowder from *Ansari*. They had also seized mobile phones from all the accused to crosscheck the numbers stored in the cell phone and also ascertain the history of calls made to and from the phones. The ATS has charged the three suspects with various sections of Indian Penal Code, including murder, attempt to murder causing hurt by dangerous weapons various sections of explosive Substance Act, Indian Explosives Act and Indian Railways Act.

A doctor who had undergone training in explosives in Pakistan, has been arrested in connection with 11th July,'06 Mumbai blasts while over 20 others were under detention for questioning. *Praveen Ansari*, a Unani practitioner from Central Mumbai who was arrested by the crime branch had been handed over to the Anti-terrorist Squad. Ansari was suspected to be the "prime motivator" of *LeT* cadres who triggered the blasts that claimed 200 lives. A post-graduate in Unani medicine from Nagpur, Ansari had been practicing Unani medicines in Central Mumbai and was popular in the city. A software engineer, *Muzzamil* and his cousin were detained from south Indian city along with Sohail who hailed from Pune. The Unani doctor has sent several youths from central Mumbai and suburbs to Pakistan and Jammu and Kashmir to undergo LeT training. On 25th July,'06 two more people were arrested in Mumbai for their suspected links to the 11th July, train bombings. They were *Suhail Sheik* and *Jameer Ahmed.* Jameer owned a key shop in central Mumbai and Suhail, a native of Pune were sent to Pakistan for training at LeT camp by Tanvir Ansari..

The hunch that the Mumbai blasts had a Hyderabad link after the ATS of Mumbai and Intelligence Bureau picked up three youths from the Tolichowki and Kalapathar of Hyderabad, Andhra Pradesh on 25th July'06. Of the three, one was Jameel of Tolichowki and another person was *Mohsin Mirza Khan* a resident of Kalapathar. The duo belonged to the banned SIMI and were reported to have supplied RDX for the blasts. The duo and another person were picked up based on the confession of *Kamal Ahmed Ansari, Khalid Ronak Sheik* and *Mumtaz Ahmed Maqbool Ahmed Chaudary* who were already in the police custody. *Ansari* and *Khalid* were arrested from Basupatti village of Madhubani district in the Bihar. *Mumtaz* was arrested from Navi Mumbai.

Faizal Sheikh, the Mira Road resident (in nearby Thane district) was arrested on the night of 27th July,'06 along with his Bangalore-based software programmer brother *Muzammil* for alleged LeT links. He was suspected to be fund raiser for the terrorist outfit in Mumbai. *Faizal*, arrested in connection with the11th July,'06 Mumbai serial blasts allegedly used the' hawala mode' to acquire funds from Pakistan and West Asia. *Faizal* and *Tanvir Ansari* arrested earlier were motivators of the Pak-occupied Kashmir-based terrorist outfit and were active in Mumbai.

The Crime Scene Observation (CSO) prepared by the Andhra Pradesh Forensic Science Laboratory revealed volumes about the *'jehedis'* planned their strategy in the minutest detail. According to the CBO report, the terrorists sought to maximize casualties. This theory was proved by the fact that they chose the side luggage racks near the emergency break chain to plant the explosives. "It was observed that the explosions in all the seven trains were sited at the side luggage near the emergency brake chain. This only proved that they wanted to have the heads of all the passengers smashed resulting in their instant death."

The sources pointed out that had the explosives been placed under the seat or any other part of the compartment, the casualties would have been fewer and the passengers would have suffered only injuries. The CSO report further stated that each bomb blast could have been carried out by two persons. "The study of the scene suggested that one person might have boarded the crowded train and managed to position himself under the emergency brake chain while another passed on the bag from a distance and walked out of the train. Since it would be risky to carry the bag through the crowd, it appeared as though some one passed the bag which, in turn, was handed over to the second person who placed it on the luggage rack seconds later, both walked out of the train."

The experts, during their visit, boarded different trains at various stations to ascertain how the terrorists planted the explosives. The report stated that the possibility of suicide bombers was ruled out as all the bodies were identified. They observed that all the explosions, except the one at Jogeswari took place in the fourth and sixth coaches, which were first-class compartments. It was further observed that while six bomb blasts took place while the trains were leaving the platform, the seventh took place after the train moved for about two km..from the station. A sketch was prepared by experts of the black rexine-canvas bag and the order in which the material was placed. It has gone like this – stainless steel container, round splinters, high explosive (RDX), electric detonator, electronic timing circuit, battery cells and the on/off switch. The team collected several pieces of black bag material from all the sites of explosions besides pieces of battery and stainless steel containers and gave them to the Maharashtra FSL analysis.

In the first indication that 11th July, serial bomb blasts in trains could be foreign funded as the police seized 37,000 riyals (approx. Rs.3,70 lakhs) sent from Saudi Arabia through *hawala* to *Faizal Sheik*, one of the key LeT operatives arrested in the blasts case. Though the money was sent by Faizal's brother who lives in Saudi Arabia, anti-terrorist squad authorities said that what was suspicious was that part of the money came a day before and remaining a day after the blasts. *Faizal* was suspected to have supervised *LeT's* operations in the region. He was alleged to have recruited people for LeT training in Pakistan and used to receive money from abroad for this purpose. He was arrested along with his brother on 27th July,'06.

The Mumbai city police arrested on 31st July,'06 a journalist working in a vernacular daily, under the Unlawful Activities Prevention Act for his alleged association with the banned outfit SIMI. *Danih Riaz Shaukatali Shaik* (28) a reporter in an Urdu daily was suspected to be associated with subversive groups operating in the city and was found to be in possession of literature concerning SIMI. *Danih* was one of the active members of SIMI and used to sell literature of this banned organization. *Danih* had close links with Etesham Kutubuddin Siddiqui, who was arrested on 29th July,'06 for his alleged connection with SIMI.

In a joint operation, the anti-terrorist squad (ATS) of Mumbai police and CID (counter intelligence) sleuths of *Jammu and Kashmir* police arrested a youth in connection with the terror bombings in Mumbai on 11th July,'06. *Abdul Hameed* was arrested from Sanei in Surankote on the evening of 4th July,'06 This was the first arrest made in insurgent-hit *Jammu and Kashmir* in connection with the serial blasts in Mumbai. The arrested youth was earlier working with an agency in Mumbai.. He was taken from Jammu to New-Delhi on the night of 3rd July,'06.

A top Pakistani militant, arrested by the Army in South Kashmir on 22nd August,'06 gave some vital clues about 11th July, '06 serial bomb blasts in Mumbai. *Toufeen Akmal Hashmi* alias *Abu Amad*, a Pakistani militant and the Al Badr divisional commander for Jammu and Udhampur areas was arrested by the troops from Nandmarg forest near Shopian in South Kashmir on 22nd August,'06. The ultra was handed over to the Kulgam police During interrogation *Hashmi* admitted to knowing the perpetrators of serial blasts on 11th July in which about 200 people were killed. *Hashmi* revealed that seventeen militants of the banned *LeT* were asked to carry out the blasts in Mumbai. While 16 ultras returned safe, one had been killed in the blasts. The militant also claimed to have worked for the Pakistani Army before joining militant cadres.

The Mumbai police solved the 11th July train serial blasts. They blamed Pakistan's Intelligence Agency ISI for masterminding the explosion that were executed by activities of the banned and SIMI of India. Fifteen persons have been arrested in connection with the blasts in which eleven Pakistani nationals were directly involved. There was no involvement of *al-Qaeda* or any link with the 9/11 attacks in the U.S. Of the fifteen arrested twelve people were directly involved in the explosions

One of the Pakistanis involved was killed in the blast in one of the trains, while another was gunned down by police in an encounter at Antop Hill later. The conspiracy was hatched in Pakistan's Bahawalpur in March,'06 with the training of the Indian LeT and SIMI members, some of whom went to Pakistan two or three times. Of the eleven Pakistanis, five had come from Bangladesh, two from Nepal and four from across the porous Gujarat border.

The police said that 15 to 20 kg..of RDX used in the bomb blasts was brought from Pakistan by *Ehsanullah*. Four kg. Of ammonium nitrate, which was mixed with the RDX, was provided by local groups. The bombs were put together in Chembur area between 8th July and 10th July, '06 at the house of *Mohammad Ali* in Shivaji Nagar then taken to mastermind *Faisal Sheikh's* home in Bandra. The conspirators had bought eight pressure cookers to put the explosives, but only seven were used, while one remained untraced. The Indians who planted the explosives were identified as *Faisal Sheikh*, who placed the bombs on the local train at Jogeshwari, *Kamal Ansari* at Matunga, *Ehteshaam Siddiqui* at Mira road and *Naveed Khan* at Khar.

The 11/7 Mumbai serial bomb blasts did have a Hyderabad, A.P connection. The police raided a ground floor apartment in Lake Shore Towers in Vidyanagar Colony in Neredmet, Hyderabad on 30th Sept.'06 and arrested one *Naveed Rashid Hussain Khan*, the man who planted a "pressure cooker" bomb on one of the trains. Twenty-six-year-old *Naveed* was an active associate of *Fasal Shaik* the key accused in the serial bomb blasts and also the Mumbai 'commander'; of *LeT*. *Naveed* too was the LeT operative. His elder brother, who works for an English daily newspaper in Mumbai, was already arrested by the Mumbai police.

With *Naveed's arrest*, the worst fears of the intelligence had come true – that terrorist are using software firms and call centers at a front. *Naveed* worked in two major companies in the city and was the man who planted bomb on one of the trains that went off near Khar station, killing many Mumbaikars. He had gone to Mumbai a few days before the blasts. He was there for quite some time after the blasts and then returned to Hyderabad. He had also visited Pakistan earlier.

Naveed was born in Kuwait and his father, *Rashid Hussain Khan* worked there. *Rashid's* first marriage was to a Pakistani woman, an Islamic teacher in Kuwait. She died after she declined a kidney transplant on the ground that it is 'unislamic'. The family then moved to Mumbai. *Rashid* married, for a second time, one *Zareena Begum* at Gorakhpur in Uttar Pradesh. She and her daughter live in Mumbai. She came to Hyderabad on 30th Sept.06 with a large amount of cash meant to be handed over to *Naveed.* She was supposed to return to Mumbai on the evening of 1st Oct. "06. "Why this short visit, that too with so much money" investigators wondered. *Naveed* who was working with RSR Sales a call center at Ameerpet, owned a Maruti Esteem car with Maharashtra registration. He also owned an apartment on Mira Road in Mumbai.

The 11/7 investigations was the first major case in which Mumbai police used the internet to track down terrorists. When, *Firoz Deshmukh* of the Islamic Research Foundation was picked up on 14th July,'06 by the Crime Branch of Mumbai, they knew they had someone who could give information on the blasts, he knew *Rahil Sheik* of Grant Road. So they got him to log in and chat with *Sheik* while they watched. In the chat-room, *Rahil* opened up and gave Firoz a Bangladeshi telephone number. That was the second important breakthrough. The number was immediately kept under surveillance. The police then began watching the mails from and to. The password for both these e-mails was Jannat. When they spied on the messages and Internet-chats on these e-mails, the police came across several phone numbers and got vital clues which finally led them to *Faisal Sheik* and *Muzammil Sheik*. But *Faisal* turned out to be a hard nut to crack. The Mumbai police were not sure of his exact role into the bomb blasts until *Dr.Tanveer Ansari* came into the picture. It was Ansari who spilled the beans on *Faisal's* proximity to Lashkar terrorist *Azam Cheema*. "In the Bahwalpur base camp, I saw Faisal using Cheema's Internet, dining with him,. They were on backslapping terms and shared a great rapport. I realized they were close to each other. The blasts are 100 percent the handiwork of Faisal", Ansari told in his statement to the Crime Branch. On interrogation, Ansari said that "Lashkar would never attempt any big operation in Mumbai without keeping *Faisal* in the loop. But as soon as Faisal was arrested, the Bangladesh number stopped working and Rahil disappeared from the cyber radar.

Faisal had managed to hoodwink an entire team of investigators till Ansari's arrest. It was after that his brother Muzammil was picked up in Bangalore. *Muzammil* told the police that *Faisal* had also sent him and his brother Rahil to Pakistan via *Zahedaan* in Iran for training. It was now clear that Faisal held the key to the 11/7 blasts case and that he was not talking. *Faisal* remained tightlipped even when he was put through lie-detector. After a series of truth serum tests, however, Faisal began to sing.

Faisal spoke of the involvement of Pakistanis in the whole operation, the manner in which they assembled the bombs at *Mohammad Ali's* house at Govandi. *Ehsanullash* imported 15 kg. of RDX to Mumbai and the bombs were kept at *Faisal's* house on 10th July,'06 a day before the blasts. *Mohammad Majid*, who played the role of a "fecilitator" for Pakistanis crossing into the Indian territory proved to solving the 11/7 case. *Majid* was identified as a key Bengal-based operative aiding terrorist outfits the LeT and *Harkat-ul-Jihadi-al-Islami* in bringing and sending youths across the border.

Investigations had revealed after the narco-analysis of three of the prime accused-*Kamal Ansari, Faisal Sheik* and *Tanvir* arrested earlier in connection with the blasts, that they have brought Pakistanis and Bangladeshis and sent tem for training. *Kamal* had told that he had brought two men from Pakistan to the city via the Nepal border. A few days later, they were joined by another group from Pakistan and were brought to the city by an "outsider". When questioned *Majid* told about his role in the blasts. He had not only helped five operatives cross the Bangladesh border and brought them to the city, he had earlier helped three youths from rural Maharashtra to get across to Bangladesh. These three youths were recruited by absconding LeT operative *Zahibuddin Ansari* alias *Zaby* and had been identified as *Abdul Samad*,resident of *Beed, Afroz Khan*, a resident of Mansalgaon and *Mustafa Sayeed*, a resident of Nagar. Majid admitted sending the trio across the border for terror training days before he was asked to escort the five member Pakistani group to Mumbai.

In a prize catch the Maharashtra's Anti-Terrorist Squad (ATS) arrested on 3rd Oct.'06 *Asif Khan* alias *Juniad*, suspected to have planted a bomb in one of the suburban trains on 11th July from Belgaum in neighbouring Karnataka and brought to Mumbai. *Junaid* was allegedly one of the key persons in the entire conspiracy and the police were looking out for him ever since his involvement came to light in the month of Sept.'06. He hails from Jalgoan in North Maharashtra and is also an accused in a case registered against *LeT* activities for subversive acts in a court there. He was one of the three absconding accused of Indian origin who had allegedly planted bombs in the suburban trains.

Pakistanis involved in the 11th July serial train bomb blasts had come to Mumbai exclusively to offer their expertise for making bombs which were subsequently used to strike terror in suburban locals. The bomb expert assembled the bombs using RDX (Research Developed Explosive), ammonium nitrate and quartz timer in pressure cookers at the residence Mohammad Ali in Shivaji Nagar slum in North East Mumbai. The cookers contained a lump of RDX placed in the center surrounded by ammonium nitrate. A detonator comprising a quartz timer was placed over the explosives to trigger the explosions.

Two to two-and-a-half kg of RDX, four to five kg. of ammonium nitrate and quartz timer were kept in a five-litre pressure cooker to cause the seven explosions which kill\ed nearly 200 persons and injured over 600. The compression of all these materials into a pressure cooker gave a high intensity to the explosions. Investigations had also revealed that the master-mind of the blasts, *Faisal Sheik*, was an expert in radio sensitive, remote sensitive and light sensitive detonators. In a light sensitive device, the detonators triggered off due to fluctuations in the intensity of light and the blast occurs in 19 minutes. RDX used in the blasts was brought from Pakistan by one *Ehsanullah* while the ammonium nitrate and cookers were procured locally. .

The Mumbai police's Anti-Terrorism Squad requested the Interpol to issue red corner notices against 10 Pakistani nationals and two Indians who were allegedly involved in 11/7 serial blasts plot. As a first step towards this, lookout notices were issued against the accused. On Oct.'06 the ATS submitted a list of absconders in the blasts case before the special court of Maharashtra Control of Organised Crime Act . The list named Indian nationals *Rizwan Daware* and *Rahil Sheik*, and specifically mentioned the names of Pakistani nationals *Azam Cheema*, *Sohail Sheik*, *Hafiz Zubeir* and *Abdul Rehman* as absconders along with other Pakistani nationals.

The ATS of Mumbai police on 20th Oct.'06 claimed that four of the six accused in the 11th July train blasts had confessed to the exact roles played by them in the incidents. The confessions of the four – *Mohammad Ali*, *Naved*, and *Majid*–

had been recorded. "The bombs were assembled at *Mohammad Ali's* residence at Govandi by an expert team of Pakistani and Indian nationals. *Majid* facilitated the movement of six Pakistanis who crossed over to India from Bangladesh in 24 Parganas district of West Bengal", *Sajid Ansari* helped the Pakistani nationals in assembling the electronic circuits used in the bombs and *Naved* served as the local guide for the Pakistanis.

Junaid, arrested from Belgaum on 3rd October,'06 handled the entire support system and logistics and was among the masterminds. It had also come to the notice of the ATS during interrogations that accused *Mohammad Sajid Ansari.* who ran a mobile phone repair shop at Jogeshwari in Mumbai, was an active member of the banned SIMI and knew the other accused including *Junaid* and *Faisal. Mohammad Sajid* had even attended a meeting at *Faisal's* Bandra house where the plan to cause a series of blasts in trains was finalized with the exact role to be played by the accused.

He actively participated in assembling the bombs by lending his expertise and knowledge of electric circuitry in making timer devices which were used to activate the bombs. The role of Mohammad was also confirmed by the other accused during disclosures before the MCOCA court.

More than 20 Indians involved in carrying out the attacks were arrested and charge-sheeted, but eight Pakistanis managed to escape to their country. The probe into the attacks revealed that the Pakistanis came to India through three different routes Bangladesh, Nepal and the sea...... and were directly involved in planning the bombs. Though the terror attacks on mass transportation systems in Mumbai were not a solitary instance, they were most serious terrorist strikes to date.

Three of the thirteen accused under arrest said in their confessional statements that all seven bombs in the serial bomb blasts in local trains in Mumbai on 11th July were planted at Churchgate station by as many teams of men who had undergone arms training in Pakistan. *Kamal Ahmed Ansari* said in his confessional statement that these teams traveled to Churchgate from the house of Faisal Sheikh in Bandra in different taxis with bombs packed in black rexin bags.

Ansari and his team members purchased tickets for them and planted the bombs in first class compartments of local trains. According to the plan, all four members of the team were to get down at Dadar station. But one *Salim*, later identified a Pakistani national, could not get down at Dadar station due to heavy rush of incoming passengers. He was among those killed in the blast.

Ansari, a resident of Basupatti village in Madhubani district of Bihar and a former worker of the Rashtriya Janata Dal, left the city the same night for his village from where he was arrested by Mumbai police on 20th July,06. According to him, he had gone to Pakistan for arms training on a fake Nepalese passport he received from Pakistani contact.

The Maharashtra Government is taking further action in the matter.

10
Malegoan Bomb Blasts

At-least 32 people including ten children died and over 300 were injured in four blasts, including three in a mosque-cum-graveyard in the communally sensitive town of Malegoan in Maharashtra on the occasion of *Shab-e-Barat*, the Muslim holy day for commemoration of the dead. The blasts occurred on 8th September,'06 just before 2.00 p.m. leaving a trail of death and destruction. Scores of people gathered for Friday prayers were among the causalities. The explosion that took place on 8th Sept.'06 occurred only four days prior to the verdict in the 1993 Mumbai blasts case due on 12th September,'06. Three blasts took place at the *Noorani mosque*-cum-graveyard where people had come to pray for the dead on the occasion of *Shab-e-Barat* and another explosion rocked the busy Mushaira Chowk.

A predominantly Muslim textile town off the Mumbai-Agra National Highway in Nashik district, Malegoan has long been on the list of communally sensitive spots in the State. The town has grown into a city of about seven lakh people and its old municipal council was upgraded into a corporation after the communal riots of 2001. One aspect of the life here is that this up-gradation, however, has not changed its history of communal flare-ups.

For reasons ranging from Muslims celebrating when India lost a game of cricket against Pakistan to the *Babri Mosque* demolition in 1992 to the U.S attack in *Afghanistan* in 2001, the town has had riots. Since three-quarters of the population is Muslim, Friday is a special day in the town. It is the day when the power-looms close for the weekly holiday and the two lakh-odd workers go for the Friday Namaz and after that either go for a movie or spend time shopping or visiting relatives. Hence, any person interested in making an impact here waits for Fridays. Most public meetings are held on this day, not on Sundays. No surprise then, that the town was shaken by blasts on a Friday. The last time the town witnessed communal riots was in October, '01 (on a Friday again) in which thirteen were killed. The reason, as revealed by the State Minorities Commission, was the desperation of an ageing local politician – *Nihal Ahmed Maulevi Mohammads Usman*, 75, leader of the Janata Dal (Secular)

When the situation was in tense, a policeman tried to snatch a pamphlet being distributed by a youth outside the town's *Jama Masjid* after the Friday Namaz. The pamphlet was an appeal to boycott American and British goods to protest against the U.S attack on *Afghanistan*. But when the youth refused to let the policeman see what it was, a scuffle ensued and flared up into a riot between the police and Muslims. Angry youths ran amok in the town pelting stones and provoking the police to open fire. The incident rather invited prompt retaliation in Hindu area, giving it a communal turn, claiming 13 lives (12 Muslims, 1 Hindu).

The incident had roots in an agitation in the town a week earlier. On 19th October,'01, *Nihal Ahmed* has taken out a *morcha* to protest against the U.S attack on *Afghanistan*. The protestors had carried portraits of *Osama bin Laden* and shouted anti-U.S slogans. The town was very tense and needed just a spark to ignite a full-fledged riot.

With no reports of untoward incidents, the authorities lifted the curfew on the next morning of 9th Sept .'06 and people in the predominantly Muslim town thronged mosques for prayers. There was anger among the kin of the dead, four of whom refused to accept the compensation of Rs. one lakh provided by the State Government, saying it was too little. They also complained that the authorities were not enough to improve Malegoan's crumbling health infrastructure as the town had a Muslim-majority population.

Surprisingly, just after 36 hours after the serial blasts, too little a time for this town to leap over its troubled past, the residents of Malegoan took first shaky steps towards normalcy, crossing over the divide that cuts across the town. They shouted not to call them a communally sensitive town. Soon after the curfew had been lifted, astonishingly, there was no war cry from either side. In fact, scenes across this divide were by tragedy. So while Muslims revisited the site of the blasts at *Bara Kabristan* to bury their dead and gather whatever belongings they could retrieve, around the same time, vendors were picking up the remains of the day, from the hurriedly abandoned weekly Friday bazaar.

The first two hours after the blasts were tense, fears of a riot loomed large when large groups of Muslims made their way to the Wadia Hospital area to donate blood. Many of the local residents thought this was a mob heading towards them. But within, seconds, the "us versus them" attitude dropped and helping hands came forward. Improper communication and misunderstanding was cause of all past riots. However, this time both Hindus and Muslims, took to the streets, positioning themselves in Hospitals and blood banks. Others hit the road armed with water, food and compassion. All the while, they kept in touch, consoling the grieving and soothing the agitated. Despite mobile lines jammed, the message, was conveyed; this was not the time for violence. Reports of Hindus lining up to donate blood and Muslims forming a human chain so that hundreds of girls stuck in the Zilla Parishad school could be safely evacuated helped soothe frayed edges.

Although investigators were not completely ruling out

the hand of the Hindu fundamentalists in the Malegoan blasts which killed over 30 people, confirmation of RDX and the discovery of an electronic circuit from the blast site have Islamic fundamentalist groups under the scanner. The Nashik forensic laboratory on 11-9-'06 confirmed the presence of RDX in the bombs that went off in the Hamidiya mosque and Mushawarat Chowk in Malegoan. The first lab reports stated that the sample contained a mixture of RDX, nitrate, ammonium nitrate, petroleum and hydrocarbon oil.

Besides the first forensic details investigating officials claimed that they have got definite leads from a number of eyewitnesses who came forward after sketches of the first two suspects were released on 10th Sept.'o6. The sketches have been circulated among residents of Malegoan through posters pasted on public transport vehicles. A third sketch was added to the list on 11th Sept.'06. Panic struck the city of Nashik once again on 11th Sept.'06 when news spread around that another bag cache of explosives have been found in one of the most crowded hospitals in the city. The textile town of Malegoan is in close vicinity to Nashik city. The bomb was detected outside Lifeline Hospital, a busy healthcare center in the city around noon and also immediately the entire premises of cordoned off. The investigating team had got some solid leads to believe that the explosives used in the blasts were similar to those used on the 11th of July train blasts in Mumbai. The police recovered seventeen gelatin sticks, four detonators and four pencil cells. The bomb disposal squad defused the bomb within half-an-hour of receiving the information.

With the Maharashtra police confirming the presence of RDX, ammonium nitrate and fuel oil in the explosives investigators were comparing the Malegoan IEDs with devices used to trigger blasts in *Varanasi*, Delhi and Mumbai blasts. The technology, investigators belief were similar. *The Varanasi* blasts carried out by three youths – *Bashir*, *Mustafix* and *Zakaria*

– from Bangladesh under directions of JeM commander *Asadullah.* Those behind the Delhi and Mumbai blasts were to be pinpointed. What shifts the focus from the Hindu fundamentalists was the level of sophistication of the device and the potent mixture used. A number of Pakistani nationals caught by security agencies have confirmed having learnt the same technology from mentors in training camps across the border and even in Bangladesh.

With the arrest of alleged prime conspirator of 8th Sept.'06 Malegoan blasts *Shabbir Ahmed Mushirullah* alias *Batterywallah,* the State Anti Terrorist Squad has stumbled upon links between Malegoan, the serial train blasts in Mumbai and the 10th May seizure of arms and explosives at Aurangabad. It emerged that what started with the RDX blast aboard the Karnavati Express on 18th February,'06 at Ahmedabad, culminated with the serial blasts at Malegoan on 8th Sept.'06. The ATS found a strong evidence linking the Aurangabad, Mumbai and Malegoan terror modules. According to investigators, they found not only had a common handler but they also happened to know each other well and had been in regular contact.

Shabbir Batterywallah found to be strongest common link between the Aurangabad, Mumbai and Malegoan modules. Batterywallah was arrested on 11th August,'06 under the provisions of the Unlawful Activities (Prevention) Act for being an active SIMI member and was subsequently arrested by the ATS for alleged conspiracy of blasts at Malegoan.

The bomb blast aboard the Karnavati Express had been the handiwork of key *LeT* operative and member of the Aurangabad module *Fayaz Riaz Ahmed Kagzi* who was believed to be in Pakistan. SIMI activist *Noor-ul-Hada* was already held for his alleged involvement in the Malegoan blasts. He was Batterywallah's employee and was named as a planter of one of the three bombs at Malegoan.

Batterywallah had not only put together the Malegoan

module but was also in know about the arms landing at Aurangabad and had been since last year been in close contact with *Kagzi* and *Zahibuddin Ansari*– prime accused in the arms haul case, the police claimed. Investigations have also revealed that *Batterywallah* had been recruited three years back by serial train blast accused *Mohammad Ali Sheik* and was sent in May,'03 for 26 days of terror training at a camp at Bahawalpur in Pakistan.

For the first time after the 8th Sept.'06 blasts in Malegoan, the State Anti-Terrorist Squad (ATS) has revealed the role of Pakistani nationals in the incident. In its application seeking police custody of accused *Dr. Salman Farsi Aimi*, 35, and *Dr. Farogh Maqdumi*, 33, the ATS stated that the duo provided shelter to their Indian and Pakistani accomplices and were conspirators in smuggling of RDX and other devices into Malegoan in May,'06 along with their Pakistani associates and some members of the banned SIMI. Aimi and Maqdumi, both unani doctors and SIMI activists, had meetings with other conspirators for trafficking RDX and other materials. Aimi had been booked by the Shivaji Nagar police in a rioting case in 2001, while Maqdumi had a case under Unlawful Activities (Prevention) Act in Aisha police station, Malegoan, in 2003. Both these case were pending trail.

Both regularly visited Malegoan and the police got their names from *Noor-ul-Huda*, who was the first person arrested in the case. *Aimi* is Huda's uncle. *Farsi*, *Shabbir Masiulla*, alias *Batterywala* and 12 other SIMI activists attended *Huda's* wedding at Malegoan. It was suspected that *Farsi* might have been in the know of the 11/7 plot, and links between the two cases of blasts.

The Mumbai police on 27th November,'06 said the banned Students Islamic Movement of India (SIMI) conceived and carried out the September 8 serial bombings in Malegoan which killed 31 people and injured 300. They successfully detected the four blasts in Malegoan and arrested eight suspects in the case all of whom belong to SIMI. Investigations suggest that the RDX used in the Malegoan blasts had been smuggled into the country from across the border. No one of the absconding suspects known to the investigators, as *Muzammil*, had sneaked into the country from across the border on 3rd July,'06 to help perpetrators to make improvised devices (IEDs) using the deadly mixture of ammonium nitrate and RDX, which were used in the blasts. Naming *Shabbir Batterwalla* and *Farooq*, a unani medicine practitioner, as the blasts' masterminds, the police said eight more suspects, including two alleged Pakistani nationals, are still at large. Investigation is still in progress.

11
Serial Bomb Blasts in London

After nearly two incident free years the terrorists raised their ugly heads and struck at Ayodhya temple and serial bomb blasts in London. In both these cases it seems they waited long enough until they concluded the security establishment had become lazy and lackluster enough for them to dare such major strikes after a long gap when the heat was on them. Britain backed the U.S. led war both in Afghanistan and Iraq and London was in high alert since *al-Qaeda's* September, 11 attacks on the United States. London, as one of the world's most powerful capitals and a hub for international finance, was long under threat. On the morning of 7th July, 2005 the inevitable had happened. The timing of the attack was too precious to the perpetrators of the crime. The serial bomb blasts in London was nothing more than a direct message to the G-8 nations assembled at Gleneagles that unvisible ghost still walks amidst them. Terrorism can cross national borders, work in tandem, lurk for the right moment to strike meticulously, commit considerable damage and then melt into the scenery. As city after city came under terror attacks – the United States, Istanbul, Jakarta, Madrid and New Delhi – London held its breath. On the 7th of July morning what was sure to come had occurred.

In the deadliest terror attack in Britain in three-decades the militants on the 7th of July, 2005 carried out co-ordinated bomb blasts in underground stations and a bus killing 54 people and injuring 700. A visibly shaken Prime Minister *Tony Blair* said the perpetrators of the serial blasts "acted in the name of Islam". "We know that these people act in the name of Islam but we also know that the vast and overwhelming majority of Muslims here and abroad are decent and law-abiding people who abhor terrorism every bit as much as we do." The first explosion took place in the underground railway tunnel near *Moorgate* on the edge of London's financial district, second explosion near *King's Cross* and the third at *Edgware* road station in *West London.* Fourth blasts took place in the bus number 30, a red double-decker that was blown in the elegant *Georgian* streets of *Bloomsbury* in the heart of London. Investigations revealed that high explosives were used in the three bombs that were detonated possibly by synchronized timers within 50 seconds of each other in the underground. Experts who examined the scene of tragedy said that high explosives were used and that would tend to suggest that these were not home-made.

Al-qaeda claimed responsibility for the serial bombing that took place on the morning of 7th July, 2005. They said through an internet statement that "a group of 'mujahedeen' from a division of the *Abu Hafs-al-Masri* brigades piled blow after blow on the infidel capital leaving dead and injured". British investigators probing the *al-Qaeda* link to the multiple bombing suspected that a London-based Moroccan, linked to terrorist attacks in *Madrid* and *Casablanca* was behind the above terror attacks. British Police had launched a hunt for *Mohammad al Gerbouzi* after he disappeared from his home and the *Scotland Yard* and M15 requested the European agencies to help track him. *Gerbouzi* who was granted asylum in Britain, was sentenced to twenty years in prison in absentia by a court in Morocco for his alleged involvement in bombings in *Casablanca* killing forty-four people in 2003. The North African, a British resident for sixteen years was also accused by the French and German security services of connection with *Abu Musab al-Zarqawi*, the Jordanian – born leader of the insurgent group in Iraq connected to *Al-Qaeda* which murdered the British hostage *Ken Bigley*. He was also an associate of *Abu Qatada* one of the detainees released from Belmarsh in the month of March, 2005. *Abu Qatada* was described by a British judge as a "truly dangerous" individual and by a Spanish judge as "*Osama bin Laden's* ambassador in Europe. According to another report, M15 believed that a fundamentalist organization linked to *Laden's al-Qaeda* network was responsible, as like the Madrid train bombing in 2004, which were the work of North African extremists.

It was suspected in some important quarters that the *al-Qaeda* chief suspect behind the 7th of July serial bomb attacks in London was secretly recruiting Muslims in colleges and especially looking for students with engineering or computer expertise. Extremists are known to target schools and colleges where young people may be very inquisitive but less challenging and more susceptible to extremist reasoning. The Iraq war one of the key causes of young British Muslims turning to terrorism.

Three Islamic groups claimed responsibility for the London blasts, which government Ministers said bore the hallmarks of the Islamic militant *al-Qaeda* network which was behind the September 11,2001 attacks on the United States. The police was at a loss to know whether the bombers were foreign extremists or "home grown" radicals from among the 1.6 million Muslims in Britain.

About thirty *al-Qaeda* fighters, including *Mustafa Setmariam Nasar* of Syria and *Mohammad Al Gerbouzi*, a Moroccan were identified by counter-terrorism officers as the most likely suspects behind the London bombings killing 54 people and injuring 700 others. The mixture of foreign and British-born suspects were investigated as part of a massive inquiry to track down those responsible for the attacks. The cell responsible for the attacks believed to number from four to twelve. Initial group of about thirty key suspects were identified from the hundreds of pieces of intelligence collected by M15 and M16, Scotland Yard's anti-terrorist branch, and the bugging center at the government communication head quarters in Cheltenham. The material included phone taps and reports from foreign agents and police forces. It was suspected that the person believed to have organized Madrid train attacks in 2004 in which 191 (one hundred and ninety One) people were killed must be behind the serial bomb attacks in London. Spanish intelligence officers flown to London to help the British police and they were among one hundred police officers from forces across the world that gathered at Scotland yard in Central London to share information. British intelligence officers were concentrating on trying to identify an individual bomber or one of their supporters which they hoped would lead to the rest of the terror unit. *Chrisopher Chaboud*, head of the French anti-Terrorism Co-ordination Unit and one of the five top officials sent by Paris to London was worried about the explosives appeared to be of military origin. He said that "we are more used to cells making home-made explosives with chemicals. How did they get them? Either by trafficking, for example, in the Balkans, or they had someone on the inside who enabled them to get them out of a military establishment."

While the British government warned the people not to expect quick break through had to give high security alert in Birmingham on the 10th of July,2005. The police had evacuated about twenty thousand people from the center of the city during the night and carried out a controlled explosion on a bus. They found no bombs. They, however, continued their hunt for those who set off three bombs on the London Underground and blew up a double decker bus. As the three subway bombs went off almost simultaneously, it was suspected that they were detonated by timers, rather than suicide bombers.

Britain was aghast of four young friends from northern England, including tear away teen and a cricket-mad sports graduate carried out the attacks in London on the 7th of July, 2005. It was suggested in media reports that the four "boy bombers" who died in the blasts on London's transport network, were British-born living in the northern England town of Leeds and aged between 19 and 30. They were said to be ethnic Pakistani origin. It was really surprising the Britishers as to why did they become the suicide bombers. Neighbours in Leeds were shocked that their young were responsible for the blasts as they were sweet guys and one of them was a science graduate and adore football and cricket. Of the four suspects, a 19 year-old also from Leeds, was said to have turned to religion after being a "bit wild". It was told that "he went off the rails and his parents were very worried. They wanted to instill some discipline in him; I don't know what happened but eighteen months to two years ago he suddenly changed and became devoutly religious".

Millions across Europe paid silent tribute to London's dead on the 7th July, 2005 as the British Government was trying to track down the mastermind behind the four bombers. In London, workers poured out of their offices to line the streets while taxis and buses came to halt. Planes at airports switched off their engines and delayed take-offs. Hundreds gathered at *King's Cross* station, site of one of the blasts detonated by a group of young British Muslims of Pakistani ethnic-origin who lived in Nothern England. Prime Minister *Tony Blair* marked the silence in the garden of his Downing Street Office. While *Queen Elizabeth* observed it at *Buckingham Palace.* The *Pope* on holiday in the Italian Alps prayed for peace.

Prime Minister *Tony Blair* urged the Muslim leaders to help root out terrorists in their communities and told the British Parliament on 13th July, 2005 that he had urged Muslim leaders to stop those who 'twist' the teachings of their own religion. He said that "there is a sense in the international community and in the Muslim world that this has to be taken on. Security measures alone are not going to deal with this. This is not an isolated act. It is an extreme and evil ideology whose roots lie in a poisonous misinterpretation of the religion of Islam."

Mohammad Siddique Khan, one of the four suicide bombers was of Pakistan-origin. His wife *Hasina Patel*, came from Bharuch in Gujarat, India. *Hasina* and *Khan*, who met at Leeds metropolitan University, were thought to have separated and *Hasina* worked in education as a 'neighbourhood enrichment Officer' and the two had a baby daughter in 2004. But the pressure on their marriage was too strong and the couple were believed to have separated. *Hasina* said to have held anti-Taliban, pro-women views at odds with her husband's extremist version of Islam. *Hasina's* mother *Farida Patel* is a Gujarati and was honoured by the British Queen, sometime before the serial bomb blasts in London, for community work. The Patels were known opponents of extremism and supporters of women's rights.

One of the men, who carried out 7th July, serial bombings in London had visited Pakistan twice spending a total of four months. Bomber *Shehzad Tanveer's* links to *Lashkar-e-Toiba* became apparent after his uncle informed police about his visit to a *Madarasa* near Lahore believed to be run by L-e-T.

British authorities had initiated a worldwide manhunt for thirty-three-year old *Magdy Nashar* who left England two weeks before the bombings. The police said that it was he who helped the bombers set up their bomb factory. He was, however, arrested in Cairo and interrogated. The British police confirmed that there was a "a Pakistan connection" to the bombings, in which three of the four suspected perpetrators were Britons of Pakistani Origin. They had also added that "there are also connections in other countries and what we expect to find at some stage is that there is a clear *al-Qaeda* link, a clear *al-Qaeda* approach. The discovery that the fourth bomber, a Jamican-born Briton, came from a different background than the other three, Britons of Pakistani Origin, suggested that the bombers were part of wider network. Intelligence Officers were trying to establish links between the two groups, whether they were both in contact with a radical cleric or had met in Pakistan. Among those investigated was a man in his mid-40s who stayed at the Leeds house where the bombs were made but left the country for Iraq months ago. Police were also hunting the mastermind and an Egyptian Chemistry student who disappeared from his Leeds home."

Pakistan President *Musharraf* expressed shock and heart felt condolences on behalf of the people and government of Pakistan over the bombings in which fifty-four people were killed. As the probe pointed to the involvement of men of Pakistani origin, President *Musharraf* assured Prime Minister *Tony Blair* of his country's full co-operation in the investigation.

Pakistan has officially 7,300 *madrassas* while unofficially the list runs into over 15,000. In connection with the London bombings the British Government has provided the details of calls made by some bombers to Pakistan. Responding to the above, Pakistan had launched investigations into the activities of Islamic seminaries run by banned militant outfits *Jaish-e-Mohammad* and *Lashkar-e-Toiba*. As a part of the probe the staff of over a dozen seminaries in the rural area of Islamabad and Rawalapindi had been questioned about the serial bomb blasts in London on 07/07/05. As a precautionary measure a state of high vigil had been declared at airports in the country and security had been enhanced at churches in the twin cities of Islamabad and Rawalapindi to ensure security of British diplomats and nationals based in Islamabad and Rawalapindi. The *madrassas* being run by *J-e-M* and *Lashkar*, both banned by President *Musharraf* were among the first to have been visited by intelligence officials in connection with the London bombings. What goes on in Pakistan *madrassas* and the thinking they inspire was of critical interest to Western security agencies after the discovery that at-least one of the London bombers *Shehzad Tanweer* visited several times to Pakistan.

The attacks of July 7, 2005, and the revelation that the bombers were British Muslims and not foreign militants, sent shock waves through the country's Islamic community. While condemning the bombings, Muslim leaders have had to accept there are radicals in their midst who advocate violence and preach hatred of the West. Some Muslims had called for reform in Britain's mosques, which they said were out of touch with young Muslims. Others had urged police to clamp down on radical Islamic groups who regularly canvas outside mosques and on university campuses. Following the attacks of July 7 bombings over 500 (five hundred) British Muslim leaders and scholars issued a religious decree on the 19th of July, 2005 criticizing the July 7 blasts in London, saying suicide bombings were 'vehemently prohibited' in Islam. The FATWA or formal legal opinion issued by the British Muslim Forum at Parliament expressed condolences to the families of the victims of the atrocity and wished the injured a speedy recovery. The decree said, that the "Islam condemns the use of violence and the destruction of innocent lives and suicide bombings are vehemently prohibited". Over 50 Muslim religious leaders stood together outside the House of Parliament to hear the FATWA read out. *Gul Mohammad*, Secretary General of the British Muslim Forum quoted the *Koran* as saying, "Whoever kills a human being..... then it is as though he has killed all mankind."

On 19th July, 2005 the Muslim Leaders and Prime Minister *Tony Blair* discussed ways to tackle radical Islamists in Downing Street for an hour. "There was a strong desire from everybody there to make sure to establish the right mechanisms for people to be able to go into the community and confront this.... evil ideology, take it on and defeat it" said *Blair* to a news conference afterwards. Muslim Member of Parliament *Shahid Malik* said:" a massive appetite" among Britain's 1.6 million Muslims to weed out radicals." He said that "we recognize we have got to work better at confronting those evil voices – as minute as they are – inside our community".

There were over 30,000 *madrassas* in Pakistan which were believed to be breeding ground for Islamic terrorists. In the wake of London bombings Pakistan arrested 125 suspected Islamic extremists in a country-wide crackdown on. *madrassas* Dozens of clerics and students, including those from Seminaries frequented by three Pakistani-origin London bombers were detained in the swoop across the country. Heavy police contingents were deployed at the main seminaries and mosques in the federal capital to arrest religious activities allegedly having links to banned militant groups. The Pakistani police said that over thirty members of banned militant groups – *Lashkar-e-Jhangvi, Jaish-e-Mohammad, Harkat-ul Mujahideen* and *Hizbul Tehrir* – were arrested in Pakistan Punjab, which had over 10,000 seminaries.

A statement issued in the name of the "Europe division" of the same al-*Qaeda* group claimed responsibility for the July 7, 2005 bombings in London's public transport system. The same group also claimed the 2004 train bombings in Madrid and the 2003 attacks in Istanbul.

According to an inter-net statement the *al-Qaeda* terror network warned European nations to pull their groups out of Iraq within a month or face more attacks like the deadly London bombings. The statement signed by *al-Qaeda* group. The *Abu Hafs al-Masri Brigades* said that "this message is the final warning to European States. We want to give you a one-month dead-line to bring your soldiers out from the land of Iraq and after August 15, there will be no more messages, just actions that will be engraved on the heart of Europe. It is a message we are addressing to the crusaders who are still present in Iraq Denmark, the Netherlands, Britain, Italy and those other countries whose troops continue to criss-cross Iraqi territory".

As Londoners were still recovering from the shock of serial bombings on 7th July, 2005 the terrorists struck again on 21st July, 2005 on a bus and a London tube station. Four explosions took place which were described as "a very serious incident". The British Police said that "at the moment the casualty numbers appear to be very low-the bombs appear to be smaller" than those denoted on 7th July.

The blitz of detentions of suspected militants and Islamists continued in Islamabad and the Pakistani security forces detained about 300 people. They said that some of those detained were believed to have links with the London bombers, three of whom were Britons of Pakistani descent, while the fourth was a Briton of Jamaican origin.

Shahzad Tanveer, one of the London bombers, idolized *Osama Bin Laden* and sympathized with militants in Kashmir according to his cousin *Asfaq Ahmed*. "*Bin Laden* was his hero and everything he did was right. He believed that America had made Muslim suffer all over the world. He used to say about Kashmir that India was committing great atrocities against the Muslims" said *Asfaq Ahmed* about *Shahzad Tanveer*. *Asfaq Ahmed* further told that "when Shahzad Tanveer father in England gave him money to buy clothes he would not spend it on himself, but for buying coats for those waging the *Jihad* in Kashmir". *Ahmed* said *Tanveer* could never have knowingly been a suicide bomber. "He was either tricked or brainwashed".

Tanveer 22 regularly offered prayers and observed fasts every Friday and Sunday, and visited Pakistan in November, 2004 and spent three to four weeks in his village. *Sadique Khan*, another suicide bomber, visited the village many a times to see him. Khan lived in the house of his maternal uncles in Rawalpindi according to *Asfaq Ahmed*.

After 7th July serial blasts and second wave of terrorist attacks on 21st July, 2005 the British Police became very cautions and serious on the suspicious movements of any individual in London. Needless to point out that the United Kingdom became a home to many immigrants from South Asian countries of Pakistan, India, Sri Lanka and Bangladesh among others. A South Asian man wearing a thick coat at a London subway station on 22nd July, 2005 was shot by Officers at the Stockwell subway station in south London. Passengers at scene described the man who was shot and killed as South Asian ran onto a train at Stockwell station where plain clothes police chased him, he tripped and police then shot him. Muslim leaders, however expressed concern at the shooting.

On the eve of four attempted bombings in London on 21st July, *Sheik Omar Bakri Mohammad*, one of Britain's most outspoken militant clerics predicted that another terrorist attack would hit London. *Sheik Bakri* blamed the British government only for the 7th July attacks by the terrorists. He said "hundreds" of young disaffected British-born Muslims felt compelled to take action in Britain to protest Prime Minister *Tony Blair's* foreign policy, especially the support of the American-led invasion in Iraq which they perceived as anti-Muslim. He said further, that "unless British foreign policy is changed and they withdraw forces from Iraq I am afraid there is going to be a lot of attacks, just the way it happened in Madrid and the way it happened in London" Britain's Home Secretary, *Charles Clarke*, has identified *Sheik Bakri* as one of several extremist clerics who could be deported from Britain, as part of a new package of anti-terror legislation.

There was enormous pressure on the British police to find the four bombers who struck London's public transport, without causing causalities, two weeks after 56 were killed in bomb attacks on trains and bus. Over-zealous to hunt down the culprits the British police admitted killing *Jean Charles De Menzes* a twenty seven old electrician of Brazil who had been living in London for three years. The police expressed regret for the tragedy of killing the innocent victim. After this shooting Muslims living in London were very much worried.

In a dramatic dawn raid on 27th July, 2005 the British Police arrested one of the four suspects in connection with the failed July, 21 attacks. The arrest of *Yasin Hassan Omar*, 24 provided a break through in the search for the other three suspects. Omar, who came to Britain from Somalia as a child refugee, was wanted in connection with an attempted attack at London's Warren Street underground station on 21st July.

On 29th July, the British Police captured all four men they were seeking over 21st July, 2005 botched bombings in three underground trains and a bus which came exactly two weeks after four bombers killed themselves and 56 people in similar attacks. Three of the men were kept in custody in Britain and a fourth was arrested in Rome. The man arrested in Italy, named by the authorities as *Osman Hussain.* Hussain was born in Ethiopia and was wanted over the attempted bombing of a train at Shephered's Bush in West London. *Hussain* confessed that "we wanted to make an attack, but only as demonstration".

Osama bin Laden's deputy *Ayman al-Zawahiri, al-Qaeda's* second in command warned Britons in a video aired on 4th July, 2005 that Prime Minister *Tony Blair's* policies will bring more destruction to London. "*Blair's* policies brought you destruction in Central London and will bring you more destruction" said *Zawahri* in a tape aired by the *Al Jazeera* television. He also warned the United States that *al-Qaeda* would continue to launch deadly attacks until U.S. troops quit all Muslim countries. In reference to the September 11 attacks he said that "what you have seen in New York, Washington and *Afghanistan* are only in the initial losses and if you (United States) continue the same hostile policies you will see what will make you forget those horrors". He said *Osama bin Laden* had offered a truce to Western countries asking them to pull out their armies from Iraq and Afghanistan in order to live in peace. *Zawahiri* said in the video tape that "to the people of the crusader coalition—— our blessed Sheik

Osama has offered you a truce so that you leave Muslim land. "As he said you will not dream of security until we live it as a reality in Palestine and until all your infidel armies leave *Prophet Mohammad's* lands", he warned. "Our message to you is clear, strong and final. There will be no salvation until you withdraw from our land, stop stealing our oil and resources and end support for infidel (Arab) rulers" *Zawahiri* stated.

Fearing backlash against the Muslim community after the London bombings, a senior Muslim cleric on 4th July, 2005 urged women to stop wearing '*hijabs*'. *Zaki Badawi*, head of the Muslim college in London and Chairman of the Council of Mosques and Imams, said, '*hijabs*' could lead to Muslim women being attacked physically or verbally. "In the present tense situation, with the rise of attacks on Muslims, we advise Muslim women, who fear being attacked physically or verbally to remove their '*hijab*' so as not to be identified by those who are hostile to Muslims', *Badawai* said. He asserted that "dress is meant to protect from harm not to invite it. He further said that preservation of life had a much higher priority than appearance, and *Koran* justified abandoning of the '*hijab*' in present circumstances.

Reacting to the reported Deoband "*fatwa*" that women should not contest poll and if constrained to do so they should come out in a veil, legal expert and former Chairperson of National Minorities Commission *Dr. Tahir Mehmood* said on the 18th of August.'05 that there was nothing in the Islamic history and Shariat to ban Muslim women from participating in public life or requiring to put on veil while doing so. In a statement *Prof. Mehmood* said the *Prophet* saying about the leadership of women reportedly mentioned in the so called '*fatwa*' of Deoband was in a particular context and did not lay down a rule, As regards the practice of wearing a veil, *Mehmood* said that the law of India does not recognize it as an essential practice of Muslim religion which according to the courts and advocates only moderation of social interaction between the two sexes and has no absolute injunction against covering of the face. The matter covering of the face by the Muslim women has come up in some European countries. The Dutch government was seeking a way of banning the wearing of *burquas* and other Muslim face veils in public places. Existing legislation in the country already limits the wearing of *burquas* and other total coverings in public transport or schools.

A court remanded in custody on 8th August, 2005 three men charged with attempted murder over failed attempts to set off bombs in London's transport system. *Yassin Hassan Omar*, *Ibrahim Muktar* and *Ramzi Mohammad* were also charged with conspiracy to murder and explosive offences over the botched attacks on 21st July, 2005. After July, 2005 bombings in London, there had been a steep rise in incidence of hate crime against Hindus and Sikhs, with most of them perpetrated because of mistaken identity. There were as many as 932 instances of such hate crimes against Indians, who were predominantly Hindus or Sikhs, as opposed to approximately 600 instances of faith-related hate crime against Pakistani and Bangladeshi Muslims. *Ramesh Kallidai*, Secretary General of the Forum said "as Asians we all look the same, and are equally vulnerable to any backlash". The Hindu leaders noted that most of the hate crimes against the community were perpetrated through mistaken identity during the backlash after 7th July, 2005 bombings. "However, our greatest concern is that there is no official recognition yet of the vulnerability of Hindus and Sikhs". The leaders of the Forum voiced their anxiety over the lack of community infrastructure to prevent hate crimes and help the victims. "Even worse is the fact that there has been very low levels of government engagement to understand what effect such high levels of hate crime is having on our confidence in the criminal justice system" said *Kallidai*. He further added that very little effort was being made to help increase reporting of hate crime.

Terrorism became a word of threat across the globe. Whenever top leaders of the countries meet each other terrorism is placed as a main agenda for discussion and they resolve in unambiguous terms that it should be curbed and banished from the globe. In the month of September, 2005 there was a Security Council meeting in the United Nations where all the top leaders of the world met. During the 15-member Security Council meeting they unitedly felt the need to ban incitement of terrorism after Britain pushed for a resolution on terrorism following the 7th July, 2005 London bombing. President *Bush* told the Security Council meeting held on 14th Septem' :r, 2005 that" we have a solemn obligation to stop terrorism at its early stage and we must do all we can to disrupt each stage of planning and support for terrorists acts".

Ayman al-Zawahiri, *al-Qaeda* group's second-in-command said in a video tape aired on Arab satellite channel Al Jazeera on 19th September,2005 that al-Qaeda carried out the July,2005 suicide bombings in London to strike at "British arrogance". "The London attack is one of the attacks that *al-Qaeda*... had the honour of carrying out against ..... British arrogance, the aggression of the crusader British against the Muslim nation for over a hundred years". He denounced Britain for "the historical crime of setting up Israel and continuing crimes in Afghanistan and Iraq. These and other attacks have revealed the true hypocritical face of Western civilization that talks about human rights and freedom only as long as it is in its interest", he said citing the planned toughening of the British security laws after the London blasts. A U.S. counter terrorism official said that the tape was "*al-Qaeda's* clearest public statement suggesting that they were responsible (for the London attack). But that in and of itself does not prove that *al-Qaeda* planned or directed the attack. They are quite happy to take responsibility for any terrorist attack".

Faced with a new challenge in the aftermath of the 7/7 London bombings the British were hoping to learn from the experience of their Indian counterparts, in dealing with terrorism and intelligence gathering. In a first of its kind exercise, the British government hosted Kolkata Police Commissioner in England for a week in the month of September, 2005 and the problem of terrorism and ways to tackle the menace topped the agenda during his visit. The Commissioner said that "after the London bombings the British police is also faced with a new challenge. They have not tackled this kind of problem earlier and they are also absorbing ideas from us since we have been dealing with it for long". He further said that "things like tracking down terrorists or dealing with the religious or fundamentalist groups was not akin to the Ireland problem which was more political in nature and continuing since hundred of years. It was, however, assumed that the British police was at a loss to track down the terrorists after the London bombings since they have no sound network with the various communities living in England unlike Indian police. Soon after the bombings, the London police messed up when they shot dead an innocent Brazilian mistaking him for a terrorist." The Commissioner of Kolkata further said that "I think they were appreciative of the ways Kolkata police dealt with the case of American Center shooting. Within a short time the perpetrators of the attack were identified, arrested and prosecuted which probably impressed them".

A British-born Muslim of Gujarati origin was arrested on 22nd October, 2005 after he told a newspaper that he was lined up to be the fifth 7-7-2005 bomber. *Imran Patel* who is believed to have had arms training in Pakistan, was cornered by a team of 20 anti-terrorist officers and taken to Leeds Police station for questioning. He had claimed that he was asked to join the attack on London by his friend terror cell leader *Mohammad Sadique Khan*. Before the 7th July,2005 atrocity, *Khan* and the other London suicide bombers *Shehzad Tanweer*, 22, *Jermaine Lindsay* 19, and *Hasib Hussain*, 18 met at Patel's home in Dewsbury, west Yorkshire. They watched extremist *jihad* videos calling for Muslims to launch holy war. And they held discussions about their "mission" to carry out terrorist attacks in Britain. Patel decided not to join them when they suggested one of their targets should be schools where the victims would be innocent children. Although he refused their invitation to join them, he did not tip off the police about their intention. He said he did not want to see Muslim "brothers" jailed. Patel also claimed he would never attack a target in Britain – though he would willingly do so abroad. But he told a *NEWS OF THE WORLD* reporter that he knew at-least half-a-dozen other Muslims from Dewsbury who have had training in camps in Pakistan and came back to Britain. He said he was friendly with another young Muslim who contemplated to launch an atrocity in London. *Patel* was introduced to Khan, 30 by a close friend who was one of the bomber's relatives. On 7th July, 2005 Khan blew himself up at Edgware Tube station, killing six people. *Patel* said that "*jihad* is valid". The British police launched a thorough investigation into this man and his activities After 7th July, 2005 serial blasts, London came again in the news after the London Police unearthed a major terrorist plot to commit "mass murder of an unimaginable scale by blowing aircraft flying from Britain to the U.S. They have arrested 24 people in the connection on the 10th of August,'06. The plot was "very significant" and was designed to bring down a number of aircraft through mid-flight explosions causing a considerable loss of life. The British intelligence agency M15 said that the threat level was critical – the highest possible – meaning thereby "an attack is expected and indicates an extremely high level of threat to the U.K." Security sources believed that some liquid explosives could be mixed during the flight into a lethal concoction. The plot was intended to be mass murder of unimaginable scale and believed that the terrorist aim was to smuggle explosives onto aero planes in hand baggage and to detonate these in flight. The plot involved to blow up passenger planes flying between the U.K and the U.S.

Twenty-four people were arrested in London, Brimingham and *Thames Valley* in the operation. Police sources said majority were believed to be of Pakistani origin but most, if not all were British Following the above revelation the U.S raised the terror threat to the highest level of 'severe' or red for commercial flights originating in the U.K and bound for the U.S. It also prohibited any liquids, including beverages, hair gels and lotions, from being carried on aircraft. The British Airways said any of its passengers who failed to comply with the government's restrictions on luggage and other items would not be allowed on its planes. Passengers were also advised that no electrical or battery powered items, including laptops, mobile phones, ipods and remote controls could be carried in the cabin and must be checked in as hold baggage.

The British Government said that although the alleged plot to blow up American planes in mid-air, using sophisticated liquid explosives was "planned" and "driven" in the United Kingdom, intelligence from Pakistan was crucial .in disrupting it. The British Government arrested 24 persons and froze the assets of 19 people. The Home Secretary of the British Government singled out Pakistan for its help saying it was "grateful" to the Pakistanis for their co-operation in foiling an attempt to commit "mass murder on an unimaginable scale."The British security agencies, which had been investigating the alleged conspiracy for several months, decided to act on the 9th August,'06 night after intelligence from Pakistan suggested that it could be executed anytime – as early as within 48 hours. This followed the arrest of two Britons of Pakistani origin in Pakistan in the first week of August,'06. The British police swung into action after reportedly intercepting a message from Pakistan suggesting that the attacks were imminent. The Pakistani Government claimed that it played a "very important role in uncovering and breaking this international terrorist network. After American criticism of Pakistan's role in fighting terrorism Islamabad appeared to have regained its credentials as a "valuable" ally in Western eyes.

However, most of the twenty-four people arrested in connection with the alleged plot were reported to be young men of Pakistani origin, though born and brought up in Britain. One of the alleged suspects was identified as young white convert to Islam who married a Muslim woman. Another suspect was said to be a woman. Most of the arrests were made in East London, High Wycombe, Brimingham and Buckingshire. As investigations continued with nationwide searches of residential and business premises a "martyrdom video" was found at one of the addresses. There was concern in the Muslim community that it might face a "backlash" once the names of the alleged suspects were published. Amin Asmin *Tariq*, who was among the 24 arrested is said to be an employee of a private Indian air carrier. *Tariq* a British national was from east London and a security worker at the Heathrow airport. He was arrested after a car chase.

Investigators on three continents worked to fill in the full, frightening picture of a suspected plot to blow the U.S jetliners out of the Atlantic skies, tracking the money trail and seizing more alleged conspirators in the teeming towns of eastern Pakistan. In Islamabad, investigators probing the plot suspected involvement of four Islamic militant groups, including the Pakistan-based extremist outfit Lashkar-e-Jhangvi. The probe revealed that funds provided by a U.K. based Islamic charity for earthquake relief in Pakistan-occupied Kashmir (*POK*) was apparently been used to target planes. The two U.K-based outfits *Al Mahajroon* and Hizbul Tehrir and two Pakistani organizations LeT and Lashkar-e-Jhangvi (LJ) were already on the watch-list.

Investigations revealed that a U.K-based Islamic charity group remitted a huge amount of money to three individuals having bank accounts in Mirpur (*POK*). In December, 2005 with the sole purpose of helping its recipients and their organizations carry out the plan to bomb the aircraft in the U.K. The links with *LeT*, which was based in Pakistan, was disquieting for Islamabad as the outfit was already blamed for the Mumbai bomb blasts in the month of July,'06. New Delhi was demanding that Pakistan take stern action against the *Jamaat-ud-Dawa* (JuD), an Islamic charity organization, which India was saying the reincarnation of the banned *LeT*. A day before the plot to blow up the planes unfolded in London, Pakistan police in a midnight swoop put the LeT founder-leader and head of *J-u-D Hafeez Sayeed* under house arrest. *Sayeed* was arrested to prevent him from taking part in a rally planned to be held by the group on August, 14. Pakistan's Independence Day. *J-u-D*, which was officially kept on the watch-list along with another banned group, *JeM*, had officially been allowed by the Pakistan government in the year '05 to take part in relief work in the quake-affected area of *PoK* and NWFP during which the two outfits reportedly received and spent large amounts of money for relief and rehabilitation.

The British police, on 21st August,'06 charged eight British Muslims with plotting to blow up planes after police found bomb-making equipment, suicide notes and 'martyrdom videos' Three others were also charged with terrorism-related offences by police investigating a suspected plot to attack several airliners flying from Britain to the United States.

Eight suspects were charged with conspiracy to murder and preparing for acts of terrorism. They were accused of plotting to smuggle parts of homemade bombs onto planes, then build the bombs and detonate them. The police had seized a huge amount of equipment and evidence, including 'martyrdom videos' in sixty-nine searches of houses, businesses, vehicles and open spaces. They had found bomb-making equipment, chemicals including hydrogen peroxide, electrical components and documents. A 17-year man was charged with possessing items useful to a terrorist, including a book on home-made bombs, suicide notes, wills "with the identities of persons prepared to commit acts of terrorism" and a map of Afghanistan. Two other suspects – including the mother of an eight-month-old-baby – were charged with failing to report the plot. Of the 23 Muslims arrested in the operation, eleven were detained pending a decision whether to charge them.

The British police arrested on 2nd Septemer,'06 sixteen men in two separate anti-terrorism operations just three weeks after uncovering a suspected plot to bring down the U.S bound airliners over the Atlantic. Fourteen of the men who were held in London in an operation focused on suspected training recruitment and encouraging others to take part in terrorist activity. Anti-terrorist police in Manchester arrested two men early on 2nd Sept.,'06 were carrying out three searches but this was not linked to the London arrests. Twelve of the London arrests were made at or near a Chinese restaurant in south London that police riot gear raided on 1st Sept.'06 night, questioning diners for hours and taking some away in handcuffs. The probe was linked to alleged 'training camps' in Britain as there had been reports of militants getting together for adventure training as a means to develop closer ties. The arrests came soon after the head of London Police's anti-terrorist branch, said in a television interview that police were keeping tabs on thousand of British Muslims who they suspected might be involved in or support terrorism higher than previous official estimates. The fourteen men held in south and east London on 1st Sept.'06 night and early 2nd Sept. morning were arrested in a pre-planned intelligence-led operations..

Al-Qaeda might be planning to attack rail and air travel in Europe, possibly targeting the busy holiday travel season, according to intelligence findings. The CBS report, citing Arab and other intelligence sources, said interrogations of al-Qaeda suspects who recently left Afghanistan and Pakistan raised the concerns. "One suspect said plans for repeating the Heathrow attempt (a plot foiled in August,'06 to bomb trans-atlantics airplanes) were all prepared", the network quoted an Arab Official as saying on 10th Nov.'06.

"It is now a matter of taking action ... *al-Qaeda's* strategy appears to be raising the pressure in Europe", the report said. The report came as Britain's intelligence agency, M15 said on 10th Nov.'06 that Muslim extremists were plotting at least 30 major terrorist attacks in Britain, and the threats may involve chemical and nuclear devices. Britain suffered its worst peacetime attack in July'05 when four British Islamists blew themselves up on London's transport network, killing 52 commuters and wounding hundreds

Britain is facing a 'very great threat' from a wave of plots among Muslim extremists and a terrorist attack on the U.K .is highly likely. Echoing a warning by the head of Britain's domestic spy agency M15, British authorities were aware of 30 active terrorist plots. "There are a lot of conspirators out there. These 30 are the ones we think are the most serious of them. They are ongoing, they are working and they have the potential....some will be nearer preparation than others." said the Home Secretary. The spy agency M15 sacked around 1,600 suspects, many of them Muslim extremists, most of whom were British-born and linked to *al-Qaeda* in Pakistan. The agency revealed that young British Muslims were being groomed to become suicide bombers. The British Government will not simply arrest or stop the suspected Muslims as it was difficult to gather sufficient information to constitute evidence strong enough for prosecution. The Home Secretary said that "information is not evidence, this is one of the great problems. You can have information, you can have suspicion, you can put a case together, but it doesn't naturally constitute evidence. And in this country we have a rule of law which says that in order to try someone you have to have evidence".

After taking over charge from *Tony Blair* as new Britain's Prime Minister, *Gordon Brown* cautioned his country-men to realize that the terrorist threat Britain faces is "long term and sustained" He said that "it was clear that we are dealing in general terms with people who are associated with al-Qaeda.

On 30th June, 2007 the terrorists raised their ugly heads

again in London. *Kafeel Ahmed*, a Bangalore born Engineer working in London rammed a flaming jeep into the main entrance of Glasgow airport, shattering the glass doors and sparking a raging fire just metres from people lined up at check-in counters on the first day of summer vacation for Glaswegian school children. The police took him into custody and admitted in the hospital with ninety per cent burns. *Khaleel* left to the U.K after doing his M.Phil and he completed a Ph.d in Aerodynamics there. *Khaleel* also completed his B.E in mechanical engineering from the University BDT College of Engineering at Davangere in 2000. He secured fifth rank in his final exam.

After ailing in the hospital for some time. *Kafeel Ahmed* succumbed to the injuries.

The Indian doctor *Mohd. Haneef* help by the Australian police on terror charges along with *Kafeel* was realeased on 27th July, "07 from custody after the case against him collapsed dramatically in Court with the prosecution admitting mistakes.

A court in London sentenced on 11th July" 07 four men to forty years jail each for plotting to bomb London's transport system on 21st July, 2005 The botched attempt was to replicate Islamist suicide bombings that had killed 52 people. They are all Muslims of African origin.

12
Blast Rock Egyptian Resort

A rapid series of car bombs and another blast ripped through a luxury hotel and a coffee shop in the Egyptian Red Sea resort of *Sharm El-Sheik* on 23rd July, 2005 killing eighty-eight people. The attacks appeared well co-ordinated. Two car bombs with suicide attackers went off simultaneously at 1.15 a.m. (0345 IST) some four k.m. apart. A third bomb, believed hidden in a sack, detonated around the same time near a beach side walkway where tourists often stroll at night. According to a hotel employee "a suicide car bomber forced the barrier at the entrance of the hotel. A member of the security staff tried to stop him but he sped towards the reception and there was a huge explosion." Several hours after the attacks, a group citing ties to *al-Qaeda* claimed responsibility on an Islamic web site and asserted that the bombings were revenge for "crimes committed against Muslims".

All the world leaders condemned the attack. Egyptian President *Hosni Mubarak* said that the killing of 88 people in the tourist resort bomb attacks would only serve to stiffen his resolve to combat militants. He said that "this will only make us more determined to pursue terrorism and dig it out by the roots. We will not give in to its blackmail or seek a truce."

A second unknown group calling itself *Mujahedeen Egypt* had claimed the deadly triple bombings in *Sharm al-Sheikh* on 23rd July, 2005. The statement posted on an Islamic website said, "Your brothers in the Mujahedeen Egypt carried out the blessed earthquake in *Sharm al-sheikh.* Do not believe what is being said about the claim made by al-Qaeda, may God protect it. The five "*martyrs*" carried out seven bombings, against hotels and tourist buses used by "*Zionists*". As long as the Zionists do not get out of the land of the Muslims, they will be digging their own graves with their own hands."

Meanwhile the Egyptian police exchanged fire with gunmen on 25th July 2005 as they hunted for six Pakistanis suspected of involvement in deadly bombings in the Red Sea Resort of *Sharm al-Sheik.* Intelligence source said that "two Pakistanis had been staying there and it is suspected that the bombs were assembled in this area." Pictures of the six Pakistanis believed to have entered Egypt in early July 2005 were distributed to police stations in the *Sharm el-Sheik* area after the attacks.

13

Simultaneous Bombing Across Bangladesh

About 400 small bombs planted by an Islamic militant outfit exploded almost simultaneously in cities and towns across Bangladesh on 17th August,'05 between 11.00 a.m. and 11.30 a.m.(local time). The ugly face of religious extremism came to haunt South Asia yet again and this time in Bangladesh. The blasts which were carried out in a co-ordinated manner only revealed how cohesive the organization of terrorist activities simultaneously in cities and towns across Bangladesh. A rickshaw puller and a child died and at least 138 people were injured in nearly 400 explosions of crude bombs. The militants targeted government offices, courts and press clubs in all but one of the 64 districts in the first such attack in the politically volatile country. Home Minister Lutfuzzaman Baber told that "this is not a scattered incident, but an organized one. In such attacks it is possible that a motive is there". The attacks were an attempt to create chaos and unrest in the country. The explosion came at a time when Prime Minister *Khaleda Zia* was away in China on a five-day visit focusing on trade.

The Government of Bangladesh detained 100 Islamic extremist A number of them were students or teachers from *madrassas* or Islamic Seminaries. Among them a Bangladeshi *madrasa* student of 18 years old was caught with a video, which showed speeches of Osama bin Laden and military training strategies. Two others found with books containing training manuals. These three were transferred to the capital for further questioning.

Two people were killed and 40 injured in a series of bombings at courts in the three districts of Bangladesh on 3rd October,'05, in an apparent repeat of the nationwide 17th August 2005 bombings. One person was killed and five others were injured when a youth hurled a bomb concealed in a book at a court in central Chandpur district. The injured included court official. In another attack in Luxmipur district, one person was killed and 30 others injured when two youths hurled bombs at a court building. In the third incident, bombs exploded in three places in Chittagong city injuring at least five people.

Security experts in Bangladesh said that the radical Islamists behind Bangladesh second bombings in less than two months targeted the judiciary to press for the introduction of Islamic laws in the mainly Muslim democracy. The simultaneous blasts on 17th August 2005 at court houses in three towns, which killed two people and wounded others including a district judge, to terrorize judges due to try people arrested for string of attacks in August, 2005. It was suspected that the militants wanted to intimidate the judiciary, as they demanded radical changes in the legal system in favour of Shariat law.

Assailants hurled homemade bombs at ruling party members in two separate attacks in southwestern Bangladesh injuring at least 22 of them, including staffers chatting in front of a party office on 8th October, 2005. Though nobody claimed responsibility for the attacks on members of the ruling Bangladesh Nationalist party in the Jessore and Chudanga districts it was, however, suspected the hand of Maoist militants who have been active in the area. On the same night 20 party members were injured when unidentified assailants hurled a bomb at the ruling party's office at Keshobpur in Jessore district. 140 km west of the capital of Dhaka.

On the morning of 1-12-2005 a powerful blast took place outside the Deputy Commissioner Office of Gaziapur town of Bangladesh killing two people and injuring 20 others. A suspected Islamic militant was caught from the blast scene with an injury. This is the second bomb attack in Gaziapur after November 2005 when Islamic militant outfit JMB's suicide squad exploded powerful bombs in a bar library in which seven people including two lawyers were killed. Simultaneous explosions rocked southeastern Chittagong court, where two people including a policeman were killed. The suspected militant *Mahmud Hossain* was trying to enter the office in the guise of a tea boy carrying a flask containing the bomb. Being challenged by the police guards, the bomber threw the flask at the police. The militant lost both his legs in the blast and died on 1st, December, 2005.

Unidentified assailants hurled three bombs at a tea shop in a market in western Bangladesh killing *Kajal Mahmud*, a local leader of the governing Bangladesh Nationalist party on 15th Dec.'05 in Meherpur district. *Mahmud* and three friends were having tea at a shop in a village market when four masked men threw the bombs at them. The friends were injured and admitted to the hospital.

14
Attack on the U.S Vessels in Jordon

Terrorist outfit *al-Qaeda* fired rockets at the US Navy ships in Jordon's Aqaba port on 19th August 2005 but they missed their targets and hit a warehouse and a hospital killing a Jordanian soldier and striking the Isreali port of Eilat. A statement carried on an Islamism website claimed that "a group of our mujahideen had targeted the US vessels in Jordon and (Israel's) Eilat port with three Katyusha rockets before safely returning to their base". These rockets were launched from an industrial warehouse area near the entrance to the city and the Jordanian Security force were searching for a Syrian and two Iraqis who were in Aqaba and used Kuwaiti number plates. Immediately after the attack, the two US amphibious assault ships, which had been on a joint training exercise with the Jordanian navy, weighed anchor and headed for the safety open water.

The US Commander of the Fifth Fleet in Bahrain said one missile narrowly missed the *USS Ashland*, an amphibious warfare ship that was designed to transport marines and to launch assault landing craft and helicopters. The Commander of the Fifth Fleet in Bharain said that "a rocket flew over the bow of *USS Ashland* and the rocket impacted in the roof of a warehouse. It was pretty safe to conclude that they were probably trying to hit one or both of the ships.

On the night of 9th, November 2005 suicide bombers attacked on luxury hotels in Jordon that killed 57 people and wounded 110. In a synchronized attack, two bombs exploded while crowds were celebrating weddings, leaving blood and destruction at Amman's luxury *Grand Hyatt* hotel and the nearby Radisson SAS. A third blast targeted a Days Inn Hotel.

Al-Qaeda in Iraq, led by Jordanian militant *Abu Musab al-Zarqawi* claimed the responsibility of the killings and said in a statement on an Islamism website that "a group of our best lions" had launched the attacks in Jordon. The message said that "some hotels were chosen which the Jordanian despot had turned into a backyard for the enemies of the faith of the Jews and crusaders". It was suspected that the blasts were the work of suicide bombers. Simultaneous attacks are an *al-Qaeda* hall-mark. Jordan's King *Abdullah* blamed a "deviant and misled group" for the blasts. The attacks targeted and killed innocent Jordanian civilians. Jordan is bordered by Iraq, Syria, Saudi Arabia and Israel. Jordan is one of two Arab countries that have signed peace treaties with Israel. It helped the United States in the war on Iraq, where *Zarqawi's* group is part of an anti-U.S insurgency.

The bombs at the hotels, all run by U.S chains, were timed to detonate almost simultaneously. The explosion at the *Radisson* tore through a banqueting room where about 250 people were at a wedding reception. A smaller wedding, attended by several dozen well-dressed young people, was going on at the Hyatt. Many westerners, including tourists, businessmen and foreign contractors working in Iraq, were staying at the three hotels. The *Radisson* is known to be popular with Israeli tourists.

An Iraqi woman confessed on Jordanian television on 13th October ,2005 that she had tried to blow herself up alongside her husband in an Amman hotel on 9th November 2005 in one of three attacks that killed more than 50 people.

She was identified as *Sajida Al-Rishawi*, appeared in a headscarf and long black coat describing her attempts to detonate an explosives-laden belt at a wedding celebration in the *Radisson* hotel. In a statement *Rishawi* said "We went into the hotel. He (my husband) took a corner and I took another. There was a wedding in the hotel. There were women and children. "My husband executed the attack. I tried to detonate and it failed. People started running and I ran with them," *Rishawi* said.

15

Attack in Bali in Indonesia

On the 1st of Oct., 2005 suicide bombers made three attacks in Bali, Indonesia and killed 26 people and wounded 122 others. Three bombs tore through restaurants packed with evening. Two attacks at outdoor seafood eateries on Jimbaran Beach and one at a bar at Kuta Beach in an area surrounded by shops and jammed with pedestrians including children.

The attacks were the latest in a number of bomb blasts in Indonesia in recent years, which had hurt tourism and raised concerns among investors about security in the world's most populous nation. Preliminary investigations revealed that the terrorists had not used vehicles and rather their own bodies. Investigators found heads detached from their bodies and all of them were around the area of blasts. All precautions were taken on the 2nd of October 2005 in Jakarta to guard pivotal points such as embassies and other public places.

Jakarta experienced deadly car-bomb attacks on a luxury hotel in 2003 and outside the Australian embassy in 2004. Security experts said that the strikes bore hallmarks of Jemaah Islamiya, a network seen as the regional arm of *al-Qaeda*. Police blame *Jemaah Islamiya* for the 2002 blasts and a series of attacks against Western tourists as targets in the world's most populous Muslim nation. Following the attacks in Bali, the U.S Embassy in Jakarta warned the Americans on 2nd

October that they and their interests could be targets of attacks in Indonesia.

Azahari Bin Husin, a British educated bomber, was suspected of masterminding the near simultaneous attacks on three crowded restaurants in the Indonesian resort island of Bali. Forty-eight-year-old *Azhari Bin Husin*, who completed a doctorate at Reading University in the 1990s before being trained with the *al-Qaeda*, was known in his native Malaysia as 'demolition man' and suspected to have masterminded the Bali attacks. Azahari learnt his bomb-making craft on one of *Laden's* Afghan training camps, and hunted by the Indonesian security services for his active involvement in Jemaah Islamiya, the group which was the most feared terrorist network in Southeast Asia. The group was behind the 2002 Bali attacks in which car bombers killed 202 people, including 88 Australians, in attacks on night-clubs in the tourists resort of Kutta, the scene of one of 1st October 2005 explosion. The group was also blamed for the bombings at the *JW Marriott Hotel* in Jakarta which killed 12 people in 2003 and a car bomb blast outside the Australian embassy in 2004 which killed eleven people.

Southeast Asia became a base and target of Islamic extremism. Indonesia has borne the brunt of many an attack, with hardly a year going by without its share of terror. The Bali bombings of 2002 were followed by the attack on Jakarta's Marritt hotel in 2003, and the targeting of the Australian embassy in September 2004. Each of these attacks, including of October 2005, bore the footprint of the *Jemaah Islamiya* which is believed to have links with the *al-Qaeda.* This was a challenge face not just Indonesia, not just Southeast Asia, but the world.

A top anti-terrorism official said the investigation into the October, 2005 attacks focused on Islamic militants blamed for previous bloody bombings in the world's most populous Muslim nation, Investigation through video footage revealed that a man in a black shirt and jeans strolling into a restaurant on the resort island, followed almost instantly by an explosion. Involvement of *Jemaah Islamiah* was suspected and the investigations moved in that direction.

Indonesian police have made their first arrest over October, 2005 suicide bombings on the resort island of Bali, picking up a man in East Java suspected of links in the attacks.

16
Convicts of Mumbai Bomb Blasts, 1993

ABU SALEEM & MONICA BEDI

After a prolonged legal battle underworld don *Abu Salem* was extradited on 11th November, 2005 from Portugal along with *Monica Bedi* and arrested him under Terrorist and Disruptive activities Act and Indian Penal code provisions for his complicity in the 1993 serial blasts case in Mumbai. *Salem* was produced amidst tight security before a special court in Mumbai which remanded him to Police custody and *Monica Bedi* was produced before a local court in Hyderabad, Andhra Pradesh for her production in a passport forgery case.

Monica Bedi, who acted, in a few Telugu and Hindi films before getting close to *Abu Salem* has a fake passport case against her. *Monica Badi's* Andhra Pradesh connection was not through movies but with a passport issued to a Kurnool address. *Salem* obtained passports from Kurnool with a fictitious names and addresses for himself, wife Shabana and *Monica Bedi* in July 2002. *Monica* alone used the fake passport to flee to Portugal, where she was detained along with *Abu Salem*.

From a PCO booth owner to one of *Dawood Ibrahim's* important henchmen, *Abu Salem's* crime career started as a taxi driver in Delhi before shifting to Mumbai where he began as a small timer in Mumbai's underworld. *Salem alias Abdul Saleem Ansari*, who was brought to Mumbai on the morning of 11th November, 2005 was wanted in more than five dozen cases by the Central Bureau of Investigation and various police stations in India.. Thirty six-year-old *Salem*, who hails from Azamgarh in Uttar Pradesh, moved to Mumbai in mid 1980's and engaged himself in petty crime while operating a telephone booth in the northern suburb of Andheri. Salem, considered one of the most dreaded underworld figures wanted in connection with more than 60 cases became a gun runner with the D-company of *Dawood Ibrahim* through his younger brother *Anees Ibrahim*.

Abu Salem, and his girlfriend-wife, *Monica Bedi* married two Protugal partners on paper to get Portugese citizenship so as to avoid any chance of extradition. It was *Salem*, who first married a Protuguese girl. Subsequently *Monica* too married a man of that nation. The marriages had taken place almost a year before *Salem* was caught by the police in 2002. *Salem* partially succeeded in his attempt as he received a permanent residency status for himself and *Monica* in Portugal, where laws allow such status to the spouses of Portuguese citizens. After the residency status, the duo planned to apply for citizenship and in that event it would have been difficult for the Government of India to have them extradited. *Salem*, ran out of luck in the intermittent period when he was caught by Portuguese authorities on the basis of a red corner notice issued by the Interpol against him. Recovery of a forged Pakistani passport added to his woes. *Salem* had cleverly decided to settle down in Lisbon as he wanted to evade Indian investigation agencies. *Salem* and *Monica* were arrested by the Portuguese authorities in 2002 and charged with possession of forged documents. *Salem* has three Indian and one Pakistani passport, while *Monica Bedi* has two Indian Passports. Interestingly none of them tried to procure passports using their true names. The passports possessed by Salem and Monica were genuine ones, but they have been procured using false information. *Salem* procured the three passports in India even though he was at large, enjoying the costly comforts in West Asia and Europe. He acquired a passport in the name of *Akil Ahmed Azmi* from Lucknow, *Danish Baig* from Bhopal and *Ramin Malik* from Hyderabad, Andhra Pradesh.

Monica Bedi, had denied that the gangster *Abu Saleem* was her husband. The underworld don refuted her claims before the CBI sleuths on 20th November, 2005 and claimed that the marriage was performed in the United States after *Monica* had changed her religion. When *Salem* was asked to produce the *'nikah nama'*, he told the CBI that he neither possessed the original marriage certificate nor its photocopy. Asked to give the address of the *maulvi* who performed the marriage, *Salem* said he did not remember him. The CBI sources hinted that there was a possibility that he was having only a live-in relation with *Monica*.

Salem had 45 cases registered against him faced charges on only eight cases that were presented by the CBI in Lisbon for the extradition process. Infact, *Salem* could not be tried even for the high profile murder of music baron *Gulshan Kumar*, and attempted murder on the lives of film producers *Rakesh Roshan* and *Rajiv Rai*. *Abu Salem* has confessed his complicity in the 1993 Bombay bomb blast case to the CBI. An envelope containing *Salem's* confession was delivered in a Tada court by the Chief Metropolitan Magistrate on 21st November,2005.

While *Monica Bedi* was in the custody at Hyderabad her family pitched in support of their daughter's claim that she had never married underworld don *Abu Salem* saying their "innocent child" had been misled by the gangster. Her father *Prem Kumar Bedi*, and mother, *Shakuntala* said that *Monica* never knew Salem's true identity until she moved to Dubai. She had never married *Salem* and was trapped. "We are calling her home because she has no future left in India". *Prem Kumar Bedi* migrated to Norway in 1975 from Hoshiarpur in Punjab. He said though his daughter had referred to *Salem* in the past, she had never revealed his real identity to the family. "She introduced him as one *Sanjay*, a friend who helped her get a few films . According to him, he met the don for the first time in 2002 in prison following the arrest of *Salem* and *Monica* . He said that "when he first met Salem he introduced himself as *Sanjay*. *Salem* never gave an impression of being a notorious underworld don".

Abu Salem, who was in the custody of Mumbai police in connection with the murder of builder *Pradeep Jain*, has confessed to his role in the case. He also confessed his role in the murder of *Ajit Dewani* former Secretary to Bollywood actress *Manisha Koirala*. This is the third case in which Salem has confessed to his role, the first one was the 1993 bomb blast case and the second was the *Pradeep Jain* murder case. He also disclosed to the magistrate the names of all those Bollyhood personalities from whom he had extorted money. The gangster also talked about his association with *Shah Alam* who was arrested in this case for helping *Salem* in extorting money from the victims in Bollyhood. *Dewani* was murdered in 2002 allegedly on the instructions from *Salem*. The alleged killers were also arrested. The *Ajit Dewani* murder case was one of the two cases on the basis on which *Salem* was extradited from Portugal.

The Ahmedabad police shot dead four men having links with the Kashmir-based *Harkat-ul-Mujahideen* on 17th March, 2005 in a house near Varva. After the Varanasi blasts and the RDX blast at Ahmedabad railway station, vigilance had been stepped up in the city. The police later found that one of the four terrorists killed in police encounter was a Pakistani and "chief commander:" of the militant outfit *Harkat-ul-Mujahadeen* in Kashmir. He was identified as *Azaan*, a Pakistani. He was the "most wanted" terrorist in Kashmir and was involved in numerous terrorist activities in *Jammu and Kashmir*. The two others were identified as *Mohammad Javed* and *Mohd.Ayub* both Kashmiris.

The Special TADA Court framed charges against extradited don *Abu Salem* and co-accused *Riyaz Siddiqui* in the 1993 bomb blast case. The Central Bureau of Investigation had proposed 14 charges against *Salem* and *Siddiqui* on 18th March, '06 before the TADA Court for the 1993 Mumbai serial blasts, which killed 256 people and injured 713. *Salem* and *Siddiqui* were charged with criminal conspiracy, abetting and facilitating commission of terrorist acts.

In the second week of January 1993, *Salem* had gone to Baruch in Gujarat with absconding accused *Aziz Bilakhia* to collect arms and transport them to Mumbai. He also collected nine AK-56 rifles, 100 hand grenades, cartridges and magazines from Sansrod village near Baruch, Gujarat and transported them to Mumbai via Bhiwandi, concealed in false cavities in a Maruti van. *Salem*, along with *Baba Chauan* and Magnum video co-owner *Samir Hingora*, delivered nine AK-56 rifles and some hand grenades to actor *Sanjay Dutt* at his Bandra House in the second week of January 1993. A few days later, at the instance of absconding accused *Aziz* and *Anees Ibrahim*, *Salem* and co-accused *Manzoor Ahmed* and *Hanif Kadawala* took two AK-56 rifles from *Dutt's* house and kept them at Zaibunnisa Kazi's house at Vindyachal Apartments at Bandra. Since the arms were in *Salem's* possession and control, and were intended to endanger lives and serious damage to property in India was charged under the TADA Act, the Explosive Substances Act and the Arms Act. These Acts also applied because of his participation in transporting arms and ammunition from Gujarat and delivering them to Sanjay Dutt.

Monica Bedi was under the judicial custody at Chanchalguda prison in Hyderabad, Andhra Pradesh. Her father *Prem Kumar Bedi* who was anxious to see her was allowed to meet her for half-an-hour. Meanwhile, *Abu Salem's* lawyer also met *Monica* in the jail. *Monica* was charged with obtaining a fake passport along with her boyfriend and underworld don *Abu Salem*, on 29th September,,2006 was convicted and sentenced by a special court for CBI cases to undergo five years rigorous imprisonment. The judge also imposed a fine of Rs.2,000/-on *Monica* on three counts and ordered she should serve simple imprisonment for three months in default. All the sentences were to run concurrently. Three others, including retired assistant sub-inspector *Shaik Abdul Sattar*, postman *Gokari Saheb* and former Revenue Inspector *Mohd. Yunus*, who helped her in getting the passport by producing fake documents, were handed down three years of rigorous imprisonment each, All the accused were present in the court hall when the judgment was pronounced.

Monica Bedi had served the remand period in the Chanchalguda Central Jail, Hyderabad ,A.P (about a year). It was considered as part of the sentence. The judge also gave *Monica* a month's time to prefer an appeal in the High Court. The sentence brought to an end to the proceedings which lasted for eleven months ever since she was brought to Hyderabad on 11th November,'05. In all 38 witnesses were examined and 79 documents were marked.

CONVICTION OF TIGER MEMON & OTHERS

Thirteen years after the serial blasts killed 257 people in Mumbai, a TADA Court on 12th September, 2006 pronounced its verdict convicting three brothers and sister-in-law of prime accused *Ibrahim Musthaq Memon* alias *Tiger Memon*, who is absconding. Three other members of the *Memon* family his mother, another brother and sister-in-law were left off by the Judge on benefit of doubt.

Tiger Memon's brothers, *Yakub, Essa* and *Yousuf*– and sister-in-law *Rubina* – were found guilty of conspiracy for thirteen serial blasts that rocked Mumbai on 12th March,1993 which left 257 people dead and 713 injured. *Tiger Memon's* father, *Abdul Razack*, was also an accused but the case against him abated after his demise during the course of trail.

The Mumbai blasts were masterminded by the underworld don *Dawood Ibrahim* with the help of his lieutenants, *Tiger Memon* and *Mohammad Dossa*, allegedly at the instance of Pakistan's intelligence agency, ISI to avenge the demolition of *Babri Masjid. Dawood, Memon* and *Dossa* were accused along with another 26 people. *Dawood* was already abroad when the blasts occurred, *Memon* and *Dossa* fled a day before.

The *Memons* had allowed the use of their garages for loading RDX into the vehicles involved in the bombing of 13 crucial points in Mumbai on 12th March, 1993. *Tiger Memon* and his brother *Yakub* also arranged for payment to two other members of the *Memon* family in the NRI account in the Bandra Branch of Hongkong Bank, in the names of *Ayub, Rubina Shababa Reshma Memon. Yakub* was also convicted for providing tickets to the co-accused to travel to Pakistan for training in arms and ammunition. He was found guilty of possessing arms and ammunition and distributing them among the co-accused besides purchasing vehicles that were used in the explosion. *Mohammad Essa* was found guilty of conspiracy and allowing the use of his flat at *Al-Hussani* building in Mahim for meetings to plan the blasts and storing arms, ammunition and explosives. *Yousuf* and *Rubina* were also convicted on similar charges. As a matter of fact, the CBI had named 199 persons as accused of which 94 were on bail and 29 in jail.

Asgar Yusuf Mukadam, a former accountant of *Tiger Memon* and accused No.10, and *Shahnawaz Abdul Khader Qureshi*, accused No.29 were found guilty of parking an RDX-laden car at Plaza theatre which exploded on 12th March, 1993 at 3.15 p.m. *Mukadam* was driving the car while *Qureshi* accompanied him. *Qureshi* was also found guilty of receiving arms and training in Pakistan. *Mukadam* and *Qureshi* were convicted for conspiracy, distributing funds for terror acts and stuffing RDX in several cars which exploded, killing 257 persons and injuring 713. *Mukadam*, whose cousin *Shoaib Ghansar* convicted for planting an RDX-laden scooter in *Zaveri Bazaar* that killed 17 and injured 37 were also found guilt and also helping other accused to plant explosive-laden bags in three five star hotels-*Sea Rock* in Bandra, *Centaur* in Juhu and Centuar Airport. There were no casualties in these blasts but damage to property was estimated at Rs.13 crore

The special TADA Court hearing the 1993 Mumbai blasts case on 19th September,'6 convicted *Abdul Gani Turk* after finding him guilty of packing an explosive-laden jeep at *Centry Bazar* in Worli area, where 113 people were killed and several others injured. He had also been found guilty of participating in the RDX planting operation at Shekadi coast in Raigad district and participating in the meeting where the conspiracy of the blast was hatched. .

Meanwhile, *Asghar Mukadam* and *Shahnawaz Qureshi*, both found guilty by the TADA Court for their role in the blasts pleaded for leniency in sentence saying they were not terrorists and were emotionally driven into the conspiracy.

While the law taking its own course to punish the guilty in 1993 Mumbai blast case, Pakistan on 20th September,'06 made it clear that it would not entertain any fresh demand from India for extradition of underworld don *Dawood Ibrahim*. "This (the new terror mechanism) will not make any difference to that because we have (already) seriously investigated those complaints". Pakistan High Commissioner to India *Aziz Ahmed Khan* told a TV channel when asked about India's demand to extradite terrorists like *Dawood*, *Mazood Azhar* and *Hafeez Mohammad Sayeed*.

Tiger Memon aide, *Parvez Sheik* accused No.12 found guilty on 17 counts for parking an RDX-laden scooter in Katha Bazaar, killing four and injuring 21, and a suit-case filled with

RDX in *Hotel Sea Rock*, Bandra causing damage to property worth more than Rs.9 crore. Before *Hotel Sea Rock* was bombed, *Sheik* had sent another person to book the room under a fictitious name. This man put his evidence on record and the court accepted it. *Sheik* was also found guilty of participating in the Shekhadi landing of arms and ammunition and taking part in the filling of RDX with pencil timer in vehicles on the night of 11th March, 1993 which were used the next day.

For the first time since the special TADA Court started deliverance of verdicts in the 1993 Mumbai bomb blasts case, it established the involvement of underworld don *Dawood Ibrahim* in the bombing. On 22nd September 2006, the court convicted *Dawood Ibrahim Phanse* and *Sharif Abdul Gafoor Parkar* and recognized that *Phanse* was found guilty on the charge that he met underworld don *Dawood Ibrahim* in Dubai and was told by him to help in the landing of arms and ammunition in India. This evidence admitted by the court on his confession established *Dawood Ibrahim's* role in the bomb blasts without any doubts. *Phanse alias Dawood Taklya* was convicted on the charges of attending a meeting in Dubai convened by *Dawood Ibrahim* to plan the conspiracy and later organized the landing of arms, ammunition and explosives on Shekadi coast in Raigad district on 3rd and 7th February,1993. Accused No.17 *Parkar* alias *Dadabhai* was also found guilty under various sections of TADA Act for organizing landing of arms and ammunition at Shekadi coast in Raigad district on 3rd and 7th February,1993. In his confession to the police, Phanse had submitted that he was involved in the landing of smuggled silver and other goods. He had said that he went to Dubai and met *Dawood Ibrahim* and that he talked about revenge and asked him to help in the landing of arms and ammunition. *Phanse* had added that after the meeting *Dawood* had sent him back to the hotel in a Mercedes car and those present received Rs.15 lakh each for their role in landing, while more than Rs.12 lakh were given in bribes to officials of the port, where the explosives landed. However, the third charge against him that he had reportedly bribed several Customs Officials did not come up in the court. *Parkar* on the other hand was also found guilty of identifying a place in village Sandheri and Borghat in Raigad where the other co-accused were given area training, by *Dawood's* men.

The TADA Court on 26th September,06 held five suspended policemen guilty of aiding and abetting terrorist acts by helping in transportation of arms and explosives used in the 1993 serial blasts from Raigad to Mumbai in consideration of a bribe of Rs.7 lakh. This was the first ever conviction of law enforcers arrested in the case, Others in the dock include Customs Officials. Among the five held guilty was *Vijay Patil*, the then Police sub-inspector posted at Shrivardhan police station who was convicted for conspiracy by allowing passage of arms from Raigad. Others held guilty under TADA (p) Act were constables *Ashok Muneshwar*, *P.M.Mahadik*, *Ramesh Mali* and *S.Y.Pashilkar*. Patil was held guilty for conspiracy as he had cleared the arms laden truck at Ghondgar checkpost in Raigad. Others were not found guilty of conspiracy as they had merely followed Patil's directives, and hence were convicted only for aiding and abetting terrorist acts.

The special TADA Court on 27th September,06 convicted the 19th accused in the Mumbai serial bomb blasts case, *Mohammad Musthaq Musa Tarani* a close aide of prime conspirator *Tiger Memon*. The judge pronounced guilty of all charges brought against him including triggering of a blast in a five-star hotel situated near the famous Jhu beach in which three persons were injured on 12th March 1993. *Tarani* in a premeditated plan, checked into a room of the famous five star *Centuar hotel* in Juhu and left an RDX-laden bag in a room there, which later exploded wounding three persons. He was also found guilty of attending a conspiracy meeting at hotel Taj Mahal along with *Tiger Memon* and others and surveying other terror targets like the Bombay Stock Exchange and Municipal Corporation of Greater Mumbai.

The TADA Court on 28-9-06 convicted *Sarfaraz Phanse* who was found guilty of involvement in the landing of arms, ammunition and RDX at Shemadi coast in Raigad. The arsenal was used in triggering multiple blasts on 12th March,1993. Sarfaraz's father *Dawood Phanse*, too had been convicted of the similar charge by the court on 22nd September,'06. While accepting his guilt the next day, *Phanse*, 82 pleaded for leniency, saying "I want to die at home instead in jail." By the end of 28th September, 2006, the court had convicted twenty accused, including the five policemen and four members of the *Memon* family and acquitted eleven, including three cops and an equal number of members of the *Memon* family.

Five henchmen of *Dawood Ibrahim*, in the 1993 Mumbai serial bomb blasts case were convicted by the TADA Court on 29-9-'06 . The five were found guilty of conspiracy and attending a training camp in Pakistan to learn handling of arms and explosives as well as making car bombs. Among the accused, *Gul Mohammad Noor Mohammad Shaik* and *Usman Khan*, were taken into custody and their bail bonds cancelled. The CBI proved that the accused had gone to Pakistan for arms training, which also revealed that the conspiracy was not only confined to India but also extended to a foreign soil.

The special TADA Court on 3rd October, '06 pronounced accused number 98, *Niyaz Mohammad* guilty for conspiracy, abetment to terrorist activities besides training in destructive weapons. He had been found guilty of visiting Pakistan for weapons training programme and also for attending meetings with the key accused in the bomb blasts case, *Tiger Memon*. He was also convicted on the charge of conducting a survey of Municipal Corporation of Greater Mumbai building, a potential target for blasts with prime accused *Tiger Memon, Javed Chikna and Mohammad Usman Jan Khan*. The court, however, acquitted the second woman in the blasts case, *Ruskhsana Mohammad Shafi Zariwala* of charges of aiding and abetting terror acts.

The TADA Court on 5th October,'06 found *Nasir Dhakla* and *Mohammad Rafiq Usman* guilty of obtaining arms, training in Pakistan and attending conspiracy meetings. *Nasir* was also guilty of participating in landing of arms and explosives at coastal Raigad district but acquitted of the charge of filling RDX in vehicles that were planted at various places in the metropolis on 12th Match, 1993. The court accepted their confessions as well as those of the co-accused while implicating the duo under various sections of TADA (P) Act. The judge also considered the evidence of an eyewitness, who had identified Nasir in arms landing operations. It was held that Nasir had participated in the blast conspiracy "up to a particular point and the duo face punishment ranging from five years to life. With the conviction of *Nasir Dhakla* and *Mohammad Shaik*, the number of persons found guilty by the court rose to 28 while 13 were acquitted.

The special TADA Court, on 6th October'06 found accused no.57 *Shaik Ali. Shaik Umar*, accused No.135 *Shahid Nizamuddin Qureshi* and accused no.100 *Parvez Qureshi*, guilty of involvement in the explosions. The judge convicted Umar on five charges, including criminal conspiracy, abetting and knowingly facilitating the terrorist acts between December'92 and April '93 in assisting the absconding of the prime accused *Tiger Memon* in smuggling, landing and transportation of arms, ammunition and explosives at Shekadi, Raigad district on 3rd and 7th Feb.1993.

Umar was also found guilty of attending meetings with other conspirators at Al-Husseini building where the conspiracy was chalked out. He, along with co-accused *Mustaq Tarani*, *Usman Khan* and absconding accused *Javed Chikna* and *Tiger Memon*, also carried out a recee of the BMC and the Bombay Stock Exchange buildings for planting bombs in the premises.

He was also found guilty of violating the Arms and Explosive Substance Act. *Umar* was found guilty of being one of the occupants of Maruti van, laden with arms and explosives for attacking the BMC building. However, the mission was aborted and the van was abandoned opposite the rear gate of Siemens company in Worli on 12th March, 1993. Umar's role in loading of RDX with time device detonators in various vehicles at Al-Husseini building and initiating co-accused Gul *Mohammad alias Gullu* into the conspiracy was proved to a limited extent.

Unlike *Umar*, accused no. 135 *Nizamuddin* was found guilty of only one charge – his role in the landing operations at Shekadi. He along with *Tiger Memon* went in a boat to fetch the consignment of the deadly explosives making him liable of abetting a terrorist act. Accused no. 100 *Parvez* was found guilty of abetting terrorist act and going to Pakistan for training in the handling of arms, ammunition and explosives.

On 9th October'-6 the TADA Court convicted *Mohammad Farooq Pawle*, close associate of prime absconding accused *Tiger Memon*, for conspiracy in the 1993 bomb blasts case and also for causing explosions at Air India building and in the vicinity of *Shiv Sena Bhavan*, killing 24 persons. He was held guilty for parking a car at the rear end of Air India building in front of Oman Bank, which exploded killing 20 persons and injuring 84 on 12th March, 1993. He was also held guilty of parking a van loaded with explosives between *Shiv Sena Bhavan* and Lucky Petrol pump which exploded killing four persons and injuring fifty.

Pawle was held guilty of 23 charges including joining conspiracy meetings, visiting Pakistan for arms training, surveying blast targets, filing RDX in vehicles and planting cars at Air India building and near Sena Bhavan. The court had accepted confessions of *Pawle* and approver *Mohammad Usman Jaan Khan* besides considering account of an eyewitness while convicting the accused.

The TADA court found guilty three blast accused, being the owners of the trawlers, helped *Tiger Memon*, the prime accused in the 1993 serial bomb blasts in Mumbai in landing the deadly arms and ammunition at Shekhadi in February,'93. *Yeswant Boinkar*, *Abbas Shekhdare* and *Shahjehan Shekhdare*, who were on bail, were found guilty under section 111 of the Customs Act. Meanwhile, another two blast accused *Ismail Patel* and *Mohinuddin Abdul Kadar* were acquitted by the court following lack of evidence.

The accused *Mohinuddin* had visited Dubai and had a meeting with the absconding Tahir Taklya. who had showed him some video clippings of riots in Mumbai in which members of a particular community had suffered. According to the charges, after seeing the video film, they had chalked out the plan for committing terrorist act in India to take revenge on behalf of the members of the community which suffered in the communal riots which took place in 1993 after the demolition of *Babri Masjid* on 6th December, 1992. However, *Patel* was charged for financing blast accused *Abdul Aziz Sheik* who had also visited Dubai for taking part in the conspiracy of the bomb blast. *Shanawaz Khan*, *Shariff Khan*, *Sujat Alam* and *Sheikh Ethesham* were found guilty by the TADA court under IPC, TADA and other acts as they were close aides of prime accused *Tiger Memon*, for their involvement in 1993 bomb blasts in Mumbai. However, *Sharif Khan* was found guilty under the Customs Act The court, however, acquitted accused *Ashfaque Kasam Hawalder* for lack of evidence.

On 11-10-'06 the TADA court convicted four blasts accused of landing a consignment of deadly RDX at Shekadi in Raigad district, which was used in the 1993 serial bomb blasts in the Mumbai that killed 257 people. The Judge held accused number 18 *Suleman Ghawte*, accused number 31 *Yusuf Khan* and accused number 34 *Abdul Aziz Gharatkar* guilty under sections 3 (3) of TADA Act. However, the court did not find enough evidence against accused number 27

Rashid Alware to convict him under TADA but he was found guilty under Customs Act.

The Bollywood actor *Sanjay Dutt*, the 117th accused in the case to appear before the court on 18th Oct.'06 along with 25 other accused had sought exemption from the court daily appearances on the ground he was acting in several films. *Dutt* was charged with possessing an AK-56 rifle that was part of the consignment meant for the serial bomb blasts. The four convicted, *Tulsiram Dhonde Surve*, *Muzamil Umar Kadri*, *Khalil Ahmed Sayyed Nazir* and *GulamHafeez Shaik*, were guilty of taking part in the landing of RDX smuggled to Shekhadi coast, transporting weapons and possessing arms. Surve, who had served as watchman of the high-security Wangani tower in Raigad, was found guilty of concealing 59 bags of RDX in his farm in Raigad district. *Anant Bhoir*, who had allowed his dumper to be used for dumping 59 RDX bags in Nagla Bunder creek, was acquitted as it was proved that he had no knowledge that the goods were RDX.

On 17th Oct.'06 the TADA court convicted three accused, including a close confidant of prime accused *Tiger Memon*, for their involvement in the serial blasts. The Judge pronounced *Syed Abdul Rehman*, *Manoj Kumar Gupta* and *Mohammad Kasim Lajpurya* guilty of helping *Tiger Memon* and his associates with the landing of the arms and ammunition at Dighi in Maharashtra. *Syed Abdul Rehman* was specifically termed as 'close confidant of *Tiger Memon* by the judge. The court held three more accused guilty for their complicity in the blasts, taking the total number of those convicted to 61. *Ashraf-ur-Rehman*, *Mohammad Yusuf Bolomiyan* and *Shaik Asif Yusuf* were held guilty under the TADA and Arms Act. However, the three were acquitted of the charge of conspirators.

After a trail spanning 13 years, *Sanjay Dutt* was on 28th November,'06 acquitted of the grave charge of conspiracy in the 1993 serial bomb blasts in Mumbai but was convicted for a much lesser offence under the Arms Act by the TADA court that ruled the Bollywood actor was not a terrorist. As with 90 others convicted in recent weeks in the blast case, the judge did not pronounce the quantum of sentence immediately. *Sanjay*, who had already spent 16 months in jail in two spells during the trail, was convicted under various sections of the Arms Act, for possessing an AK-56 rifle and a 9mm pistol, and faces a prison term ranging from five to ten years. The judge while giving reasoning not found *Sanjay Dutt* a terrorist. Considering matters in his confession and also taking into account certain admissions from other evidence accepted the stand of *Sanjay Dutt* of acquiring and possessing weapons for self-defence. In his confession, *Dutt* had said that he had asked Magnum film owners, Samir Hingorani and Hanif Kadawala (he has since died) to arrange for firearms from Anees Ibrahim as he feared for the safety of his family, mainly father *Sunil Dutt*, who was actively involved in relief work among victims of the December 1992 and January 1993 riots.

On 30th November, '06 *Sanjay*, who was convicted under the Arms Act was sentenced to six years rigorous imprisonment for possessing arms illegally.

The Supreme Court in regard to *Monica Bedi* granted bail, released the bail conditions on 24th July, '07 after Monica's counsel stated that her client had lost the passport.

After 14 years the Special Tada Court handed down death sentences in the serial blasts case to *Abdul Ghani Ismail Turk, Mohd. Musthaq Musa Tarani, Pervez Ahmed Nasir Shaik, Asghar Yusuf Mukadam, Shahnawaz Qureshi, Mohd. Shoaib Ghansar, Farooq Pawle, Zakir Hussain Noor Mohd. Shaik, Abdul Khan, Feroze Amani Malik, Mohd. Eqbal Yusuf Shaik and Yakub Memon. Bashir Ahmed Usman Ghani Kharirula, Somnath Thapa, Tiger's brothers Yusuf and Essa and his sister-in-law Rubina Memon were awarded life imprisonment by judge P.D. Kode.*

17
Revenge Killings

The U.S. Government in order to capture *bin Laden*, *Omar* and to crush the *al-Qaeda* movement lionized President *Musharaff* and showered plenty of funds in the names of economic aid and other aids to Pakistan. In response to the above, President *Musharaff*, despite opposition from the extremist Islamic Organizations within his own country has offered support to the United States and allowed Pakistan airspace and territory to be used for anti-terrorist operations.

The *Taliban* was a creation of Pakistan and it has disowned its own child at an hour of crisis of retaliation by the U.S. and its allied forces. President *Mushraff* not only turned his back on the *Taliban* but without any reservation denounced them as harbourers of terrorists. He claims, all that was necessary to protect the Kashmir cause. The way he supported the U.S. led forces in *Afghanistan* taking shelter under the Kashmir cause it appears that he may one day sell entire Pakistan for the sake of Kashmir.

The betrayal of Pakistan, obviously piqued the *al-Qaeda* linked militants. They, therefore, turned against President *Musharaff* and couple of times made suicide attacks on his life in Pakistan itself. In this way, the tides of *al-Qaeda* linked militants turned against President *Musharaff* and his Government and started fighting with Pakistani forces. President *Musharaff* deployed several army posts bordering

Afghanistan which, came under rocket attacks by the militants. Pakistan forces were, however, trying to flush out foreign and local militants from mountain hideouts of Shakai area, South Waziristan, 400 km South-east of Islamabad.

After heavy bombings in and around *Afghanistan* by the U.S. lead forces the *al-Qaeda* militants appears to had shifted their bases to Pakistan along with their top leader *bin Laden* who is believed to be hiding in Pakistan's mountainous tribal region. Pakistan said up to 600 foreign militants including Arabs, *Chechens* and Uzbeks linked to *bin Laden's* network have been hiding out in the semi-autonomous tribal areas protected by Pakistani tribesmen. Pakistan forces were targeting suspected training camps and houses of militants. The houses of residents supporting militants were also destroyed

In the second week of June, 2004 the Pakistani police smashed a major *al-Qaeda* network and arrested 13 hardcore militants including nephew of the terrorist leader *Khalid Sheikh Mohammed*, who was responsible for recent violence in Karachi and the bid on the life of a top Army General. While an eleven member gang of *al-Qaeda* saboteurs responsible for various attacks in the port city, including on the army Corps Commander *Ahsan Saleem*, Pakistan police said two most wanted *al-Qaeda* militants – *Mosad Aroochi*, nephew of *Khalid Sheikh* and *Dawood Badini*, a leader of Laskhar-e-Jhangvi were also held. The Southern Sindh chief said that they had identified a new al-qaeda-trained terror organization '*jund allah*' (God's Brigade) as responsible for the violence. *Aroochi*, who had a two million dollar reward for his arrest, along with eight others were part of the group.

While *Aroochi* was wanted by the U.S. for various terrorist attacks in Karachi, *Badini*, who had .two million re-ward for his capture was wanted by the Pakistani police for various sectarian attacks in southwest city of Quetta. *Aroochi's* capture along with the eight member gang comprising Uzebks, Chechens and Arabs was announced by Pakistan Information

Minister, *Sheikh Rahid* and Interior Minister *Faisal Saleh Hayat* on the 13th of June, 2004. In a separate statement the Director General of Pakistan Rangers *Maj. Gen. Javed Zia* announced the arrest of *Badini*. He said that *Badini*, who was arrested during a raid on a house in Karachi on 13th June, 2004 had during initial interrogation revealed that he was one of the important leaders of the banned *Lashkar-I-Jangvi*, a banned Sunni extremist body and confessed involvement in various sabotage activities. *General Zia* said that *Badini* had planned attack on the vehicle of the Balochistan Police, killing twelve Shia police recruits on the 8th of June 2004. He also said that *Badini* had planned a suicide attack on a Shia mosque where 51 worshippers were killed. In the same week, the Pakistani officials questioned a senior *al-Qaeda* operative linked to September 11 2001 mastermind *Khalid Sheik Mohammed* over a Christamas Day attempt to kill President *Musharaff* and other attacks. A security official said that *Musabir Urumchi*, who had a one-million dollars bounty on his head, was also being interrogated about an attempt to kill a senior General in the southern port city of Karachi in the first week of June 2004. The official further said that they strongly suspect an *al-Qaeda* role in the two suicide attacks on President *Musharaff* and deadly attack on Karachi's Corps commander.

As the sabotage activities of the *al-Qaeda* militants were increasing day by day the Pakistani forces engaged in the search of them even in a remote tribal regions bordering Pakistan. There, they raided on a mud wall compound and killed a top tribal warrior and his four comrades on the 18th June 2004, who sheltered *al-Qaeda* fighters. *Nek Mohammed* who protected *Al-Qaeda* linked foreign militants in the semi-autonomous South Waziristan tribal belt, was killed near the region's main town of Wana. Military spokesman Major General *Shaukat Sultan* said that the military attacked *Mohammad's* hide out after receiving reports that he had taken refuge there. The Major General said that it was a big success in the war against the terror. Pakistan has been battling *al-Qaeda*-linked militants and tribesmen sheltering for months in a campaign to rid the country of Islamic radicals. Up-to 600 foreign militants who joined the U.S. funded insurgency against the Soviet forces in Afghanistan in the 1980's are believed to be living in tribal areas, although dozens have been killed in the recent clashes.

The Saudi Arabia withdrew the citizenship of *bin Laden* in 1994, when he indulged in the terrorist attacks and criticism of the Royal Family. Bin Laden, therefore, left his birth place and lived in Afghanistan as a "guest" of the *Taliban* militia since 1996 and led the *al-Qaeda* terrorist organization. With the help of *Mohd Omar* and others he developed the net-work of the organization having international ramification. Though, he left Saudi Arabia in 1994 the terrorist movement nursed by him never disappeared there. They terrorized Western residents of the Kingdom and severed the head of the American aeronautics engineer Paul Johnson. The beheading which sparked international outrage, climaxed a spate of fatal attacks against the westerners in Riyadh and other parts of the kingdom since May, 2004. The Interior Minister of the Kingdom read a statement on the State Television that *Abdul Aziz Bin Issa al-Muqrin* who claimed to head the gang of "*takfeer*" (holding others as infidels) and bombings and issued statements (claiming responsibility for assassinations and kidnappings) was one of the four gunmen shot dead by the security forces on 18th June, 2004. The four were said to have been besieged in a gas station in the Al-Malaz district in Riyadh by security forces, and a heavy exchange of fire took place. The television also showed the photos of the bloodied dead bodies of at Muqrin and the other slain militants. The above statement was first denied by the militants and a communiqué was posted on the site http/alsaha.Fares.Net stating that "following the lies....about the death of *Abdul Aziz al-Muqrin*, we affirm that such allegations, spread by the tyrants in Saudi Arabia, are intended to undermine the morale of the *mujahedeen* on the Arabia peninsula.

The Ministry has however, identified the other slain gunmen as *Faisal bin Abdul Rahman al-Dakheel*, a militant on a top wanted list who appeared in footage on websites showing the killing of an American. It did not name the U.S. national but appeared to be referring to video footage of the killing of *Robert Jacob* a Riyadh resident who worked for the Vinnel corporation that helps to train the Saudi National Guard. The third was named as Turki *bin Fuhaid al Mutairi*, one of the three gunmen who escaped after a shooting and hostage-taking rampage that left 22 people dead in the eastern oil city of al-Khobar in the month of May ,2004. The fourth was *Ibrahim bin Abdullah al-Draihem*, who helped in planning the bombing of a residential compound in Riyadh in Nov. 2003 and committed other crimes. A Security man was also killed in the clash and two were wounded.

The militant organization which first denied the killing of *Abdul Aziz al-Muqrin* confirmed his death a couple of days later. A statement posted on an Islamabad website stated "fighting commander *Abdul Aziz al-Muqrin* fell as a martyr on 18th June, 2004 in an ambush laid for him by the soldiers of tyranny in the Malaz district of Riyadh. The *Mujahideen* are continuing the *jehad* (holy struggle) that they have pledged to God and killing of their brothers will not weaken their resolve but only increase their determination and commitment."

After the elimination of *Abdul Aziz al-Muqrin* the Saudi Arabia warned Muslim militants that they would share the fate of their slain leader unless they repented,. "We tell this deviant group and others that if they do not return to the right path, they will meet the same fate or worse" said the Saudi Arabia's de facto ruler Crown *Prince Abdullah* on 19th June, 2004. "Security forces will deal with them, God willing, and with every aggressor inside or abroad" he added. The State television showed the bloodied corpses of the four militants, saying they had been behind a wave of violence against foreigners in the Gulf State, a key U.S ally and the world's biggest oil exporter. "The Government is strong and will eradicate the enemy and cleanse the country of them," said "Saudi Interior Minister *Prince Nayef*. He also said "God willing, we will be victorious.

Al-Qaeda led by the fugitive *Osama bin Laden* who is responsible for the September 11, 2001 attacks on the United States had vowed to expel "infidels" from the birth place of Islam. The Saudi Arabia government also arrested twelve other militants on the 18th June, 2004, including a senior figure suspected of involvement in the bombing of the U.S. warship *Cole* off the coast of neighboring Yemen in the year 2000. The Foreign Policy Advisor of the Saudi Arabia said that Riyadh would pursue the Islamic extremists without mercy. We believe with this blow to *al-Qaeda* in Saudi Arabia on 19th June, 2004, we have substantially weekend their organization. We will continue to pursue them with vigor until we eliminate them from our midst". "We will show no mercy".

Amjad Farooqui, Pakistan's most wanted militant was shot dead at his rural hide out near Karachi on the morning of 26th September, 2004. President *Musharraf* has termed the death of *Farooqui* as a major blow to terrorism. The dead man was suspected of being the mastermind behind the two assassination attempts on President *Musharaff* and was indicted in the kidnapping and beheading of the American journalist *Daniel Pearl* in 2002. The U.S. has described the killing of a top Pakistan militant linked to *al-Qaeda* as an "important development" but stated that Islamabad needs to do more to nab terrorists hiding in that country. "It is an important development. But there is clearly more to do "said *Adam Ereli*, Deputy spokesman of the U.S. He further said that "we welcome the news over the weekend that Pakistan apprehended several *al-Qaeda* suspects, including a suspect in the *Daniel Pearl* case".

Russia denounced the western countries for granting asylum to the *Chechen* leaders who are linked to violence. It started pushing the United Nation to take tougher action against terrorists and circulated a draft in the third week of September, 2004. The draft condemned all acts of terrorism and stressed the need for the 15- Council Nations to 'co-operate fully' in tracking down the perpetrators and organizers of terrorist attacks. The Russians had also sought the Committee monitoring governments to consider how to draw up a new list of "individual groups and entities involved in or associated with terrorist activities. They also wished the committee to consider sanctions to be imposed against those on the list, including freezing assets, a travel ban and an arms embargo and to consider the "expedited extradition of anyone named in the list.

At least 70 persons were killed and several injured when Pakistan's fighter planes and gunship helicopters bombed the hideouts of *al-Qaeda* militants and their local supporters on 9th September, 2004 in a major offensive in the tribal region close to Afghanistan border. Pakistan's private television channels *Geo* and *Ary* reported that a guided missile hit a meeting of the foreign militants in Khunkhela mountains in South Waziristan tribal region killing forty people. Ten others were killed when the fighter planes dropped bombs when the people were collecting bodies of the dead. The operations, part of efforts by Pakistan's military to flush out *al-Qaeda* militants holed up in the region, came a day after a landmine blast hit a Pakistani military convoy near Wana, the headquarters of south Waziristan, injuring three soldiers.

Two days before the third anniversary of September 11, *Osama bin Laden's* right-hand man emerged for the first time in a year to warn Americans of imminent defeat for their armies in Iraq and *Afghanistan.* With Americans needing no reminder of their vulnerability to potential terrorist attacks, al-Qaeda number two *Ayman Al-Zawahiri* was shown on *Al-Jazeera* television on the night of 9th September, 2004". Americans will no longer be safe while their government does not stop committing its crimes against Muslims in Iraq and *Afghanistan* and Palestine" said the fugitive Egyptian cleric, shown on the tape with an assault rifle at his side. He said that "the American defeat in Iraq and *Afghanistan* has become just a question of time, God willing". "In the two countries, the Americans are between two fires: if they remain there they will bleed to death, and if they withdraw they will have lost everything". *Zawahiri* said that armed Islamists whom he described as *al-Qaeda's Mujahedden* had foiled U.S. forces in Iraq and left them hiding in the trenches in *Afghanistan*.

The U.S. death toll in Iraq hit the 1,000 mark by the first week of September, 2004 as American troops fought a deadly insurgency that had also set its sight on taking hostage any foreigners perceived as collaborating with the U.S. led forces. "In Iraq, the *Mujahedeen* foiled the American plan after the interim government showed such weakness" said the 53 year old Zawahiri, considered by Washington to be *al-Qaeda's* ideologue and main strategist. *Zawahiri* claimed that in the terror network's *Mujahedeen* were in control of "the entire East and South of Afghanistan" with the support of the people. "The Americans are dug into their trenches and refuse to come out to face the *Mujahedeen*, despite their provocations by bombing and besieging them."

As the sounds of silence had fallen on the third anniversary of 09/11, the events of the tragic and fateful day seared into the hearts and minds of every single American and the kith and kin of those, who lost the lives, in the twin towers of the *World Trade Center, New York*. President *Bush* observed a moment of silence on 9th September, 2004 on the lawn of White House that has begun at 8.46 a.m. the time the first plane struck the *World Trade Center*. That was also the time when silence was observed State-wide in *New York* and houses of worship struck the *bells*. *New York* city observed the day with a programme "*Tribute in Light*" at the site of the *World Trade Center* towers. According to the plans released by the Governor *George Pataki* and *New York* City Mayor, Michael Bloomberg there was an early morning observance at the low Manhattan attack site and 200 readers of the victims' names, including parents and grandparents. The reading paused for four moments: Twice to mark the times that each plane hit the towers and two more times to mark each time the towers fell. Relatives of the victims walked to a ramp to the lowest level of the Trade Center site where they laid flowers. The Port Authority which lost 84 employees in the 2001 attack on the *World Trade Center*, held a memorial service in a church near the Twin Towers Site.

The *al-Qaeda* linked militants in Islamabad kidnapped two Chinese engineers, who were working on Pakistan's Gomal Zam Dam project for China's State-run Sino Hydro Corporation. They were identified as *Wang Ende* and *Wang Teng*. Pakistani officials said the engineers were kidnapped with one or two Pakistani security men on 9th October, 2004. *Abdullah Mehsud*, leader of the kidnappers holding the engineers in Pakistan's South Waziristan region, has insisted that the kidnappers and hostages be allowed to join him in a nearby area, or one of the Chinese would be killed. The kidnappers, with explosives strapped to their bodies, were holed up in a mud house surrounded by the security forces and the armed tribesmen in Chagmalai of South Waziristan. Brigadler *Javed Cheema*, Director General of the Interior Ministry's Crisis Management Cell informed that talks were going on with them and they were waiting for the outcome. *Abdullah Mehsud*, Pakistani tribal commander, who kidnapped the two Chinese Engineers is a former inmate of the U.S. military prison in *Guantanamo Bay* in Cuba.

Shi, the wife of *Wang Ende* after learning the incident on the State Television and the internet spent sleepless nights that her husband spirits hit bottom when she learned on 09-

10-2004 that her husband and another Chinese were kidnapped by the Islamic militants in Pakistan. She, however, sighed a sense of relief, when the Chinese media reported that the hostages would be released soon.

A tribal delegation sought on 12th October, 2004 to secure the release of the two Chinese engineers taken hostage by the *al-Qaeda* linked militants near Pakistan's border with *Afghanistan*. The militants, who number four or five, have threatened to blow up themselves and their hostages, who include a Pakistani driver and Security guard, if any rescue attempt was made. *Maulana Mirajuddin*, a local member of the national assembly led a tribal delegation in a convoy of 50-60, cars, for talks with *Abdullah Mehsud*. *Mehmood Shah*, chief of Security of the tribal region warned *Abdullah Mehsud* on phone that the tribe as a whole would suffer unless he freed the hostages and he would face tribal justice. A senior security official said that they are considering many options, including the use of force. He further added that "we are operating via various channels, that is why we are confident no harm will come to the engineers and I remain optimistic". He also said that the kidnappers had refused an offer of safe passage if they freed the engineers. Pakistan's North-West Frontier Province Governor *Syed Iftikhar Hussain Shah* assured the Chinese diplomats at an emergency meeting that the hostages were in the same room as the kidnappers and that no explosives were strapped to them. The Governor said that on negotiations with *Abdullah Mehsud*, a former *Taliban* Commander who claimed responsibility for the abduction, thirty elders of the *Mehsud* tribe had conferred with political representatives of the provincial government to seek negotiation measures. Even after protracted negotiations the militant group of *al-Qaeda* did not release the Chinese engineers. *Abdullah Mehsud* the kidnap leader did not also spell out the demands, but repeated a demand for safe passage for both the captors and the captives to join him. Pakistani Officials, however, said that *Abdullah* has demanded an end to military operations in the semi-autonomous tribal region, where hundreds have died in the year 2004 in battles between Pakistani troops and *al-Qaeda* linked militants and freeing of two Uzbek militants, *Mehmood Shah*, the head of security in the tribal region and another. They hoped for a peaceful solution to the crisis but warned the use of force could not be ruled out.

Two rounds of talks between tribal elders and militant leader *Abdullah Mehsud* who was hiding in mountains while five of his men held the hostages in a nearby village failed on 13-10-04. After which, when they heard gunshots and feared that the captors might have killed one of the Chinese, Commandoes who were alert, stormed the remote hideout killed five *al-Qaeda* linked kidnappers on 14-10-04 and rescued the other Chinese hostage.

On hearing the news, President *Pervez Musharraf* condoled the death of the Chinese captive during rescue operation, and vowed to track down those responsible for the hostage drama. Stepping up hunt for *Abdullah Mehsud*, who master minded the kidnapping of two Chinese Nationals, the Pakistan Security forces cordoned the tribal region bordering Pakistan. The government has also stepped up security for the Chinese Nationals working in different projects in Pakistan following the hostage drama.

As the Presidential election in Afghanistan got underway after driving out *bin Laden*, *Omar* and other top militants of *al-Qaeda* group from Afghanistan. Their sympathizers were still threatening on one pretext or the other. On 15-10-2004, the first day of the Muslim holy month of *Ramadan*, an Islamism group threatened to attack the producers and broadcasters of a televised love story set during the Taliban rule of Afghanistan, if it insults the former hard-line regime. Several Arab television stations began broad- casting the series, 'The Road to Kabul', on 15-10-2004. "This is a warning for all those who contributed to making this soap opera, actors, producers, cameramen, if it contains insults to Taliban" said an internet statement by a previously unknown group calling itself the Mujahedden brigades of Iraq and Syria. The statement continued said that "we will strike, God willing, satellite Channels showing this soap opera and their correspondents as well as their offices in Iraq and Syria".

Iraq's most-wanted militant, *Abu Musab al-Zarqawi*, a Jordanian was responsible for a number of bombings and beheadings in Iraq wrote a message on 17th October, 2004 posted on Islamism websites agreeing with *al-Qaeda's* strategy and the need for unity against "the enemies of Islam". The message said that *Zarqawi*, leader of the group believed bin *Laden* is "the best leader for Islam's armies against all infidels and apostates"

There is a lot of concentration of militant group in South Waziristan bordering Afghanistan. The Pakistani military was engaged to flush out *al-Qaeda* militants from the tribal region bordering *Afghanistan* and had left 246 insurgents and 171 soldiers dead by the third week of October 2004. Among 246 militants killed 100 were foreigners belonging to Uzbeks, Chechens and Arabs, and 100 more foreigners were still hiding in the region in the area of Mehsud tribe, one of the major tribes in Waziristan. They, however, denied that *Osama bin Laden* was in Pakistan tribal region and there was a strong possibility of the presence of Uzbek militant Tahir Yuldesh in the area.

The gun battle between the Pakistani Security forces and the *Al-qaeda* militants continued in Azam Warsak area in South Waziristan bordering Afghanistan. A group of militants opened fire on security forces there forcing the troops to return fire in which three militants were killed and three more militants injured, were captured. Three soldiers of Pakistani forces were also injured in the battle.

India which is determined to continue to work closely together to counter the menace of terrorism discussed the issue at the level of External Affairs Ministers of India and France. *Michel Barnier*, who was in India in the last week of October 2004 noted that international terrorism was one of the serious challenges faced by open democratic multilingual and multi-cultural societies.

The fifth Indo-European summit was hosted by Netherlands Prime Minister *Jan Peter Balkenende* wherein the Prime Minister *Manmohan Singh* addressed the Inter active Session of Prominent CEOs of European Union business industry and senior representatives of Indian Industry. In recognition of India's growing stature and influence the European Union has passed a strategic partnership with India. The Summit after due deliberations resolved on 8th November 2004 to strengthen co-operation in combating terrorism by seeking among other things to jointly address issues which create an environment conducive for the growth of terrorism. After the fall of *World Trade Center* and attack on *Pentagon*, the World has realized that any slackness and negligence on the part of the nations would lead to mass destruction. Therefore, after the end of the Summit, the leaders of the European Union and the Indian team lead by Prime Minister *Manmohan Singh* identified co-operation in the fight against terrorism as a priority area. This issue would be included in the Indo-EU action plan for strategic partnership to be adopted at the next year's Summit in New-Delhi. The statement said that both the European Union and India would explore ways to expand counter-terrorism dialogue bringing into its ambit other appropriate security related issues.

India has got the bitter experience of terrorism in its territory and it is still losing many valuable lives in *Jammu and Kashmir*. The perverted acts of terrorists took the lives of eminent leaders and many were killed in Bombay blast and in Godhra train. Therefore, it is high time a consensus approach is evolved to contain terrorism in India and in the World. The stress on co-operation during the course of the fifth Indo-EU Summit to combat terrorism is a diplomatic victory to India which has been a victim of cross-border terrorism for long.

After nearly four weeks in captivity, three U.N. workers kidnapped in Afghanistan were released unharmed on 23rd Nov. 2004. An official said that there was no deal had been made to secure their freedom. The release was a relief to foreign aid workers and the U.N. Staffers among Kabul's 2000 strong expatriate locked down since the kidnapping. Large tracts of the country were already off-limits to aid organizations because of a stubborn *Taliban*-led insurgency. Afghan Interior Minister said discussions had been held with the kidnappers, whom he declined to identify, but insisted no deal was done and that the releases were – unconditional. Afghan officials said that a criminal gang carried out the abductions and ransom was demanded. In contrast to the above, a *Taliban* splinter group claimed that it had freed two of the U.N. hostages in exchange of 24 *Taliban* prisoners, while the third was freed because of an appeal by a Muslim Kosovar man.

Everyone expected that bin Laden would be caught and handed over to the U.S. during the course of its Presidential elections in November, 2004. Even after *George W.Bush* was been reelected the where about of *Laden* and his key men are not known. However, his threats continued to haunt the U.S. and other nations. Following the reports that the American interests in Mumbai and in New-Delhi could be the target of terrorists the U.S. Consulate and the American Center in the metropolis were closed on 23rd Nov. 2004. A Consulate spokesperson in Mumbai said that "all the staff members who reported on duty were asked to go home". Mumbai police have deployed" additional forces, wherever necessary, to foil any attack on the U.S. establishments. The DCP with the anti-terrorist squad of the Maharashtra Government said, "we are taking utmost precaution to foil any possible attack on the consulate and various other buildings, having sizeable number of U.S. citizens.

A couple of days after President *Musharraf* acknowledged the U.S.A. that *bin Laden* is alive and after a brief lull of about a month, dozens of militants armed with assault rifles and rockets attacked an Afghan military base in Khost province, sparking a firefight that left four Afghan soldiers and at-least six militants dead, according to an Afghan commander. The attacks on the first day of second week of December, 2004 near the Pakistan frontier that left ten dead provided a reminder of threats to Afghan stability. Added, to the above killings, bin *Laden's al-Qaeda* claimed on the 7th of December, 2004 that the attack on the U.S. consulate in Jeddah, was a serious blow to the Saudi Government's attempts to wipe out Islamism militants behind a wave of terror strikes. The broad-daylight attack took place on the 6th December on the fortified compound in the Red Sea city claimed some lives, including consulate staff, gunmen and Saudi guardsmen. The U.S. President Bush said the attack showed that terrorists were still at large in the oil-rich desert kingdom and the Saudi Government vowed there would be no let up in its fight against extremists. But there were fears foreigners could take fright, and flee the kingdom, which has seen scores of people killed in a renewed violence since May 2003 despite a government crack down.

The Saudi branch of the *al-Qaeda* claimed in a web site statement that it was behind the attack and said some assistants had managed to flee before security forces regained control of the compound "Your brothers of the squadron of the martyr *Abu Annas al-Shami* stormed one of the bastions of the American crusaders in the Arabiaṇ peninsula in Jeddah", "They were able to withdraw from the consulate and reach a safe place, after losing two martyrs who covered the retreat of the *Mujahedeen*, three of whom wounded and are being treated," said the statement signed by the *al-Qaeda*

Organization in the Arabian Peninsula.

The Indian who was one of the five American Consulate staff killed in Jeddah, was identified as *Mohammad Basheeruddin*, a procurement clerk who joined the Consulate staff 18 months ago from Hyderabad, India.

Abdul Razzak, a rebel Commander had organized many subversive acts in Kandhar province. He again ventured to attack the Mayor's Office in Alghar district of Zabul close to Pakistan border. A gun battle, therefore, took place between the government forces and the militants in the first week of January, 2005 that left five people dead including *Abdul Razzak*.

America needed President *Musharaff* as Pakistan needed the U.S.A. to capture *bin Laden* and his aides who are said to be hiding in the mountainous areas bordering Pakistan and Afghanistan. President *Musharraf* had at high risk of assassination, although no known attempts on his life since December 2003. Pakistan's extremist group Islamic leaders gain power if President Musharraf was assassinated or replaced. Pakistan's new leader would be less pro-*U.S. Musharraf* who is key ally in the U.S. war on terrorism and provides critical support against *al-Qaeda* and *Taliban*. The Americans support him even though Pakistan continued to be under the military rule.

Seething with vengeance, *bin Laden* had spread the network of *al-Qaeda* to the other countries like Iraq where the U.S. dethroned *Saddam Hussain* and incarcerated. In Iraq, the *al-Qaeda* was pursuing the war against "infidels" (those who were supporting the cause of the U.S in Iraq). According to an internet statement posted on 04-03-05 attributed to the military commander of the *al-Qaeda* organization for Holy war in Iraq said *al-Qaeda's* wing in Iraq carried suicide attacks in March '05 proved the group was still strong and capable of pursuing its war against "infidels". The group said its leader, *Abu Musab al-Zarqwi*, would soon issue a message to the faithful. *Abu Musab Al-Zarqawi*, a Jordanian militant said on 29-04-05 through a tape that *Jihad* was still going strong two years since the U.S –led war on Iraq. The *al-Qaeda* leader through audio tape from Iraq called for more suicide attacks on the U.S. forces and vowed not to let President Bush enjoy "peace of mind".

After the fall of *Saddam Hussain*, the *al-Qaeda* spread over its wings to Iraq and the militants were engaged in fighting with the American forces. *Abu Musab al-Zarqawi* who was behind most of the attacks against the U.S forces had sustained serious injuries. Washington had offered a $ 25 million bounty for *Zarqawi* whom it considered No.1 enemy in Iraq.

The influence of the *Taliban* has not waned away totally in Afghanistan even after their regime was crushed by the U.S-led forces in 2001. A suicide bomber blew himself up inside *Maulvi Abdul Rab mosque* on the 1st of June, 2005 killing atleast twentyseven people including the police chief of Kabul. The blast occurred as mourners gathered to pay respects to an assassinated anti-*Taliban* cleric, *Maulavi Abdullah Fayaz* was shot dead by the Taliban militants at the weekend. A correspondent at the scene said he saw "at least 27 dead bodies" at the mosque in central Kandahar a city known as the birth place of the ousted Taliban regime. "One man entered the *Maulvi Abdul Rab* mosque and blew himself up. *General Akaram*, Police Chief in Kabul was also killed". This was a big explosion and there was blood everywhere in the mosque and outside "Human limbs were scattered all over the mosque compound". *Fayaz* served as the head of the Islamic Scholar's Council, a government-appointed body and criticized reclusive Taliban leader *Mullah Mohammad Omar. Fayaz* survived a bomb attack at the *Abdul Rab Akhunzada mosque* in 2003. Attacks on mosques in *Afghanistan* were rare, and until 2005 suicide attacks were unheard of.

The chemircle concept of *Al-Qaeda* network had been

taken very seriously by the Australian Government. Therefore the Memorandum of understanding was signed in the presence of visiting Pakistani President *Pervez Musharraf* and Australian Prime Minister *John Howard* on 15th June,2005 on counter-terrorism in a bid to rein in militant activities and the *al-Qaeda* network. The MoU envisaged joint training exercises between the Security forces of the two countries as well as sharing of sensible information.

Al-Zarqawi was accused of *al-Qaeda's* man operative in Iraq and responsible for many of the terrorist attacks there. On 15th June,2005, the Spanish police said that they had arrested eleven people linked to the Islamic terror network run by *Abu-Masab al Zarqawi* and another five suspects in Madrid train bomb blasts in 2004. The ministry said the first group of eleven people belong to a terrorist network that was established in Spain and linked to *Ansar al-Islam*, which it called the group run by Zarqawi. They were arrested in Barcelona, Valencia and southern city of Cadiz. The other five were linked to commuter train bombing in Madrid in 2004 which killed one hundred and ninety one people and wounded more than one thousand five hundred.

The U.S. military forces chasing the *Taliban* rebels pounded suspected rebels in air-strike on 19th June, 2005 that killed as many as twenty. Fierce fighting between the *Taliban* rebels and the Afghan security forces took place o 20th June, 2005 in which eighteen insurgents and three others dead. On 21st, June 2005 the fight broke out in the restive Deh Chopan District of Zabul province after Afghan and coalition units were attacked with small arms and rocket-propelled grenades. About forty suspected rebel fighters and an Afghan policeman were killed and five U.S. Soldiers injured in an eleven hour battle. To take away enemy sanctuaries coalition warplanes and helicopters hammered enemy positions.

In order to eliminate terrorism, the United States was bombing all possible hideouts of *al-Qaeda* in *Afghanistan* and other places. After the attacks on World Trade Center and other parts of the U.S. and its continued veiled threats from al-Qaeda network the Americans became wary and took many measures to counter the menace. Though *President Musharraf* promised to wipe out terrorism from Pakistan and was signing Memorandum of Understanding with other countries, the fact remained that he had not cracked down harder on militant groups in his own country. In the month of June, 2005, the United States detained some Pakistani men and felt that Pakistan was having hundreds of *Jehadi* training camps and failed to dismantle them. Since post-9/11 military strikes against *al-Qaeda* strong holds in Pakistan's tribal territories the Jehadist training effort had scattered and gone underground, where it was much harder to detect and destroy. Many U.S. officials said that "it was not surprising that President *Musharraf* has not cracked down harder on militant groups".

On the 3rd of July, 2005 the Security forces in eastern Riyadh raided a suspected militants' hideout and during the clash they killed *Yunis Mohammad Ibrahim al-Hayari*. He was Saudi Arabia's most wanted man and suspected *al-Qaeda* front man, born in Morocco. Along with him two other militants were also wounded.

The U.S. war planes bombed a suspected militant hideout at Chichal village in troubled Kunar province in the last week of June, 2005 amid the search for the small team of elite soldiers. The U.S. squad was missing since June, 2005 when rebels shot down a helicopter sent to extract them, killing all sixteen on board. One team member was rescued on 2nd June, 2005 but three remained unaccounted for. Seventeen civilians died in the U.S. bombing including women and children in the village.

The U.S. suspected that number of Islamic militants were hiding near Lowara Mandi, a border village situated in the north Waziristan tribal region on the Pakistan side of the Afghan border. The encounter took place on 14th July, 2005 and the U.S led forces in *Afghanistan* killed twenty four suspected militants. The Pakistani forces also suspected that the militants were hiding in two houses near Miranshah, the main town of the North Waziristan tribal region and after surrounding the houses appealed them to surrender. Instead the militants opened fire on Pakistani troops on 17th July, 2005 and in the clash seventeen people, including suspected foreign militants and a Pakistani soldier were killed.

Saleh Mohammed al-Aoofi was considered as the top leader of *Osama bin Laden's* militant network in t Saudi Arabia which was rocked by multiple terror attacks since 2003. He was among two at large members of a list of 26 most wanted militants issued in December 2003. The other militant was *Talib Saud Abdullah.* On 18th August, 2005 there were clashes between the militants and the police in the western city of Madina. During the police raids on numerous locations in the holy city of Madina and the capital of Riyadh al Aoofi many reported to have been killed. Sporadic incidents were reported on the fight between the US soldiers and the *Taliban* in *Afghanistan.* In Kabul four US soldiers were killed and three others wounded in a bomb blast in southern *Afghanistan* on 21st August, 2005. *Taliban* insurgents shot dead a pro-government Islamic cleric *Mullah Abdullah Malang* and his companion in Kandahar on the morning of 21st of August, 2005.

After 10 days of the parliamentary elections, 12 people were killed and 29 wounded when a suicide bomber dressed in an army uniform rammed a motorcycle into a convoy of buses carrying the Afghan army officers in the capital of Kabul on 28th September, 2005. The *Taliban* claimed responsibility for the attack at the Kabul Military Training Center, set up by the U.S. led forces to train a new national army. It was the bloodiest of several suicide attacks in Kabul since the U.S.

led forces overthrew the *Taliban* in late 2001. A statement posted on an Islamism web site used by *al-Qaeda* group urged Sunni Muslims on 4th October, 2005 to step up attacks on the U.S. forces during *Ramadan*, the holy month which had seen some of the bloodiest attacks by militants hoping for rewards in paradise. The group by Jordanian *Abu Musab al-Zarqawi*, said in a statement that the "gates of heaven are open" during the fasting month for most Sunnis in the West Asia. Further it said that this is "a month of serious work, *jihad* and initiative. Gather your strength and we incite the believers to kill the slaves of the cross who have demolished mosques and houses, burnt the *Koran* and sowed corruption in the land".

In 2003, major attacks were launched during *Ramadan* in Turkey and Saudi Arabia, bearing the hall marks of *al-Qaeda*. *Zarqawi's* group had already declared an all out war on Iraq's majority Shirite Muslims. It had intensified all attacks ahead of the 15th October, 2005 referendum on the new constitution, opposed by most Iraqi Sunni Arabs. The statement posted on an Islamism web site was in sequel to a new offensive launched by the U.S. troops in Western Iraq near the Syrian borders to hunt for *al-Qaeda* militants.

The threat of the *al-Qaeda* was still haunting the U.S. even after five years of the attacks on *World Trade Center* and *Pentagon*. A high alert was sounded in *New York* in the second week of October, 2005 following "credible and "specific" threats of terrorist attack on its underground local train system. The city was put on alert which is second highest in the color-coded system developed by the U.S. Department of Homeland Security and commuters had been advised against bringing backpacks, heavy packages and baby strollers as far as possible in the subway stations. According to the U.S. authorities, this was first time that they had received specific threat against attacks on subway system and information showed that baby strollers packed with explosives could be used in the attack.

Commuters took the threat seriously in view of earlier attacks by the terrorists in London underground trains and in Spain. No one was arrested or detained in *New York* but the threat was most specific. In the spate of violence by suspected Taliban militants eighteen German-trained Afghan national police were killed in an ambush by insurgents in the southern province of Helmand. The ambush occurred in the Helmand's Registan district on 10th of October 2005 and was followed by a clash that went on until 11th October, 2005.

Roads are important to Afghans wants to go, to schools, health care centers to banks factories, and to provide security to the people who were become accustomed to fear and helpless. As long as there were no roads, inaccessibility will keep all the dangerous elements safe. The people of the country showed courage and came out to vote on September 2005. They trudged along hilly paths avoiding minefields and thorny bushes and rocks in the direction of progress and self-expression. But they need the roads for the fast development of their country.

There were about 300 Indian nationals working in *Afghanistan. Maniappan Raman Kutty* was one among them. He was working as a driver on a road project of the Border Roads Organization. He was abducted by the *Taliban* on 19th November 2005 from the strategic Zaranj-Dalaram Road which the Border Road Organisation was constructing. The *Taliban* killed Kutty with his throat slit, after a deadline passed for his company to pull out of *Afghanistan.* The dead body of *Kutty* was found on 23rd November, 2005 with the note pinned on the body by the Taliban stating that "This *Afghanistan* is not India or America and India should get out of the country." The Prime Minister of India *Manmohan Singh,* calling *Kutty* a "soldier of peace" condemned the murder.

Abu Hamza Rabia, an Egyptian ranked among the top five in Laden's network was killed on 1-12-2005 along with other five militants in an explosion at a hideout in North Waziristan. *Rabia* filled the gap left by the capture of *Abu Faraj*

Farj al-Liby. Al-Liby was dubbed by the United States as the network's third-most important leader after *Bin Laden* and his deputy *Ayman al-Zawahir*. Pakistani security agencies were looking for *Rabia* for sometime, as he was involved in two assassination attempts on President Musharaff in December 2003. *Rabia* had escaped an attack by Pakistani Security forces on 5-11-2005 in the same region but eight people, including his wife and children were killed in that operation. Many *al-Qaeda* members took refuge in Pakistan's semi-autonomous tribal belt after the US-led forces ousted Afghanistan's *Taliban* rule in 2001 for refusing to hand over bin Laden, architect of the September, 11 attacks on the United States. While Pakistani security forces had killed hundreds of *al-Qaeda* members over the past four years, several of their key leaders were arrested and handed over to the United States.

The United Nations report revealed that Afghanistan had seen a wave of nineteen suicide attacks in 2005 including thirteen in the months of December , 2005 and January, 2006. From an undisclosed location the *Taliban* Commander *Mullah Dadullah* said by satellite telephone that "hundreds of Afghan Taliban *Mujahideen* were ready for suicide attack across Afghanistan to drive out foreign forces." The *Taliban* insurgents launched four attacks in the southern Afghan province of Helmand on 3rd February, 2006 killing three policemen. Sixteen *Talibans* were also killed. About 200 insurgents had been in the fighting. Helmand was plagued by insurgents since the U.S forces and their Afghan allies ousted the Taliban regime in late 2001. It is also a major opium-poppy growing and drug smuggling region.

After the murder of *M.R.Kutty* by the *Taliban* by the guerillas in November, 2005 the Government of India contemplated to deploy a protection force of 100 paramilitary commandos from the Indo-Tibetan Border Police to beef- up security for Indians working in *Afghanistan*.

Saudi-born *Osama bin Laden's* group always wanted to prevent the theft of Muslims wealth by 'crusaders and Jews' and to force 'infidels' out of the peninsula and topple the monarchy of Saudi Arabia's U.S allied monarchy. Two suicide bombers tried to attack the world's biggest oil processing complex and were killed on 24th Feb.2006. Sensing the danger from the *al-Qaeda* net work the Saudi Government and Saudi Armco enhanced the security of oil facilities throughout the kingdom and the facility at Abqaiq was fully protected. The attack made by the militants on 28th Feb.2006 on the *Abqaiq* complex near Saudi Arabia's eastern Persian Gulf coast could have been devastating as nearly two-thirds of the country's oil flows through the facility for processing before export. Foiling the attack demonstrated Saudi Arabia's success in putting tough security around the oil industry. The suicide bombers in explosive-packed cars traded fire with the police at a checkpoint before a gate in first of three fences around the sprawling, heavily guarded complex. One member collided with the closed gate exploding and blowing a hole in the fence. The second bomber drove through the hole before the police fired detonating his car. Gunmen outside the facility after the explosion chased for other attackers. On 27th Feb, 2006 Saudi forces killed five suspected militants linked to an *al-Qaeda* attack on the World's biggest oil processing plant.

The fighting erupted on 3rd March 2006 after militants launched a massive rocket on government installations in Mir Ali, the headquarters of North Waziristan. At least 46 militants and five soldiers were killed in a major offensive launched by Pakistan's security forces to wrest control of areas from the extremists in the country's tribal region coinciding with U.S. President *George Bush's* visit. The militants had challenged the government writ and the security forces had to use force as the action became necessary. After the fierce clashes the militants have vacated the government buildings and the government took control of them.

In a fresh blood-letting in Pakistan's strife-torn tribal region, at-least 30 pro-*Taliban* militants, including many foreigners were killed on the night of 10th March, 2006 as army backed by helicopter gun ships pounded their hideout in North Waziristan near the Afghan border .The military acted on intelligence reports indicating that terrorists had gathered at a Madrassa run by pro-Taliban cleric in Khatta Killi village near Miraanshah, 400 km southwest of Islamabad with a large cache of arms and ammunitions.

On 12th March, 06 at least four people were killed in the Afghan capital, Kabul in a suicide attack apparently targeting Sebghatullah Mujadidi, the head of the upper house of Parliament but escaped unharmed. His car was damaged but no one was hurt. *Qari Mohammad Yousuf of Taliban* said on 13-3-06 that on the orders of the *Taliban* leader *Mullah Mohammad Omar four Albanians* were killed and their bodies had been dumped in the Kandahar-Helmand area of the south. Omar's order was read by telephone on 12th March,06 at the border town of Spin Boldak in Kandahar. The orders of Mullah were that "these people had come to Afghanistan at America's behest, therefore, they should be sentenced to death".

As part of an effort to suppress Islamic militancy in North Waziristan , Pakistan authorities arrested at-least 30 people, and banned sale of weapons. The North Waziristan tribal agency was the scene of military strikes before and after 3rd and 4th March visit to Pakistan by U.S *President Bush* in which 200 pro-Taliban militants were killed. On 15-3-06 the para-military frontier constabulary blew up the town's *Anwar-ul-Uloom* (Light of Knowledge) Madrasa, which served as a sanctuary for militants. The religious school was built by Afghan refugees in the 1990s and no one was in it at the time it was destroyed.

Afghan government forces killed sixteen *Taliban* insurgents after surrounding them in mountain near the border with Pakistan. Another *four Taliban* fighters were killed on 22nd March 2006 after they fired rocket-propelled grenades and rifles. at a convoy of *Afghan* troops in the central province of Uruzgan. None of the government or foreign troops were hurt. In the months of February and March, 2006 *Afghanistan* had seen a surge in bombs and other attacks by *Taliban* and their militant allies.

President *Musharraf* ordered on 23rd March, 2006 that all militants to leave the country or be killed. Facing pressure to crack down on foreign extremists hiding out in Pakistan, President *Musharraf* told a rally of some 80,000 people in the eastern city of Lahore that "all foreign militants should leave Pakistan, otherwise they would be crushed". *Musharaf* comments came amid increased tension Pakistan and Afghanistan over allegations Islamabad was not doing enough to prevent *Taliban* and *al-Qaeda* forces from launching cross-border attacks from within Pakistan. Washington which saw Islamabad as a key ally in its war on terrorism had also urged Musharraf to flush out Islamic militants from its remote tribal region. It was estimated that hundreds of foreigners including Arabs, Uzbeks, Chechens and Afghans were hiding in the North and South Waziristan tribal regions bordering Afghanistan. In the month of March, 2006 Pakistani forces backed by helicopter gun-ships attacked a suspected *al-Qaeda* hideout in the rugged frontier and killed dozens of suspected militants mostly foreigners The slain militants included *al-Qaeda* linked Chechen commander. President *Mushrraf* said foreign militants were involved in acts of terrorism within Pakistan.

In November, 2005 *Maniappan Kutty* of Kerala was brutally killed by the Taliban.. Taliban militants again kidnapped *K. Suryanarayana* and his Afghan driver. *K.Suryanarayana* an Indian Engineer from Hyderabad was working with the *Almoayed Company*. He was held hostage in southern *Afghanistan* and threatened to kill him if all Indians did not leave *Afghanistan* within 24 hours. Even before the dead line of 24 hours struck the engineer was beheaded in southern *Afghanisatan* on 30th April"2006. *Suryanarayan's* body was found near the main road between Qalat, the Zabul provincial capital and Ghazni to the north about 300 km southwest of the capital.

In the months of February and March '06 *Afghanistan* had seen a surge in bomb and other attacks by Taliban and their militant allies. On 22-3-06 they, therefore, surrounded the Taliban insurgents in mountains near the border with Pakistan and killed sixteen of them. Another four *Taliban* fighters were killed on 21st March'06 when they fired rocket-propelled grenades and rifles at a convoy of *Afghan* and foreign troops in the central province of Uruzgan. Some of the fiercest violence since the *Taliban's* ouster erupted on 18th May'06 across Afghanistan with coalition forces engaging in multiple firefights, two suicide car bombs and a massive rebel assault on a small village where 105 people were killed. Much of the violence occurred in Helmand and Kandahar provinces where thousands of extra NATO troops were deployed to counter an increasing number of attacks from a stubborn insurgency. Taliban rebels were made up of ethnic Pashtuns, the majority in Afghanistan';s southern and eastern regions near the border with Pakistan.

On 22nd May, 2006 the government convoy, which included the provincial police chief was traveling in the north Helmand when it came under attack. *Taliban* guerillas attacked the convoy in Southern Afghanistan and eleven *Taliban* and three policemen were killed. In a separate incident, four Afghan aid workers were killed in a road -side blast west of Kabul. The attacks came after several days of some of the heaviest *Taliban* attacks since they were ousted in 2001 and just as NATO was bringing thousands of extra troops into the country. More than 250 people were killed since 17th May, 2006 - more than the number reported killed in Iraq during the same period. Most of the dead were militants but dozens of Afghan police soldiers and civilians were also killed, along with four foreign soldiers.

Anger burned among many Afghans over the behavior of the U.S troops when a fatal road accident involving a U.S army truck sparked unrest in many parts of the city. The troops patrolled the streets of Kabul and it was put under curfew for a second night on 30th May,'06 after at least seven people were killed in the worst anti-U.S riots. However, heavy security presence restored order on Kabul's streets. In Northern Afghanistan, Taliban gunmen shot dead three Afghan women working for a Western agency, while a road- side bomb killed two Afghans employed by a U.S firm.

There was widespread disillusion among people that billions of dollars in aid from the international community had failed substantially to improve standards in Afghanistan. At the same time the *Taliban* insurgency in the south and east was going through its bloodiest phase, with more than 350 people killed, including civilians in April and May,2006 alone. Hundreds of suspected Taliban fighters attacked a remote Central Afghan town on 31st May, 2006 and occupied a district police headquarters after a battle drove out the security forces., The militants took control of the police compound in the Uruzgan province town of Chora around dawn on 31st May,2006 after hours of fighting with 100 policemen inside the headquarters.

The *Al-qaeda* chief in Iraq *Abu Musab al- Zarqawi* was killed in an air strike on 7th June,2006 along with one of his key lieutenants, spiritual adviser *Sheik Abdul Rehman* and with eight to ten of partisans. *Al-Zarqawi* and his associates were conducting a meeting approximately eight kilometers north of Baquba which is located about 60 kilometers north of capital with the .U.S forces dropped 500 pound bombs on the safe house. The joint operation involved the Jordanian intelligence, the U.S intelligence and American special operation forces. *Zarqawi*, was blamed for a string of attacks, kidnappings and beheadings that bedeviled Iraq in its transition after the fall of *Saddam Hussain*.

Zarqawi was the son of an elder tribesman, his childhood shaped by poverty and the politics of Zarqa in Jordon,home to mostly downtrodden Palestinian refugees and Bedouin tribes. His real name was *Ahmad Fadhil al-Khalayleh Abu Musab al-Zarqawi.* He was one-time street thug involved in petty crimes and was introduced by radical mosque preachers in the city and left for Afghanistan. *Osama bin Laden* named him as his deputy in Iraq and a $25 million U.S bounty was on his head. *Bin Laden* called him the 'prince of *al-Qaeda* and inspired militants for suicide missions. He was jailed in Jordon in 1993. Jordon accused him of masterminding the 2002 assassination of U.S diplomat *Laurance Foley* in Amman and sentenced him to death in absentia in 2002.

Fascinatingly, the father of *Nick Berg,* a U.S business man allegedly beheaded by *Zarqawi* said on the 8th June, 2006 that he regretted the death of his son's murderer and lashed at President *Bush.* "The death of every human being is a tragedy" Michael Berg said. "The death of *Zarqawi* means a continuation of violence and revenge that took the life of my son."

Abu Musab al-Zarqawi older brother said on 8th June, 06 that the family had anticipated the death of *al-Qaeda* leader in Iraq for some time. "We expected that he would be martyred" he said, in a low voice, signaling his grief over the death of his brother. "We hope that he will join other martyrs in heaven" he added. In Zarqa *al-Zarqawi's* three sisters, all dressed in black, arrived at the one-story family home looking grief stricken. Accompanied by a man who was the husband of one of the sisters.

The *Al-Qaeda* in Iraq said its new leader *Sheik Abu Hamza al-Muhajir* would keep up a campaign of beheadings begun by *Zarqawi.* The warning came on a day when violence, including two car bombs, killed at least 34 people. The Shura council of *al-Qaeda* in Iraq unanimously agreed on *Sheik Abu Hamza al-Muhajir* to be a successor to *Zarqawi.* Although the U.S and Iraq leaders hailed *Zarqawi's* death in an American air strike as a major blow against the *al-Qaeda*, no one had suggested that it would halt the violence ravaging Iraq.

Al-Qaeda's new leader in Iraq vowed on 13th June,'06 to avenge the killing of his predecessor *Zarqawi*, saying Americans and their Iraqi allies would not be safe in their strongholds. "The day of vengeance is near and your strong towers in the Green Zone will not protect you" said the statement posted on a website often used by the Islamism militants and signed by the new leader *Abu Hamza al-Muhajir*. "Coming battles will reveal the falseness of your power and the cowardliness of you and your soldiers, Do not rejoice that you killed (*Zarqawi*), he has left behind lions that ......trained under him. You will see what we have in store for you because of your betrayal and apostasy. Our swords are poised above your necks",

Major strikes by Afghan and coalition troops killed up to 37 Taliban fighters, including a man believed to be related to the movement's leader. Two Afghan civilians were also killed and nine others including two children were wounded in the bomb attack on 12th June,'06 in Paktia province. Fifteen of the militants were killed when Afghan security forces attacked their hideout in Uruzgan on 11th June,'6.

The *Taliban* militants killed 32 friends and relatives of M.P. *Dad Mohammad Khan* in southern Afghanistan and ten others were missing. *Mohammad Khan* said that 27 of the men had been killed in Helmand province when they had gone to the scene of an earlier attack in which five others were shot dead. One of the five men killed in the earlier ambush was a brother of *Khan* named Juma Gull.former governor of Helmand's Sangin district. On hearing the news his other brother *Gull Mohammad* and other relatives rushed to the site of the incident. They were ambushed by Taliban again. Some of them were killed at the site, and some were killed in different locations.

In the month of May,'06, al-Qaeda No.2 leader *Ayman al-Zawahiri* issued a new videotape calling on Afghans to rise up against the U.S and other coalition forces in *Afghanistan*, in the wake of rioting in May,2006 in Kabul . The video by *Zawahiri*, which would be his sixth in 2006, was reported by Intelcentre a Viriginia-based contractor that provides counter terrorism intelligence services to the U.S government.

"I am calling upon the Muslims in Kabul, in particular, and in *all Afghanistan*, in general, and for the sake of God to stand up in an honest stand in the face of the infidel forces that are invading Muslim lands" *al-Zawahiri* said. He also said that "I direct my speech today to my Muslim brothers in Kabul who lived the bitter events yesterday and saw by their own eyes a new proof of the criminal acts of the American forces against the Afghan people" *Zawahiri* appeared to be referring to violent anti-U.S. protests that broke out in the *Afghan* capital on 29th May,'06 after U.S military truck crushed into traffic. The vide appeared to have been by the day after.

In the video, *al-Zawahiri* appeared to be wearing a white turban and sitting in- front of a black backdrop with an automatic rifle next to him. The new message was part of a dramatic increase in videos and audio-tapes by bin- Laden also had issued three tapes in 2006, along with six from his deputy, the Egyptian-born al-Zawahri.

The U.S anti-terrorism agents arrested seven people on 21st and 22nd June,'06 suspected of planning attacks on federal offices in Miami and the landmark *Sears Tower* in Chicago. The *Sears Tower* is strategically located at the hub of *Chicago's* affluent financial district in Wacker Drive, West Loop. It is one of the most recognizable landmarks in the Chicago skyline and in the world. This *110-story architectural marvel* which rises to a *height of 1,450* feet was completed on 3rd May, 1973. *The Sears tower* held the record for the world's tallest building for 25 years until the *Petronas Towers* in *Kuala Lampur*, Malaysia were built in *1998*. The *Sears Tower* is home to its largest corporations and commuter railway stations.

The suspects were dealing with the international *al-Qaeda* group but had been infiltrated by a U.S government informant. No weapons or explosives were found, in a raid at a warehouse in the poor Miami suburb of Liberty city. The suspects were trying to buy weapons to carry out attacks. The U.S government had an informant with whom the suspected conspirators had discussed their plans.

On 30th June,'06 through an internet audiotape *Osama bin Laden* praised the slain leader of Iraq's *al-Qaeda* wing, *Abu Musab al-Zarqawi*, and vowed that the al-Qaeda will continue to fight the U.S forces and their allies 'everywhere'. He said that " the lion of *Jihad–Zarqawi* was killed in a U.S raid. We hope to God he accepts him as a martyr". Addressing the U.S *President Bush*, *bin Laden* said that "don't be too happy, for the banner (of *al-Qaeda* in Iraq) has not dropped but has passed from one lion of Islam to another lion. We will continue, God willing, to fight you and your allies everywhere, in Iraq and *Afghanistan* and Somalia and Sudan, until we waste all your money and kill your men and you will return to your country in defeat as we defeated you before in Somalia" . He also called on the U.S forces to release the body of Jordanian-born *Zarqawi* to his family and demanded Jordan's king *Abdullah* to allow *Zarqawi's* family to hold a funeral in his home town. He said "You (King Abdullah) prevented *Abu Musab* returning to his country alive,. What scares you about *Zarqawi* after his death is that his funeral will be huge and will show the degree of sympathy, Muslims have for the *Mujahdeen*." *Laden* also defended *Zarqawi's* killing of Iraquis who fought with the U.S-led forces against Muslims. "*Abu Musab* had clear instructions to focus his fighting on the occupying forces first of which are Americans. But whoever fought in the trenches of the crusaders against Muslims, then regardless of his faith or his tribe it is acceptable that he may be killed by anyone."

Coalition air strikes killed *eight Taliban* terrorists in

southern *Afghanisatan* on 2nd July,'06 after two British soldiers, an interpreter and 12 other rebels diesd in a major battle. The deaths came as operation Mountain Thurst, the biggest anti-Taliban operation since the extremists were removed from Government in 2001, pushed on in the South. Warplanes dropped bombs on a group of rebels in Sangin district of Helmand province early on 2nd July,'06. The movement and the group of Taliban were detected first in the area and then the planes bombed them. The bombing followed an attack on a British base in Sangin late on 30th June,'06 with small arms and rocket-propelled grenade fire in which two British soldiers and an *Afghan* interpreter were killed.

A plot to bomb *New York's Holland Tunnel* in an effort to flood the wall -street financial district had been uncovered by the FBI with a suspect arrested in Lebonon. Lebonon confirmed on 7th July,'06 that it had arrested a suspect in connection with a plot to bomb a tunnel in New York. An unidentified counter -terrorism sources, said the investigation involved what officials considered a 'serious plot' to detonate enough explosives inside the landmark tunnel to destroy it and send devastating floodwaters through lower Manhattan. The 79-year-old tunnel runs under the *Hudson River* between *New Jersey* and *Manhattan* and carried almost 34 million vehicles in 2005. At the request of the U.S officials one of the suspected conspirators was arrested and identified as Amir Andalousli.

The *Al-qaeda* deputy leader *Ayman al-Zawahri* warned that his group would not stand by and watch Israel bombard Lebanon and the Palestinians. He called Muslims in a video aired on 27th July, 2006 to fight attacks on their countries. Zawahri, in the tape aired by *Al Jajeera* television, did not say how al-Qaeda would respond to the fighting. "How can we remain silent while watching bombs raining on our people"he asked. "Oh Muslims everywhere, I call on you to fight and become martyrs in the war against the Zionists and the Crusaders."*Zawahri* said in the statement which was entitled "*The Zionist-crusader war on Lebonon and the Palestinians*" Zawahri's statement was the first comment by the Sunni Muslim dominated *al-Qaeda* against Isreal's war on Lebonon which was sparked by the capture of two Isreali soldiers by Shite Muslim guerilla group Hizbollah.

Pakistan's claim that it does not have terrorist training camp in its territory was strongly contested by FBI which has told a U.S court that satellite pictures pointed towards such a camp. In the trail of 23-year-old Pakistani American *Hamid Hayat* who has been accused of terrorism-related charges, Defense Intelligence Agency's expert *Eric Benn* has stated that there was such of seventy percent "probability" that the satellite images pointed to a militant training camp near Balakot in North-east Pakistan. Much to Pakistan's embarrassment, *Benn* told the district court in California that although he did not "detect any formal weapons training", including firing ranges, targets, rocket launchers or explosives testing it did not mean that they were not taking place. The structures and trail in the remote terrain fit the "signature" of "militant training", as opposed to regular training of Pakistani Armed Forces. The Federal prosecutors wanted to nail their suspect-and indirectly Pakistan- in the terror training camp case. The defense has argued that Hamid never attended any terror facility but only made up the story to satisfy agents of the FBI who grilled him in June,2005. Hamid's jury was shown satellite images taken between 2001 and 2004 of a Pakistani national forces which was on a mountainous terrain and about 10 kms from Balakot.

India has stepped up its battle against terrorism and was keeping international community updated about the existence of 52 terrorist training camps in Pakistan and *Pakistan-occupied Kashmir*. The Govt. of India had, in its interaction with Pakistan at all levels, continuously stressed the fact that Pakistan needed to take some effective action to dismantle terrorism on a permanent basis. Pakistan has always denied the presence of terrorist training camps in Pakistan and in the territory under its control. The Government of India has been keeping the international community informed of developments in this regard on a continuing basis as part of the global war on terrorism.

The disclosure about the 52 terrorist camps operating from the territory in Pakistan's control was meant to send a strong signal to Pakistan that the peace process will not move forward unless it gives a categorical commitment to end cross –border terror. Pakistan had asked India for evidence of its alleged complicity in the Mumbai terror attacks on 11th July, 2006 that killed at least 200 people. India had responded by saying that it was ready to offer evidence but when it had done so earlier Islamabad did not act on it.

Four Canadian soldiers were killed on 3rd September '06 in a major *anti-Taliban* operation in southern Afghanisatan. The rebel death toll was around 200. The new deaths raised the figure to 19 the number of Candadian soldiers killed in enemy action in 2006, more than 30 were killed since Canadian forces deployed in *Afghanistan* in 2002, months after the ousting of the *Taliban* government.

The Deputy *al-Qaeda* leader *Ayman al-Zawahiri* had urged a militant Algerian Islamism group to punish 'Crusader nation' France, even though it vehemently opposed the U.S-led war in Iraq. He called on the Algerian GSPC group to become 'a bone in the throat of the Americans and French Crusaders'. He also urged the GSPC – the Salafist group for preaching and combat to sow fear 'in the hearts of the traitors and the apostate sons of France' and to crush the 'pillars of the Crusader alliance. The expression 'crusader' refers to medieval military campaign waged in the name of Christendom to recapture the Holy Land from Muslims and is frequently used in Islamism circles to designate enemies of Islam. The GSPC group emerged from the armed Islamic group blamed for a massacre of civilians during the bloody insurgency against Algeria's military backed government in the 1990s. It is viewed as a major threat by the French security services as it has switched its focus to taking part in the international jihad. *Ayman al-Zawahari* called U.S President a lying failure for taking of progress in the war on terrorism. According to a video posted on the Internet on the 29th Sept.'06 *Zawahri* said "Bush , O failure and liar, why don't you be courageous for once and confront your people and tell them the truth about your losses in Iraq and Afghanistan". In a second portion of the tape, *Zawahri* labeled *Pope Benedict* a "charlatan" because of his remarks on Islam. He also compared the Pope to the 11th century Pope Urban II who backed the first crusade.

The *Taliban* extremists shot dead eight laborers working on a U.S base in eastern Afghanistan as they were driving home for an upcoming Muslim holiday. A group of 10 workers had left the base in Kunar in a minibus late on 19th Oct.'06 when they were stopped by a group of gunmen. The gunmen sprayed the vehicle with bullets. Two laborers managed to escape. Fugitive *Taliban* leader Mullah *Mohammad Omar* had used the holiest Muslim holiday of the year' 06 to warn that his men will intensify their fighting in Afghanistan to "surprising " levels to drive out foreign forces. In a message to *Afghans* for *Ed-ul-Fitr*, which marks the end of the fasting month of *Ramadan*. Omar also urged NATO to withdraw its almost 20,000 troops and stop sacrificing soldiers for the U.S, adding the nation stood with him. "With the grace of Allah, the fighting will be increased. and it will be organized in the next few months," he said in a Pashto message to media also posted on the internet and signed 'Leader of the faithful in the *Afghan* resistance'. "I am confident the fighting will be a surprise for many," said the one-eyed leader, who has a $10 million bounty on his head.

The Aarhus (Denmark) court ruled on 26th Octo.'06 that a Danish newspaper did not libel Muslims by printing cartoons of the *Prophet Mohammad* that unleashed a storm of protests in the Islamic world. Seven Danish Muslim organizations brought the case, saying the paper had libeled them with the images, which included one depicting the Prophet with a bomb in his turban, by implying Muslims are terrorists. Many Muslims believe it is blasphemous to depict the Prophet.

Jyllands-Posten, which published the 12 drawings in September,'05 hailed the ruling. Saying any other outcome would have been a catastrophe for a free press. "Of course it cannot be excluded that the drawings off-ended some Muslims." The Aarhus court said in its ruling. "But there is no sufficient reason to assume that the cartoons are or were intended to be insulting...or put forward ideas that could hurt the standing of Muslims in society," .The court ordered the seven organizations to pay the paper's court expenses. The plaintiffs had appealed to a higher court. But the court did find that three of the cartoons fell within what the law could deem as insulting.

Clashes between insurgents and NATO-led and Afghan troops left 34 Taliban and three policemen dead in the second week of Oct.'06. Eight policemen, *eight Taliban* and three civilians were also wounded in clashes in the volatile southern provinces of *Kandahar*, Zabul and southeastern Khost. On 8th Oct.'06 twenty-two *Taliban* were killed during a joint operation by Afghan army, police and NATO forces in the Pashmole area of *Kandahar* province. Most of the casualities occurred as a result of NATO air support. Fighting erupted on 9th Oct.'06 again in Pashmole when insurgents attacked a police vehicle, prompting a gun battle which let six Taliban dead. In neighbouring Zabul province, *Taliban* fighters ambushed a police patrol in Shahjoy district on 8th Octo,'06 killing two policemen.

A purported audio recording by the leader of Iraq's *al-Qaeda* wing gloated over the resignation of Defense Secretary *Donald Rumsfeld*, as a top U.S General said the military was preparing to strategy changes. *Abu Hamza al-Muhajir*, also known as *Abu Ayyub al-Masri*, said in the recording posted on the Internet on 10th Oct.'06 that the group had 12,000 armed fighters and 10,000 others waiting to be equipped to fight U.S troops in Iraq. "I tell the lame duck (U.S administration) do not rush to escape as did your defense minister ...stay on the battle ground," he said. He said his group would not rest until it had blown up the Presidential mansion in Washington. "I swear by God we shall not rest from *Jihad* until we. blow up the filthiest house known as the White House,"

Mullah Akthar Mohammad Osmani , a close associate of *bin Laden* and a senior member of the *Taliban's* inner circle was killed on 19th December,'06 in Hlmand province. *Osmani* was in the top ring of the Taliban leadership and he was also a close associate of *bin Laden* and Gulbuddin Hekmatyr. After receiving credible intelligence coalition force located *Osmani* in Hemland province near the border with Pakistan and a coalition air strike hit *Osmani's* vehicle which was traveling in a deserted area, killing him and two unidentified associates.

The fight between the U.S allied forces and Taliban is still continuing claiming the lives of many people on both the sides. We, in India wish that normalcy is restored in *Afghanistan* soon and the Afghans live in peace maintaining good relations with all the neighbouring countries.

18
Settlement of Jammu and Kashmir Issue

The State of *Jammu and Kashmir* joined the Union of India, after India's independence formally and legally. The then popular leader, *Sheik Abdullah* endorsed the Maharaja's action of accession of the State to the Indian Union. The matter had been messed-up subsequently giving rise to subversive activities blissfully carried out by Pakistan and other militant groups. Kashmir valley became the bone of contention between India and Pakistan for the last sixty years. There were three wars between the two countries and Pakistan is resorting to an endless terrorist attacks. Thousands of civilians and military personnel sacrificed their lives and yet there is no peace in the valley. Time without number, discussions took place at the highest level of India and Pakistan and there is nowhere near a solution. Successive governments in Pakistan after partition, either headed by the civilians or by the military men continued in their office voicing concern about the settlement of *Jammu and Kashmir* issue. The people of Pakistan were inveigled and their attention has been diverted from the main issues of crippling economy and internal bickering. They are over dosed with the hate-campaign against India and in their enthusiasm to attack India, failed to improve their economy and settle internal issues. Very frequently, the Pakistanis indulged in crossing the Line of Control (LOC) and infiltrated into Kashmir valley and encourage the local militants in killing innocent people and damage their properties. Afraid of, terrorism unleashed by the militants thousands of Kashmiri Pandits left the valley and staying in refugee camps for more than a decade now. Their plight is clear violation of human rights which people in the valley justifiably decry.

After assumption of Office, Prime Minister *Manmohan Singh* had taken a positive step ordering cuts in troop deployment, which has a along term effect. Some 9,000 jawans were withdrawn with a view that demilitarization presupposes a level of confidence. It is a known fact, that India and Pakistan are not trusting each other. Trade and travel are bound to generate understanding and goodwill which may make the Kashmir problem easier.

For any government in India who rule at the center, they have to bestow their attention first for resolving the Jammu and Kashmir problem. After winning the elections and forming the government under the Prime Ministership of *Manmohan Singh*, the Home Minister *Shivraj Patil* visited Jammu and Kashmir in the first week of November, 2004 and met there a cross-section of people. He also visited Ladak and also the Line of Control. The delegation which met the Home Minister renewed the demand for Union Territory Status for Ladak and inclusion Ladhak in the talks while resolving the Kashmir issue. The Home Minister did not give any assurance but said that "this issue can bifurcate or unite the State." Soon after the return of Prime Minister *Manmohan Singh*, from Denmark the Home Minister briefed him of his visit to the Kashmir valley and Ladhak

After taking the necessary information from the Home Minister. *Manmohan Singh* also visited Jammu and Kashmir in the third week of November,2004 and offered to hold unconditional talks with "anyone and every one" who abjure violence and announced Rs.24,000 crores for economic revival plan in the State. He promised a new Kashmir of peace, hope and prosperity and help the State in ending the problems of unemployment and work for building infrastructure and bring in new investment. Peace is essential for economic rebuilding of Jammu and Kashmir. Kashmir needs prosperity with peace and peace without dignity is meaningless. During the maiden visit of .Manmohan Singh, after he became the Prime Minister reduction of troops began in the State. The Prime Minister assured the people of Kashmir that if, conditions improved, and infiltration brought under control there would be further cut in the troops deployment. Although his visit to Jammu and Kashmir was successful in creating a new opportunity for progress it had left some key issues unresolved; like who should be taken as legitimate representative of Kashmir: whether to allow Hurriyat to travel to Pakistan and to set up a frame-work for linking the dialogue between Indian, Pakistan and Kashmir. His visit, however, shows a continuity of the peace process in the State. During the course of his visit, he made it quite clear that "Kashmir is in our hearts... in the Constitution, or that they could be on Indian citizens" were free to meet anyone and they were in any way in touch with Pakistan Government. This could be interpreted as an insistence on a dialogue within the four corners of the Constitution, even though the Prime Minister said quite categorically that he was willing to have unconditional talks with anyone.

In contrast to the above, President *Musharaff* suggested to divide Kashmir on both sides of the Line of Control into seven "regions" demilitarizing them and granting them the status of independence or putting them under joint control or U.N.Mandate. He also insisted that both the factions of *Hurriyat Conference* should be included in the dialogue aimed at solving the Kashmir issue. He considered them as true representatives of the people of Kashmir.

Under a deal with a group of Islamism parties *Musharaff*

promised to shed his military uniform by the end of 2004 in return for support for constitutional changes validating his rule as President and expanding his power. General *Musharaff* who seized power in a bloodless coup in 1999 pushed through a new law in parliament in the first week of December 2004 to continue as military chief as well as President, despite his early pledging to relinguish his dual post. He is taking shelter donning military uniform, as it was crucial for him in his highly complicated campaign against the *Al-qaeda* network and other Islamic militants within Pakistan and to seek a settlement of the Kashmir issue with India. The United States who are called the champions of democracy taking softer line of the assumption of dual role by President *Musharaff*, as they are more interested in capturing bin Laden and his men than demand for full democracy in Pakistan.

Pakistan from its inception on the midnight of 14th August, 1947, is the best ally of the U.S in South East Asia. India on the other hand distanced itself from the U.S because of the socialist pattern of policies of *Jawaharlal Nehru* and the closeness with the Soviet Union. The U.S and Pakistan before and after the iron curtain years remained steadfast in their relations.

The U.S up-graded its relation with Pakistan in March, 2004 and accordingly it the status of the major non-*NATO ALLY* had also gained significant access to conventional arms from the U.S, world's only super power. The post September 11 attacks on the U.S.A. became a blessing in disguise to Pakistan as the U.S.A. considers it as a key ally in the fight against *al-Qaeda*. Therefore, after the Presidential election was over in the U.S.A., President *Musharaff* met President *Bush* on 5th December and congratulated on his re-election and praised his commitment to establish a Palestanian State. During their meeting President *Bush* emphasized Middle-East peace and praised President *Musharaff* in his efforts in the war against terrorism and the search for bin Laden. In this way, they admired each other, and strengthened their relations.

While the peace process between India and Pakistan was underway, supply of sophisticated arms like F-16 and missiles to Pakistan by the Bush administration angered India. It, therefore, conveyed to the United States its concern over repercussions of American arms supplies to Pakistan. It obviously, cause bout of negativism in the process of peace in Kashmir. Unconcerned with the heart burnt problem of India in regard to the sophisticated arms supply to Pakistan, the U.S. argued that it was being done to curtail the threats of *al-Qaeda* and *Taliban* forces but it would not as such weapons were for big wars. Experts in the field ridiculed the above plea, as nobody uses F-16 aircraft to fight terrorism. At the Government of India's level it was construed that the U.S. administration might have taken this stand since Pakistan happened to be its major non-NATO ally. In spite of the fact, the U.S. is pampering Pakistan with sophisticated arms supply supposed to curtail the threats of al-Qaeda and Taliban forces India on its part was sincere in the peace process of Kashmir and withdrew two battalions from *Jammu and Kashmir* on the 15th December. Troop reduction of one battalion also took place in Kalakote area of Rajori District. Further, one battalion of troops comprising 700 personnel left for an undisclosed destination from the old airfield security camp in the outskirts of Srinagar City on the morning of 15th December.

Some of the militant organizations, in the State were not interested in the peace process going between India and Pakistan. They were bent upon creating some troubles to unsettle the issue. On 22nd December, the militants hurled grenades at CRPF bunker, which exploded injuring ten civilians and five CRPF personnel.

The attacks of the terrorists on 11th September, 2001 on the *World Trade Center*, *Pentagon* and *Pennsylvania* lasted for only fifteen minutes. In this relentless gap of time, the *World Trade Center* vanished completely and about 3,000 people lost their lives. Damage was also caused to one of the portions of the building of Pentagon, the military headquarters of the United States. The trauma and travails felt by the United States was for about forty five minutes though the tragedy that took place remembered long. To avenge these attacks and to capture bin Laden and his militia group, President *Bush* declared war on Afghanistan on 7th October, 2001 and the fight took place for nearly 40 days . Though the fight between the United States and the *Taliban* ruled *Afghanistan* looked like between a ferocious lion and emaciated lamb, it became inevitable as the *Taliban* regime declined to surrender *Laden* in spite of repeated warnings given by the United States. The United States used their mighty force and sophisticated weapons and decimated the regime of *Taliban*.

On 13th December, 2001 when, the Indian Parliament was in session the terrorists hoodwinking the security personnel entered the premises of the Parliament and tried to assassinate the important national leaders of India. This was, however, foiled by the alert police personnel by killing them.

In *Jammu and Kashmir* thousands of people died in the last ten to fifteen years by the subversive acts of terrorists and still there is no peace in the region. The State of *Jammu and Kashmir* is an integral part of India and any attack on it is an attack on India. Terrorists not satisfied with their numerous destructive acts tried to attack the Assembly building of *Jammu and Kashmir* on 1st October, 2001. In this regard, it is important to note that under the benign policies of the successive governments in India, the terrorists have been carrying out their destructive acts blissfully for the last fifteen to twenty years. An attempt was also made to storm into the Parliament and shake the very foundation of democratic set-up in India. The Parliament building is a temple of democracy and it is as inviolable to the Indians as Pentagon for Americans. It is also pertinent to point out that the Americans could not tolerate the trauma of terrorist attacks on their soil for about forty five minutes and devastated almost all the camps of *al-Qaeda* in pursuit of bin Laden in Afghanistan, while killing several persons. In contrast to the above, Indians are experiencing the menace of terrorists for about fifteen to twenty years and still under the gracious attitude of our leaders, a pitch is set up for the peace process with Pakistan.

A study by the International Center for peace Initiatives, the stand off between India and Pakistan following the attack on Parliament in the year 2001 has cost the two nations on estimated total of three billion U.S. dollars. While the cost to India was estimated at 1.8 billion dollars, Pakistan had to cough up the remaining $ 1.2 billion. New Delhi's spending amounted to 0.38 percent of its Gross Domestic Product, while Pakistan's cost of a whopping 1.79 per cent of the GDP. The closure of each other's airspace cost Pakistan three billion dollars per month and India's losses ran as high as $ 4.3 million till the resumption of air links in the summer of 2004. In 2002-03, India was spending Rs. 14 billion each year on its Saichan operations, compared with Pakistan's Rs.4.3 billion. The study made by the Center said Pakistan officially lost 270 soldiers in the Kargil conflict, though "the U.S. State Department put the casualties at roughly 700".. The findings of the study has been corroborated by reports of the Asian Development Bank. "This is ironic, especially for Pakistan, considering that over 50 million Pakistanis live on or below the poverty line". These statistics translated into real, on-the-ground situation means that large populations in the two countries have been badly impacted by misplaced priorities" the Pakistani weekly the *Friday Times* said. It said Pakistan's Official defence budget of $ 2.8 billion is astronomical compared to the annual collective allocation of less than $ 300 million for health and education sectors". The weekly quoted the analysts as suggesting that Pakistan's strategy now "must focus on forging a working relationship with India rather than basing policies on the presumption that India is an eternal enemy not amenable to the idea of friendly Pakistan". The weekly also said that Islamabad should find a way to push forward a mutually beneficial coexistence with India "rather than formulating futile reactionary responses on issues like the Indian desire for a U.N. Security Council seat".

The differences between India and Pakistan which are of decades old may not be solved in a day. The meeting between the Foreign secretaries of India and Pakistan on 28th December, however, avoided a slide back and kept the ball in play. They offered each other reassurances on the basic assumption of the peace process. The two sides agreed to act on the promise by *Manmohan Singh* and *Musharaff* to "explore all options for a peaceful settlement of *Jammu and Kashmir*". As if, to dispel that India is reluctant to move forward the Foreign Secretary of India came with a bold proposal to the families divided by international policies to meet each other at five specific points of Tangdhar, Poonch, Mendhar and Uri along the Line of Control (LOC) and Suchetgarh along the international boundary on designated days. While keeping the options open, Pakistan raised concerns about Kashmiris having to travel all the way to the respective High Commissions at New-Delhi and Islamabad to obtain the permit. New-Delhi, however, felt that the two countries could agree upon a system of pre-verification individuals.

The tangle on travel documents for the proposed bus service between Srinagar and Muzaffarabad across the Line of control in *Jammu and Kashmir* remained unresolved. It was left to the two Prime Minister of India and Pakistan to sort out the wrangling over the eagerly anticipated bus service when they meet in Dhaka during the course of South Asian summit.

To thwart the peace talks that were taking place between India and Pakistan some militant outfit like *al-Mansoorian* stormed the three storyed building having Income Tax Office in Barbarshah locality on 7th January. The terrorists stormed it hurling grenades and firing indiscriminately. There was a fierce gun battle between the security personnel and the two militants that left three security men including a BSF deputy Commandant and both the ultras dead, while four others including three senior officers wee injured. The CRPF, however, rescued the employees of IT Department and other people trapped inside the building, which engulfed with flames.

There was no stop of militants making bids to cross over from across the border and damage the public properties and enter into fight with security forces. On 16-1-05 two militants of al-Mansoorian gained entry into the passport office adjacent to the Bakshi Stadium through the compound of the vacant youth hostel hurling grenades indiscriminately. The CRPF personnel guarding the indoor stadium returned the fire which left three jawans injured and two missing. The guns fell silent as dusk descended and the security forces adopted wait and watch tactics to prevent militants from escaping taking advantage of the darkness. After 26-hour gun battle the security forces gunned down both the militants of *al-Mansoorian* who stormed the passport Office in which two CRPF personnel were also killed and five injured. The bodies of the two CRPF personnel were also recovered from the passport Office on the 16th morning ending the suspense over the whereabouts of the two who had gonc missing after the encounter had broken out.

Though the Pakistan Government is shedding crocodile tears to end terrorism its reluctance to handover hard -core terrorists like *Dawood Ibrahim* and *Azar Masood* raises doubts about its sincerity. *Azhar Masood* is well-respected person amongst the *al-Qaeda* cadres and is close to terrorists like *Osama bin Laden* and *Mullah Omar*. *Azar Masood* was involved in the kidnapping of American tourists in *Jammu and Kashmir* and had links with the hijackers of Indian Airlines plane IC-814 on 24th December 1999 and he was released by the Indian Government among the three released in exchange of the hijacked plane. India had also secured an Interpol red corner notice against *Azar Masood* in connection with the 2001 Parliament House attack. Since Azhar Masood is involved in the kidnapping of American tourists in Jammu and Kashmir the U.S. asked Pakistan to hand him over to them. Pakistani authorities refused on the grounds that he was not a hijacker and his incarceration in India had been illegal.

In the early hours of 9th January, 2005 a team of police and BSF personnel resumed operation and a gun battle took place for 24 hours at the Income Tax Complex with Security forces killing a militant holed up inside the building. There is no stop of militants making a bid to cross over from across the border and damage the public property and enter into fight with security forces.

While the peace talks between India and Pakistan were going on it is quite ironical that Pakistan was contemplating to acquire from the U.S. F-16 fighter planes capable of delivering nuclear weapons, repair and up gradation of existing systems and licenses for the import of spares. Pakistan under plausible scenarios might use nuclear weapons to counter by the larger Indian conventional forces particularly given Islamabad's lack of strategic depth.

Advances in modern weaponry of longer ranges, precision delivery and destructive conventional munitions create circumstances encouraging the pre-emptive use of military force. The increased range of new missiles and aircraft delivery systems provide sanctuary to their possessors. The Indian Government should, therefore, prevail upon the U.S. to stop delivery of F-16 fighter planes and other modern weapons to Pakistan, if they are really interested in the peaceful settlement of Kashmir issue and end terrorism across the world.

There is no abatement of terrorist acts even though both Indian and Pakistan wish to settle the Kashmir issue peacefully.

On 23-1-05, an explosion took place near the Line of Control in Jammu and Kashmir's Rajouri District where troops recovered 19 Pakistani mines, besides a large quantity of explosion, triggered by detonation of a Pakistani mine in Nargis Madian area in Noushera sub-sector on 22-1-05.

After the attack on the Income Tax Complex, the militants lobbed a grenade targeting the *Jammu and Kashmir* Finance Minister *Muzaffar Hussain Baig* in Baramullah District of North Kashmir. The Minister, however, escaped the attempt on his life as the grenade fell on the road side and did not explode.

In violation of the ceasefire agreement of 25th November 2003, there were two incidents of alleged trans-motor fire on 18-01-05 and 20-01-05 and the situation appeared to have gone out of control. Between India and Pakistan, charges and counter-charges flew thick and fast across the Line of control. Just after a week of these incidents a meeting took place on 23rd January 2005 at the commanding level and 'both sides reaffirmed the ceasefire and there was no firing bringing the situation back to normal.

Though the militants are engaged in damaging the public properties and threatening the civilians, *Jammu and Kashmir* registered 60% turn-out in civic poll. Dealing a blow to the separatist groups and defying militant threats, over 60% of the electorate in Baramulla and Kupwara districts of Jammu and Kashmir on 30th January 2005 cast their votes in the municipal elections held in the State after 27 years. The first round of the six-phase elections held under tight security passed off peacefully. The municipal committees in Kupwara district witnessed a massive turnout of 86 percent while those in Baramulla registered a turnout of 56.6 percent. This is the highest turnout in any election in the Valley since 1990 where civil polls were held after a gap of twentyseven years. The Govt. of India was very much enthused by the amount of voters in the first phase of civil polls in *Jammu and Kashmir* and felt it could be a turning point in the situation in the State.

After successful completion of civic polls in Baramullah and Sopore confidence of people increased in *Jammu and Kashmir* though infiltration was down to a trickle. The number of militants in the valley had gone from 3500 to 1700. Though there was no immediate cause of anxiety, in so far as militant activities were concerned India is, however worried over the existence of terrorist training camps, launch pads, communication linkages and other apparatus in Pakistan. India asked Pakistan to dismantle terrorist infrastructure in that country. India made it very clear that terrorism should be abandoned and Pakistan should not allow its territory to cross-border terrorism to thwart the settlement of Jammu and Kashmir issue.

Ignoring militant threats and poll boycott calls by separatists, a moderate 44 per cent voters cast their franchise in the civic polls in *Jammu and Kashmir's* Anantnag and Pulwama districts on 06-02-05.

After successful completion of the civic polls in *Jammu and Kashmir* without violence further steps were taken to ease the situation in the valley. Road for bus to Pakistan Occupied Kashmir (POK) was under the consideration of India and Pakistan from a long time. There was a long moment when the Srinagar-Muzaffarabad bus service appeared to have been lost to seemingly irreconcilable postures. Pakistan was set firmly against India's insistence on passengers carrying adequately stamped passports. New-Delhi, in turn, could not countenance Islamabad's case that the service should be only to Kashmiris from both sides of Line of Control. Displaying flexibility, India and Pakistan on 16-02-05 decided to revive the bus service from Srinagar to Muzaffarabad across the divided Kashmir from 7th April, 2005 for all their nationals and agreed on discussions to reduce the risks of nuclear accidents and unauthorized use of weapons as part of confidence building measures. Travel across the LoC by this 170-km-long bus link is by an entry permit system, after verifying the identities of the passengers.

Describing the announcement on the Srinagar-Muzaffarabad bus service as "a small but significant step" a prominent Hurriyat leader said on 18-2-2005 that he and his colleagues wanted to be on the first bus across the LoC, but were willing to delay a visit to Pakistan if talks with New Delhi were to push forward the peace process. However, Jaish-e-Mohammad a militant outfit threatened to disrupt the bus service. The *Hizbul Mujahideen*, a terrorist organization, too said that the bus link is "unimportant and won't improve the plight of the people".

As if, the nature has cursed *Jammu and Kashmir*, many people feared killed and trapped as a series of avalanches triggered by the heaviest snowfall in two decades in the State. Several houses were damaged and Kashmir valley remained cut off from rest of the country as the snowfall hit mountainous areas in the State since 18-2-2005. The *Jammu and Kashmir* government had to sound a red alert and requested the Defense forces to rush essentials to the affected areas. Ironically, ignoring these traumatic conditions prevailing in the State, a two member militant suicide squad from Pakistan stormed the Divisional Headquarters of the *Jammu and Kashmir* government on 24-02-05. There were 250 people inside the building. A gun battle between the militants and security personnel took place for three-and-half hours in which four persons including three security personnel were killed and two were injured. The two militants were, however, shot dead.

As the *Jammu and Kashmir* government was engaged in supplying 1,500 truck loads of essentials including 450 carrying petrol to the Kashmiris living on depleted food and fuel due to highest snow fall in fifteen years, the militants set ablaze a house in Jammu and Kashmir on 28-02-05. Fierce gun-battle took place between the security forces and the militants in which two security men and a militant was killed and four others got injured. The incident took place at Matribugh near Shopian in Pulwama district.

A week before the first bus service started on the Srinagar-Muzaffarabad road, Pro-Pakistan militants like al-Nasireen, Save Kashmir Movement, *Al Arifeen and Farzandan-e-Milat* issued a threat on 30th March, 2005 to its passengers asking Kashimiris to refrain from boarding this "coffin" and becoming "traitors". They criticized the Srinagar-Muzaffarabad bus service as "a conspiracy to keep Kashmir permanently under the Indian occupation". The statement also included a list of 40 passengers from Kashmir waiting for Pakistan's approval and sought the news agencies to carry all the names",so that they refrain from boarding the bus". In view of the new threat, the government has increased the security cover to the bus all along 180 kms stretch. In spite of repeated threats given by the militants, the State Government of *Jammu and Kashmir* determined to make the Srinagar-Muzaffarabad bus traveling a success. Terming the militants threats as a desperate and anti-people act, the State Government envisaged the proposed resumption of service as a key confidence-building measure.

It was quite unfortunate Pakistan turned down the Indian request for allowing politicians from *Jammu and Kashmir* to be on board for the inaugural run of the bus from Srinagar to Muzaffarabad on the 7th of April, 2005. Islamabad had narrowed the eligibility requirements drastically, saying the bus service was intended "only" for families divided on both sides of the Line of Control. Both countries shed decades of misunderstanding to get the Srinagar-Muzaffarabad bus moving and to move further they should remove, bit- by- bit, the curbs on movement.

Before flagging off of the bus service on the 7th April, 2005, large-sized hoardings of Prime Minister *Manmohan Singh* and his Pakistani counter-part Pervez Musharaff accompanied by messages of peace and friendship were erected by the Jammu and Kashmir Government along the 180 km – long route of Srinagar – Muzaffarabad bus service. This was for the first time in the history of *Jammu and Kashmir* that a photograph of Pakistani leader had been prominently displayed on a hoarding in the Valley reflecting the changing scenario in the border State hit by insurgency.

Ignoring militant threats India and Pakistan on the 7th April, 2005 bridged a 57 year-old divide by starting a bus service between Srinagar and Muzaffarabad to send spirits soaring on either side of the Line of Control. At 2-00 p.m. 30 passengers of a bus from Muzaffarabad in Pakistan occupied Kashmir took what Prime Minister *Manmohan Singh* called "small but significant step" as he flagged off the corresponding service from Srinagar by crossing the Aman Setu or peace Bridge into Indian territory in the Valley. Nearly three hours later, 19 Indians crossed into PoK through the same bridge to complete a highly emotional day for Kashmiris on either side of the LoC.

The bus to Muzaffarabad has put education in the State on top gear. As a build-up to the Prime Minister's Srinagar visit, the Center and State got their act together to build 14-degree colleges. Under the Reconstruction package for *Jammu and Kashmir* the State Government notified in the month of March, 2005 13 locations – mainly militant-infested border areas-where these colleges could come up. The Planning Commission released Rs.49 crore for building these colleges. Six of these institutions are exclusively for women. Also on the anvil are to establish central schools with emphasis on primary education in the English medium. The attempt is to use education to bring back the restive Kashmir Valley into the national fold.

Promising to usher in an era of peace and prosperity in Jammu and Kashmir, Prime Minister *Manmohan Singh* flagged on 13th April, 2005 the first train connecting the mountainous town to the rest of the country in the first phase of the project that would provide a rail link to the Kashmir valley. He announced that the first train into the valley would start by 2007 when construction of the rail track from Jammu to Baramullah via Udhampur, Katra, Qazigund and Srinagar is completed.

President *Parvez Musharraf* came to India on the 16th April, 2005 nearly four years aftcr the failed Agra Summit to watch cricket match between India and Pakistan and to hold one-to-one talks with Prime Minister *Manmohan Singh* started the visit by offering prayers at the Dargah of famous *Sufi Saint Khwaja Moinuddin Chisti* in Ajmeer, India. He said to have prayed for peace and prosperity of the people of India and Pakistan, for resolution of differences and improvement in relations between the two countries. He further maintained that he came with an open mind and expressed the hope that his meetings with the Indian leaders would help strength the peace process.

On 17th April, 2005 President *Musharaff* and Prime Minister *Manmohan Singh* had a 40 minute one-to-one meeting after a two long delegation meeting during which they came up with a broad vision to co-operate more effectively in providing cross border exchange including along the LoC. It is one of the curiosities of India and Pakistan relations that even when hostilities between the two countries were at their height the smuggling of goods carried on uninterrupted. This illicit activity between the two neighbors was causing concern and had figured prominently in the talks between *President Musharaff and Prime Minister Manmohan Singh.* After all, if buses can ferry people across the borders, it follows that lorries can transfer goods. And an increased movement of goods across the borders is a good market of the state of Indo-Pak ties just as the unleashing of entrepreneurial energy is an effective way to help wind down hostilities. Therefore, Prime Minister *Manmohan Singh* and President *Musharaff* issued a joint statement reiterating their commitment to people to people contact and the need to identifying further areas for trade and economic co-operation. The joint statement issued at the close of *President Musharaff's* visit on the 19th April, 2005 committed the two countries for working towards mutual settlement of the *Jammu and Kashmir* issue and the scope for movement and contact by putting travel and trade at the center of India and Pakistan engagement. In short the joint statement enunciated that

Peace process is irreversible.

To continue discussions on Kashmir sincerely

To allow movement across the LoC.

Trade consulates to be opened in Mumbai and Karachi by year end.

To reactivate joint economic commission and

Additional bus routes from Poonch and Rawlakot in PoK..

On the above, joint statement, the Kashmiri militant outfits and hardliners like *Syed Ali Shah Geelani* lashed out at Pakistan President *Musharaff* for 'kneeling down' before India. A statement by four other groups – *Al-Nasireen*, Save Kashmir Movement, *Farzandan-e-Milat and Al Arifeen* – castigated President *Musharaff* for what they called a "sellout of Kashmir in lieu of trade, tourism and satanic cultural ties with India". These outfits which had earlier opposed the Srinagar-Muzaffarabad bus service claimed Musharaff had compromised on the Kashmir issue.

With both India and Pakistan declaring that the on going peace process is "irreversible", militant outfit *Hizbul Mujahideen* said that it is ready to consider a ceasefire provided security forces implement it on the ground. The self-styled Chief Commander, Operations, of the outfit, *Gazi Misbahuddin* told a local news agency on the 23rd of April,2005 that "if New Delhi announces a ceasefire and ground situation reflects the same, *Hizbul Mujahideen* will consider it seriously. Demanding a role for militants in the final settlement of the Kashmir issue, he said that his organization is not only active on the militancy front but also on political front.

On the 25th of April, 2005 the *Hurriyat conference* also asserted that it was keen on return of Kashmiri Pandits to the valley and invited representatives of the displaced community in the month of May, 2005 to discuss the issue. *Syed Salim Geelani*, President of Jammu and Kashmir Freedom Party told reporters that a meeting of the representatives of Kashmiri Pandits from Jammu and other parts of the country would be held in Srinagar in the second half of May, 2005 with the Kashmiri leadership of the *All Party Hurriyat conference* where threadbare discussions expected to take place on the issue of the return of the Kashmiri Pandits. He said that "Kashmir is incomplete without Kashmiri Pandits and present Kashmiri leadership is trying to fill this gap". He further asserted that "Kashmiri Muslims miss their Pandit brothers in the Valley on every occasion, so do Pandits feel nostalgic about their motherland". Welcoming the recent confidence building measures taken by India and Pakistan, Geelani said that they were expected to bring peace and prosperity for the people of South Asia. He, however, urged the leadership of both India and Pakistan to take steps to help find a viable and amicable solution of Kashmir imbroglio by taking into confidence the genuine leadership of Jammu and Kashmir.

To commemorate the fifteenth death anniversary of former Prime Minister *Rajiv Gandhi* a rally was held on 21st May,'06 at Srinagar's Sher-e-Kashmir Municipal Park. A terrorist wearing police uniform tossed hand grenades and simultaneously opened indiscriminate fire from an AK-47 assault rifle at the rally, and killed seven persons and wounding twenty-two others, including the valley's top police officer. The police and security forces personnel acted swiftly and eliminated the terrorist. Another terrorist was spotted in the nearby Polo Grounds who also was killed in the encounter. The sneak attack was carried out minutes before Chief Minister *Ghulam Nabi Azad* was due to address it. The *LeT* and the obscure *Al-Mansoorium* outfits both claimed responsibility for the attack which left security officials stunned as they had claimed that the security arrangements were foolproof.

In order to disturb the peace talks between India and Pakistan some terrorists set ablaze a 700 year old shrine of a revered Kashmiri Sufi saint, *Hazrat Zianuddin Reshi*, in Aishmuqam area of Anantnag District, on the night of 23rd May, 2005. The shrine is believed to be the first halting point of the Sufi saint who has places of worship named after him across the Kashmir valley. In another major incident, militants have blown up a bridge on the route to the Hindu holy cave shrine of *Amarnath* in Pahalgam area of the same District.

After successful implementation of Bus service between Srinagar and Muzaffarabad, Hurriyat leaders began historic trip to Pakistan-occupied Kashmir on 2nd June, 2005 in another confidence – building measure. Pakistan rolled out the red carpet for the moderate leaders of the *Hurriyat Conference* when they crossed into the Pakistan-occupied Kashmir from Srinagar to interact with various leaders, including President *Musharaff*, in Islamabad. *Mirwaiz Umar Farooq*, who lead the delegation arrived with six others of his faction. The Pakistan Government kept its promise of according a warm welcome to the group. *Sikandar Hayat*, Prime Minister of Pakistan – occupied Kashmir was at hand as was the Pakistani Army band to welcome the leaders when they crossed the Aman Setu (Peace bridge) linking the two parts of Kashmir. The cross over was described by *Mirwaiz Omar* as a 'big step' in the peace process which he said that it could form the basis for a 'triangular dialogue' between India, Pakistan and the Hurriyat Conference.

As expected President *Musharraf* met the visiting Kashmiri separatist leaders on 7th June, 2005 hours after Foreign Minister *Kasuri* told them that Pakistan "can't force" India to include them in the Kashmir talks. *Musharraf* was understood to have shared with them ideas on the resolution of Kashmir, while the separatist leaders emphasized the inclusion of Kashmiris in the Indo-Pak talks. Earlier the leaders held a luncheon meeting with Kasuri who made it clear to them that "we can't force India to include Kashmiri representatives in the dialogue. Pakistan had been trying to persuade India to include "genuine" representatives of Kashmiris in the talks, but had not been successful.

Moderate Hurriyat action leaders who met *President Musharraf* endorsed his assertion that religion cannot be the basis for resolving the Kashmir issue. They favoured the division of Kashmir on "geographical grounds" to settle the Kashmir problem. Hurriyat chairman *Mirawaiz Umar Farooq* said that "we want Kashmir to be divided on geographical grounds. We do not want Kashmir to lose its identity and integration. We do not want to further separate Hindus, Buddhists and Muslims." The moderate faction of *Hurriyat Conference* Chairman *Omar Farooq* issued a statement that they favoured fresh options other than the U.N. resolution for resolving the Kashmir issue as the U.N. had miserably failed over the past fiftyseven years. He said that "when we talked about Kashmir it means the entire territory of Kashmir and the artificial lines drawn-between Kashmir must be dismantled".

On his fourth visit to Jammu and Kashmir since assuming power in May, 2004, Prime Minister *Manmohan Singh* announced on 11th June, 2005 a slew of proposals for better connectivity of Ladakh region with the rest of the country besides giving a grant of Rs.ten crores each for the Autonomous Hill Councils of Kargil and Leh. *Manmohan Singh* visiting the Ladakh region for the first time, also laid foundation stone for a 44 mw hydel power project in Kargil and 45 mw power plant in Leh. He also unveiled the Ladakh Vision 2020 document.

Prime Minister *Manmohan Singh* created history on 12-06-05 by becoming the first Prime Minister to visit the inhospitable Glacier, the world's highest battlefield. In the process of peace with Pakistan he favoured conversion of

Saichan Glacier the highest battlefield in the world into a "peace of mountain". He hailed the contributions of the soldiers to the unity and integrity of the country and assured that all their needs would be met. Emphasising that India wanted peaceful relations with Pakistan the Prime Minister, however asserted that in pursuit of this "we are not ready to accept any change in the drawn and established boundaries of the country. We feel these boundaries are important not only for our security but it relates to the country's honour also. For this prestige, Indian soldiers are happily bearing difficulties here in Saichan".

Giving a cold response to Prime Minster *Manmohan Singh's* statement favouring the conversion of Saichan glacier into a "peace mountain" Pakistan maintained its stand on 13th June, 2005 that India vacate its "aggression" and withdraw its troops to positions held at the time of 1972 Shimla agreement. The spokesman of the Pakistan foreign Office while referring to a joint statement issued after the Defence Secretaries talks in 1989 in which both sides "unconditionally" agreed to withdraw from Saichan" on the level of the troops that were deployed at the signing of Shimla agreement" said that" once that takes place, Saichan would certainly become the mountain of peace. He further maintained that "Pakistan stand is that people of *Jammu and Kashmir* have to decide about their future. India continues to say Jammu and Kashmir is its integral part. India has to accept the disputed nature of Jammu and Kashmir and accept the right of self-determination, instead of referring to agreements with the Maharaja's.

The Pakistan President who was on his way to Australia said on 13th June, 2005 that the Kashmir problem could be resolved in "two weeks" if India and Pakistan showed political will. He said that "the most important thing for the leadership is to have the will to reach a conclusion. I see that at this moment, the leadership does have and I am optimistic that it would be resolved in a certain time frame".

While India and Pakistan were exploring the ways for the peaceful settlement of the *Jammu and Kashmir* issue militants detonated a car packed with nearly 40 kg of RDX at Pulwama district of Srinagar killing fourteen people, including two students and three CRPF Officers on 13th June, 2005. In the above blast over a hundred were injured and the death toll went up later. The blast that occurred just outside a government school and barely fifty meters from a CRPF camp at around 11-30 a.m. Several buildings including eighteen residential houses, twenty shops and many parked vehicles were damaged in the explosion. Several political parties and separatist organizations including the *National Conference* and the hard line faction of the *Hurriyat Conference* condemned the blast and demanded an impartial probe into the incident.

After a fortnight of Pulwama blast Pakistan backed militants of the *Hizbul Mujahideen* struck in a big way in the heart of Srinagar on 24th June, 2005 when they targeted an Army convoy exploding a car bomb in which six jawans died on the spot and nineteen others, including the bus driver and conductor were injured. The jawans were on their way to Mansabal via Ganderbal when militants detonated a powerful car bomb at Nishat Bagh The jawans were traveling in a civil bus and were being escorted by a Quick Reaction Team of the Army. The attack that took place near Nishat Bagh on the banks of Dal lake was swarmed with large number of tourists who had flocked to Kashmir during the summer.

The troop of 15 RR and BSF's 90 battalion personnel were carrying out a joint operation on 30th June'06 at Nowpora market in Bandipora town. The security forces cordoned off a residence-cum-mini shopping complex at Nowpora market on the information that some militants were hiding in the first floor of the three-storyed building. As the security forces stormed the house, the militants, 15 RR Lt.Colonel was hit by the bullets resulting in his on-the-spot death. In a more than five-hour fierce encounter two militants and a civilian were also killed while a constable of 90 battalion was wounded. Two AK-47 rifles and seven magazines were recovered from the encounter site.

There was a proposal to permit *Sheikh Rashid*, Minister for Information of Pakistan to travel to *Jammu and Kashmir* by the Muzaffarabad-Srinagar bus on 30th June, 2005. There were some serious allegations that he ran terrorist camps aimed against India. The allegations against him acquired more significance in light of the fact that independent Pakistan journalists and no less a figure than General *Aslam Beg* corroborated the above charges. In view of the above the Govt. of India on 24th June, 2005 denied permission to Shaik Rashid Such a stand bound to risk jeopardizing the gains of the peace process.

Barely 24 hours after the attack on Ayodhya temple, militants in *Jammu and Kashmir* made an unsuccessful attempt on the life of *Syed Bashir Ahmed*, Minister of State for Public Health Engineering, at crowded Budsha chowk on 6th July, 2005. He, however, survived a close shave when militants attacked his vehicle. Two of his security officers and a civilian were injured in the incident.

Afraid of attack by the militants the *Tripur Sundari Temple* nestled in the dense woods and narrow valleys of South Kashmir was closed for fifteen years. As the peace talks between India and Pakistan were going on a positive note the doors of the temple had been opened again amidst chiming of bells and aroma of incense sticks. Over two thousand Kashmiri Pandit migrants visited this 600 years-old complex popularly known as '*Khunbarian Mata*' located in highly militancy-prone Devsar forests of Anantnag district in South Kashmir during 2005.

A *Hizbul Mujahideen* module of the pro-Pakistan militant outfit was floated by a "dreaded militant" named Jehangir and had fixed targets. This militant organization was suspected to be behind the assassination of Jammu and Kashmir Chief

Minister *Mufti Mohammad Sayeed's* nephew in Anantnag District. The police on 15th July, 2005, therefore, arrested eleven militants who were also involved in the murder of the State Home Minister *Abdul Rehman Veeri's* brother in an abortive attempt on Veeri and grenade attacks at various places in Anantnag District. One of the arrested, *Sajad Ahmed Bhat*, disclosed during interrogation that he was given Rs.6,000/- for the killing of *Veeri's* brother *Mohammad Ismail Veeri. Sajad* and another militant, Bilal Ahmad Magray said that they were indoctrinated by *Jehangir* who told to hurl grenades at crowded places to cause maximum harm to the general public. *Magray* lobbed a hand grenade at Marhama on 27th June while another militant, *Fayaz Ahmad Bhat* served as a "courier" who brought the explosives to the venue. He said that the *Jammu & Kashmir* Chief Minister's nephew *Attiquallah Shah*, was assassinated in May by *Manzoor Tooti* and *Mohammad Saleem* who were killed in an encounter in the Anantnag District.

Taking advantage of incessant rain, intensive cold and low visibility large group of militants tried to infiltrate into the Kashmir valley and the Indian troops had to launch the operation on 12th July,2005. The gun-battle between Indian security forces and the militants took place in the snow-bound Gurez sector near the LOC and the Security forces killed nine militants. They had also surrounded the militants at a height of over 14000 feet and used heavy fire power to flush out the militants from rocky and snow-bound areas.

It has been established beyond doubt even in the western world that Pakistan has become a hub of terrorist activities and the *madrassas* run there are imparting hatred against India and other western countries to carry out terrorist activities. The *madrassas* instead of teaching virtues of Islamic religion are indulging in misinterpreting the holy of *Koran* tenets and brain washing the young Muslim generation to carry subversive activities.

Piqued by the serial blasts in London, attack on make-shift temple at Ayodhya, Kashmiri militant activities in Jammu and Kashmir and infiltration across the Line of Control, the U.S. has again reiterated to Pakistan in the third week of July, 2005 to close all terrorist training camps and also block infiltration across the LoC.

In the meanwhile, the pro-Hurriyat Kashmiri American Council began a two-day conference on Kashmir on 15th July,2005 with speakers including Pak-occupied Kashmir's Prime Minister *Sardar Sikandar Hayat Khan*, Pakistan ambassador to the U.S,. *Jehangir Karamat* and former Pakistan Foreign Secretary *Riaz Khoker* and also *Subramniam Swamy*. The non-Pakistani speakers stressed the importance of peace, ending the violence and restoring the rights of the Pandits, while the Pakistanis demanded that the Kashmiri people should have a voice in the Indo-Pak dialogue.

Following the outbreak of militancy in the Kashmir valley, the Kashmir Pandits migrated to Jammu and other places leaving their hearth and home. Their urge to return home on the 19th July, 2005 took them to the separatist headquarters after fifteen years. Forty Kashmiri Pandits stepped into the Hurriyat Office which marked a leap for Hindu-Muslim reconciliation in the strife-torn Valley. As the Pandits arrived there were warm hugs and smiles all round. Within fifteen minutes the 15 years of separation and communal divide were overtaken by the shared Kashmiri tradition and language. *Mirwaiz Umer Farooq*, Chairman of the moderate faction of the Hurriyat Conference said that "this is truly historic day and a humble beginning to remove the bitterness of the past. This is the first step. More meetings will follow". The meeting lasted for over four hours and described as "fruitful". Veerji Biloo, President of the Kashmir Pandits Co-ordination Committee said that "this is a good initiative and as the international scenario is changing we have to change our minds, our stances. There will be some positive outcome if flexibility is shown by both the sides." However, right-wing outfits like *Panun Kashmir* stayed away from the meeting. The Pandit organizations, which attended the meeting were also critical of the hardliners. At the end of the meeting they supported the on-going Indo-Pak peace process and called for greater involvement of the Kashmiri people in the peace process.

In this regard, it is necessary to mention that the Pandits were marginalized many times over targeted by the militants, unprotected by the State and used as pawns in politics. If a reconciliation with the Pandits and a commitment to help them to get back to Kashmir was part of the *Hurriyat Conference* strategy, this is all for good. If the Pandits can repossess at least some of what was rightly theirs there is confidence that there is hope for Kashmir Valley.

As the meeting between the Kashmir Pandits Coordination Committee and the moderate *Hurriyat Conference* marked an important step in the process of reconciliation in the Kashmir Valley, the *Hizbul Mujahideen* militants exploded a powerful car-bomb at a military convoy near a missionary school on the high security Church road in the heart of Srinagar killing three army personnel and one civilian instantly, and injuring seventeen persons including four soldiers. The blast took place in a parked explosive-packed Maruti car around 9.00 a.m. when the army vehicles were passing by Sher-e-Kashmir cricket stadium. The attacker had managed to escape from the scene shortly before the blast. The blast also damaged eight vehicles and rattled the Burnhall school and nearby buildings. However, no harm was done to the students. Several high-profile politicians live in the vicinity.

A fierce gun battle took place in Gulabgarh area of Udhampur district between the security forces and self-styled commander of the *Hizbul Mujahidden Abu Usman*. In the gun battle the security forces killed Abu Usman and recovered on AK rifle, four magazines, seven grenades and some ammunition.

The militants struck again in the busy business area of Badshah Chawk in the heart of Srinagar city setting off a fierce gun battle with security forces. The militants hurled a grenade and opened fire at a BSF armoured vehicle at the bus stand in the close vicinity of Akhara building targeting security personnel. The bullets fired by the militants hit the petrol tanker of a police jeep setting it on fire. The militants also hurled two grenades at the security forces during the encounter. When the militants struck two security personnel were killed and eighteen others, including seven media persons and six security personnel were injured. In the exchange of fire four CRPF men two BSF personnel and a police constable and five civilians were also injured. The injured civilians included a woman and son of a Congress worker. After a 24 hour operation, the encounter between the militants and the security forces came to end on 30th July, 2005 as a crack team shot dead two ultras holed up inside two buildings. The jamiatul Mujahideen militant outfit claimed that two of its members and two of al-Mansurian got involved in the exchange of encounter.

After a comparative lull of two years in Udhampur district the militants killed five Hindus and injured nine others in Shajroo Village, on 12th August, 2005. The injured include three minor girls. The attack came just two days before the 59th Independence Day when the victims were sleeping in the village. The militants twenty in number, first killed two village defence committee members sleeping on the roof of a house. After this, they entered the house and hurled hand-grenades, besides resorting to indiscriminate firing. Had other village defence committee members not retaliated the toll would have been higher said the villagers who accompanied the injured to the hospital. Due to the fear of the militants, seven families used to sleep in one house.

Further just an hour before the 59th Independence Day Function to commence at the Bakshi Stadium an improvised explosive device went off outside the high security stadium. An IED planted in Iqbal Park, adjacent to the stadium exploded while security forces were conducting a routine surveillance of the area. However, there was no damage caused by the explosion. Another IED blast took place near a stadium at Pattan in Baramulla district without causing any harm. *Al Mansoorian* and *Hizbul Mujahideen* militant groups separately claimed responsibility for the blasts. However, the explosions had no effect on the enthusiasm and gaiety with which the Independence Day was celebrated in *Jammu and Kashmir.* Chief Minister *Mufti Mohammad Sayeed* unfurled the tri-color amidst cheers from nearly 5,000 people who had come from different parts of the Valley at the stadium despite unprecedented security arrangements. The highlight of the celebrations was the dare-devil stunts by jawans of Jammu and Kashmir Armed Police on motorcycles.

The terrorists in *Jammu and Kashmir* were in a frenzy mood with explosives. They have resorted to indiscriminate use of explosives to cause maximum damage to the security personnel. In June, 2005 as many as 27 security personnel including 17 Armymen were killed and 35 others injured in three car bomb blasts and 16 IED explosives carried out by the militants. Within three months, commencing from June, 2005 eleven civilians also lost their lives and 74 others wounded in the blasts. According to the reliable sources there were 1,500 militants active in Kashmir, 43 per cent of them were foreigners who have resorted to use of explosives to harm the security forces avoiding open gun battles in which militants suffered maximum causalities. The changed strategy adopted by the militants was to get less exposed and cause more harm to the security forces. It was, however, backfired as people have raised voice against car bomb blasts and IED explosions in the densely populated areas.

To scuttle the attempts of the terrorists to carry out IED explosions, the security forces and police conducted intensified searches and recovered 2155 kg of explosives from hideouts of the militants from June, 2005 to August, 2005. In June, 2005 when the militants resorted to car bomb blasts 31 kg of explosives were seized followed by 159 kg in July,2005 and 1965 kg in August, 2005.

In Anantnag district two persons were arrested on 28th August, 2005 in connection with the recovery of over seven quintals of assorted explosives from the basement of a building. The owners of the building, *Mohd. Sidiq Najar* and his brother *Iftikhar Hussain Najar* were arrested. It was the second major recovery of explosives in Anantnag town within 24 hours. On 26th August, 2005, 428 kg of explosives and material used in preparation of IEDs was recovered in a joint operation by the Army and police. The recovery was made just after seizure of 1,300 kg of explosives from a private transport company in Anantnag city, the sources said, adding the explosives seized in the city included 68 kg of aluminum powder 688 kg of sulphuric powder and 50 kg of black RDX.

In order to end violence and infiltration, the Prime Minister *Manmohan Singh* had talks with Hurriyat leaders on the 5th September, 2005 and promised to create conditions for reduction of armed forces in the State of *Jammu and Kashmir* if there was a cessation of violence and infiltration. The Prime Minister also agreed to review all cases of those held in detention and promised all necessary measures to safeguard human rights violations in Kashmir. For the All party Hurriyat Conference, which had its first meeting with the Prime Minister after seventeen months, it was a welcome opportunity. Their major demand of continuing the dialogue process further was agreed upon by the Government of India. On its part the Hurriyat Conference agreed that all forms of violence at all levels should come to an end.

The Sixth India-European Summit took place in Delhi on 07-09-2005. British Prime Minister *Tony Blair* arrived in New Delhi along with his wife *Cherie Blair* to attend the summit.

Speaking in his capacity as the President of the European Union, Blair said that as the "world becomes integrated, both sides (European Union and India) will benefit" and added "it is better to open up rather close down".

Both Prime Minister *Manmohan Singh* and British Prime Minister *Tony Blair* met at Udaipur on 08-09-2005, a day after the land mark India-European Summit and agreed to co-operate in civilian nuclear energy sector and finalized accords covering co-operation in hydrocarbons and four other key areas. They also decided to work together to bring about an international norm of "zero tolerance" to fight terrorism. Both the Prime Ministers agreed that "there can be no justification for terrorism on any grounds, religious, political, ideological or any other and with the international unity and resolve we can meet the challenge of this global scourge". Jammu and Kashmir dispute had been described as the most dangerous dispute in the world. A just solution of the dispute holds the key to peace and security in South Asia.

As if the nature has cursed, there was full magnitude of the devastation caused by 9th October, 2005 killer earthquake unfolded with death in P.O.K estimated at up to 50,000 while on the Indian side of Kashmir it has crossed 1,000. Thousands of people on both sides rendered homeless as thousands of houses collapsed injuring yet another 60,000 people.

Describing the tragedy as the "worst ever" in Pakistan's history, President *Musharraf* sought international assistance in the form of medicines, blankets, tents and helicopters to provide succour to the affected people in POK On the Indian side, more deaths occurred in Kashmir Valley than in Jammu. Using spades and bare hands, thousands of security personnel looked for survivors and dug out the dead in worst-hit Uri and Tangdhar areas and Army and IAF helicopters ferried the injured to hospitals in Srinagar.

Neither the devastating earthquake in the region nor the holy month of *Ramadan* had stopped the terrorist actions in *Jammu and Kashmir*. In gruesome pre-dawn strikes, militants belonging to pro-pak *Hizbul Mujahideen* outfit, killed ten members of two Hindu families by slitting their throats in Rajouri district of *Jammu and Kashmir* on the 10th of October, 2005. The brutal killing of ten Hindus appeared to be a well-orchestrated campaign insurgency. The above sinister motive to such dastardly acts appeared to force the Hindu population flee the areas like the Kashmiri Pandits who were forced to flee the Kashmir valley seventeen years ago. In what considered a first in the seventeen years of militant violence in the Valley a suspected woman suicide-bomber blew herself on the Srinagar-Jammu National Highway at Swantipora on 13th October, 2005 and created panic in the town as several nearby houses were damaged. The suicide bomber was moving near Awantipora where the police were conducting a routine check. She tried to run and entered the compound of a nearby house and in a fraction of second a massive blast took place. In Srinagar, Pakistan-based *Jaish-e-Mohammad*, the banned militant group, claimed that the woman was *Hafsa*, a suicide bomber of its women's wing *Banati Ayesha* (daughter of Ayesha.

Following the mass murders by the militants lakhs of Kashmiri Pandits left the Kashmir valley in 1989-90 to save their lives and settled down in various places like Jammu and Delhi etc. The *Mufti Mohammad Sayeed* Governmcnt was working overtime to start the process of the return of the Pandits to the valley. There was a feverish building activity in progress at Sheikhpura in Badgam where a new colony with 204 flats was constructed to rehabilitate Pandits who left the valley seventeen years ago leaving their hearths and homes. In Mattan, in Anantnag district near Pahalgam eighteen well-built modern houses were constructed and in the Kheer Bhawani temple seventysix one-bedroom flats were ready for occupation, Chief Minister *Mufti Mohammed Sayeed* believed that their secularism and Kashmiriyat loses its meaning if they do not ensure the return and rehabilitation of the Pandits. As a matter of fact, Muslims have helped to look after the temple complex traditionally and even today it is a Muslim who hands over the thali with flowers and 'prasad' to worshippers at the entrance of the temple. Even when the tension was at its peak nobody harmed the temple. There is a legend and both the Pandits and Muslims believe that when a crisis is imminent the waters of the *Kheer Bhawani* spring turn dark, Many Muslims do not eat meat and onion the day they visited Kheer Bhawani. At the 500-years-old sun temple at Mattan, Pandits supervised the construction of the second storey of the Surya Bhavan, for tranvelers, and those who wish to spend a few months in a year.

As if replying to the buzz over that many terror camps were destroyed by the earthquake, militants chose high-profile targets on the morning of 18th October 2005 reminding of their presence. Two of the militants sneaked into a fortified VVIP residential colony in the heart of Srinagar killing *Ghulab Nabi Lone* the *Jammu and Kashmir* State Junior Minister for Education of the People's Democratic party, along with three others, including a CRPF guard. The assailant escaped leaving behind his AK-47 and a jacket.

Barely 300 yards away, another militant got into the residence of CPM leader and MLA, *M.Y.Tarigami* but was killed in an encounter with his guards, killing one of them. Both militant groups the *Al Mansoorian* and the Islamic *Jihad* Front claimed responsibility for the attacks. Eyewitnesses said that at around 9.00 a.m. on 18th October 2005 each militant knocked at the doors of *Ghulab Nabi Lone* and *Tarigami*. Lone was reading the newspaper while other family members of the Minister were watching the TV then, a sentry walked in and said to the Minister that some guests wanted to meet him. Lone stood up and went to the adjoining room. A militant forced his entry into the house of the Minister and fired indiscriminately. The Minister was hit in the abdomen, leg and arms and died in the hospital.

While the attack on the Minister was on, the second militant tried to sneak into *Tarigami's* residence. A guard, at the entrance found the militant trying to hide his gun. As soon as the guard noticed the gun the militant opened fire. Another guard who was involved in the encounter retaliated and the militant was hit and killed.

The assassination of *Ghulab Nabi Lone* and the attack on *M.Y.Tarigami*, M.L.A has caused strong disgust even among those who profess the sentiments of separation. It came at a time when the entire administration was pre-occupied in reaching succour to those whose lives were rendered hellish, after 8th October 2005 earthquake. The strike was in tandem with last heinous killing of members of two families in Rajouri and the slaying of a CPM leader in Matan on 17th October 2005.

Unconcerned about the disastrous effect of earthquakes in Jammu and Kashmir and in POK the militants threatened to kill as many as 31 Hindus from seven families on the 23rd of October, 2005 in a mountainous hamlet in Rajouri district. The minority community members decided to leave their remote village after a group of militants headed by a deserted special police officer-turned ultra Ayoub entered into the house of one *Ravinder Singh* in Khah village in Rajouri district. On hearing the commotion, one of the village defence committee members took out his gun and fired at them. After a brief gun battle the ultras escaped with the looted money.

There was a change of guard in *Jammu and Kashmir* as per the agreement between the Congress party and the people's Democratic party. *Ghulam Nabi Azad* took over charge as Chief Minister of Jammu and Kashmir on 2nd, November 2005. Hours before he was sworn in as the new Chief Minister a powerful explosion took place at Nowgam when a car strapped with explosives was detonated by a militant on being challenged by traffic policemen. The militant, two policemen and three civilians were killed at the spot. Two of the 14 wounded later succumbed to their injuries. Had the militant entered the city he would have inflicted a lot of causalities.

After the serial blasts in Delhi, the militants on 14th November 2005 struck in the Lal Chowk, nerve center of Srinagar, killing two CRPF men and two civilians while wounding 13 others including a foreign journalist. The ultras hurled a grenade at the CRPF company headquarters in Palladium Chowk and then fired at the security forces posted there and at the clock tower nearby triggering a gun-battle. No student was injured or killed in the attack of the school who were celebrating the Children's Day near which the militants struck.

For the first time in the history of Kashmir's militancy, a member of a suicide squad was captured alive on 15th, November 2005. *Azaz Ahmad Bhat* alias *Abu Sumara* aged 20, infiltrated into the valley just 21 days ago. A resident of Mansoorabad, Faisalabad, in Pakistan, he belonged to the *fidayeen* group of L-e-T (*Jamiat-e-Dawa*). He was caught amid a fierce gun-battle, his accomplice was shot dead hours later, ending a 25 hour stand-off at Lal Chowk. The arrest of Bhat helped the police to understand the psyche and the modus operandi of the suicide squads of L-e-T. Bhat tried to escape from the backside of Punjab Hotel (adjacent to Hotel Peak view where his accomplice Furqan was killed).

Bhat told the police that they were given the task of attacking security forces. He hurled a grenade and then ran into the hotel. He was trained further by L-e-T to be suicidal militant. He further told the police that he had infiltrated on October 2005 and the group had been hiding in Ari Pathan forests for a week. Then the group dispersed into smaller units and these two finally landed in the city. These two entered Srinagar on 13th November. The two *fidayeens* were brought by a guide. They were unarmed and were given the weapons once they reached Lal Chowk. The guide had already dumped the weapons in a nearby mosque.

Former *Jammu and Kashmir* Minister and senior PDP leader *Ghulam Hassan Mir* was injured on 15th November 2005 when a grenade lobbed by militants exploded at the site of his rally at Tangmarg. Three persons were killed, while others, including Mir, were injured. Several policemen, including a DSP, an SHO, and some constables were among the injured. Mir was taken to a hospital for treatment of his back and leg injuries. The grenade exploded when, Mir after completing his address at Sher-I-Kashmir Park, had boarded his vehicle. The vehicle was about to leave when SHO spotted the grenade close to the vehicle. The SHO shouted just before it exploded and people ran helter-skelter to save themselves. Al-Arifeen, a little known militant outfit, has claimed responsibility for the attack. It was the second grenade attack at Tangmarg in two years. The last was hurled in 2003 in Tangmarg bus stand injuring a few people.

The level of infiltration from Pakistan-occupied Kashmir (POK) has not picked up, mainly due to strict vigil maintained by the Indian troops. The arms and ammunition and RDX was enough to cause major damage to life and property. Militants have created some hideouts in the dense forest and dumped their arms and ammunition to be used against security force and politicians.

In a major haul, the Indian Army on 16th December,'05 seized a big cache of arms and ammunition including 40 kg of RDX after busting three militant hideouts in the Kupwara region of *Jammu and Kashmir*. It was laudable endeavor of the Indian Army to break the back of militancy.

Sending a wake-up call to security forces in the valley, the Special Operation Group (SOG), the elite counter insurgency unit of the J & K police had arrested two of their own members for links with Pakistani militants. The arrested men were constable *Mohammad Rafiq Dar* and SPG *Nazir Ahmed*, who were part of the SPG in Pulwana district. They were working for Harkat Commanders, providing them information about the operation of SOG. This was on for a long time and during interrogation, they told their involvement in three murders. They stole an AK-56 rifle and sold it to militants for Rs.40,000/-. It was "sheer luck" that led to discover the nexus between the two policemen and the militants.

The earthquake in October, 2005 in *Jammu and Kashmir* was not only a huge tragedy for the civilians of Pakistan and Pakistan-occupied Kashmir but also for its army as well. Estimates by the Indian military intelligence put the toll at 2,400 soldiers and 200 officers including five brigadiers. The Indian Army lost an Officer, an NCO and 42 other personnel in the quake which killed a total of over 80,000 people and brought the two armies together in an unprecedented way to aid in the rehabilitation work.

Prime Minister *Manmohan Singh* flagged off a bus service on 24rh March,'06 from Amritsar to the historic town of Nankana Sahib in Pakistan establishing the fourth road link between India and Pakistan. He firmly conveyed to the Pakistani leadership that a step-by-step approach had to be adopted by the two countries given the inherent difficulties in finding practical solutions to outstanding issues between them. Waving the green flag, the bus, carrying forty passengers shortly before the noon of 24th March,;06 to the cheers of hundreds of people who had gathered there despite rain. He termed the occasion as a memorable day for Punjab. He said that "this is a historic day for the entire Sikh community, both in Punjab and elsewhere. This is a historic day for the Panth. In many ways it is historic day for both India and Pakistan.." The 130-km .road link, connecting the holy sites of the Sikh religion had been a long-standing demand of people of both sides in Punjab. The two countries had decided in January, 2006 to begin the service.

Ahead of the Assembly bye polls in *Jammu and Kashmir* militants, carried out grenade attacks in busy areas of the city killing five civilians and injuring 20 others including four security personnel. The attacks took place at Exchange Road,Magarmal Bagh, Hari Singh High Street, Batamaloo and Dalgate. Several militant groups claimed responsibility for the attacks saying their targets were security forces. The highest number of deaths were caused at Badyari Chowk in Dalgate area where three persons were killed and seven injured. The BSF jawans and three civilians were injured in the attack at Exchange road in the Lal Chowk area. The ultras also attacked two security forces bunkers at Magarmal Singh and Hari Singh Street areas in which two persons, including a Napalese woman, were killed and six others injured. The fifth attack was carried out by the militants at 12.45 p.m. in Batamaloo, who hurled a grenade at a police vehicle in which three persons, including two policemen were injured

To derail the peace process of India and Pakistan, militants stepped up their violence against the minority community in *Jammu and Kashmir*. The militants gunned down thirty- two Hindus on 1st May,'06 ahead of crucial meeting between the Prime Minister of India and the Hurriyat Conference. In the first major strike against the community since 2003 *Lashkar-e-Toiba* militants shot dead nineteen people, including a nine-year-old girl, after herding them out of their homes in Kulhund village of Doda district in the wee hours of 1st May,'06. The militants also killed the 13 Hindus they had abducted on 30th April'06 from a village in adjoining Udhampur district. The bodies of nine of them were found on 2nd May,'06 in the higher reaches of the Basanthgarh area. Four bodies had been recovered on 30th April,'06.

There were ten heavily armed LeT militants wearing army fatigues, came to Kulhund village, 200 km. from Jammu and ordered people out of their homes in the two localities of Panjoli and Thave. They were herded into the houses of two village heads. The militants then bolted the doors of the rooms and opened indiscriminate fire killing nineteen and injuring nine. While ten were done to death in Thave nine were gunned down in Panjoli. The militants took village chief *Gopi Chand* into one of the rooms and shot him dead.

Five persons were killed and 30 injured when the militants on 8th Julu,'06 lobbed a grenade at the entourage of the former *Jammu and Kashmir* Minister *Sakina Ittoo*, who escaped with minor injuries. The dead in the attack at Kulgam in Anantnag district included a former *National Conference* Legislator, while Ittoo, two police men, a CRPF jawan, a special police officer and two children were among the wounded. The attack took place when *Sakina Ittoo*, stopped at a shrine in Kulgam, while on way to her constituency at Dhamhal Hanjipora, which was granted Tehsil status by the State Cabinet on 6th July,'06. Five of the injured, including *Ghulam Nabi Dar* who won Assembly elections for the opposition National Conference in 1977 and 1983 from Kulgam constituency succumbed to injuries later. A top Kulgam police official said Ittoo had violated the security drill by moving into Kulgam town against the advice of the security agencies. She was supposed to address a rally at Damhal Hanjipora but on the advice of some people, who had conspired the attack, urged her to go one km. Into the Kulgam town. Ittoo, whose father was killed by the militants in 1990, had survived nearly a dozen attacks since joining politics in 1996.

In a fresh wave of terrorist violence eight persons including five tourists from West Bengal were killed and 37 injured in a string of grenade attacks in the heart of Srinagar on 12th July, '06. In the first of five such attacks, the militants hurled a grenade at a vehicle carrying tourists near Sultan Bakery at Dal Gate at 11.50 a.m. killing six persons—five of them from West Bengal—and also injuring twelve. The condition of two of the 12 injured was critical. Nine of the injured were from West Bengal while two were locals and another, a resident of Udhampur.

Another person was killed and 11 persons were injured when a vehicle caught fire following two grenade attacks at

19
Elections In Afghanistan

After the seizure of power *Afghanistan*, by the Taliban in the year 1996, the Afghans were living under their oppressive rule of that imposed strict religious codes and reduced them to live in isolation with starvation and poverty. To ferret out *Osama bin Laden* and his aides like *Omar*, the United States and their allied forces launched a series of attacks from the 7th of October 2001. After thirty eight days of fierce battle, Kabul was taken over by the Northern Alliance forces aided by the Americans forces pounding from the sky. After the crushing defeat of the Taliban Government a new Government in Afghanistan has constituted the next political phase of the campaign against terrorism. Towards, lasting political stability in Afghanistan, a historic conference was convened in Bonn, Germany on the 27th of November 2001 where a total of twentyfive delegates took part in the talks including several from the mainly ethnic Tajik and Uzbek, *Northern Alliance*, the ethnic Hazara community as well as the supporters of the former Afghan king, *Mohammad Zahir Shah*. After hectic parleys between different factions of *Afghanistan* for eight days, they signed a pact under the auspices of the United Nations to create a new interim administration headed by an *anti-Taliban* leader *Hamid Karzai*, a moderate Muslim, whose fighters were part of the campaign to push out the *Talibans*. *Hamid Karzai* was sworn in on 23rd December as leader along with 29 other members of the cabinet including two women.

After 34 months of installation of the interim government under the aegis of *Hamid Karzai*, first ever Presidential election took place on 9th October, 2004. An independent research group described this as "the last line of defence against fraud goes entirely to India." This is a landmark that over 10.6 million people, went to vote in the polls what is undoubtedly a trial-blazing exercise in democracy. Around a million more will also vote in refugee camps in Pakistan and Iran. Though the ink marked on the left thumb cuticle is the same as that used in India's Parliamentary election, it is packaged differently to ensure easier handling. Fifty thousand marker pens that were supplied to 20,000 polling stations. All the attention was paid to the ink primarily because of fears of massive `fraud in the elections, since away from Kabul, warlords and tribal chiefs still continue to call the shots. The responsibility for ensuring that the electoral process is free and fair was vested an Indian, K.J.Rao, who, like *M.Ratta* a retired official of India's Election Commission.

On the 9th of October, o4 the enthusiastic Afghans, resisting openly and boldly, the threats of violence turned out in large numbers for their first chance of directly choosing the leader of their war-shattered land, hoping for an end to decades of conflict. This election was a milestone in Afghanistan's road to recovery after more than two decades of drought and war capped by five years of harsh rule by the Taliban Islamic fundamentalist militia, which gave sanctuary to *Osama bin Laden's al-Qaeda* net-work. Interim President *Hamid Karzai* cast his vote under tight security in the capital Kabul, *Hamid Karzai* said that "for the first time we are electing our President so it is not important who wins". "What is important is that Afghanistan is deciding its fate. If I win or someone else, the main winner will be the Afghan nation and we will accept it." The U.S – backed *Karzai* contested against seventeen other candidates, but was widely tipped to win.

Queues formed early at polling stations to choose their own leader and the voters expressed their desire to put an end to the rule of the gun behind them. Around 100,000 armed security personnel, including 27,000 foreign troops from the U.S. – lead coalition and NATO were deployed to protect the voters.

A 19 year old, *Moqadasa Sidiqui*, a science student whose family escaped from Kabul in 1992 during civil war cast her ballot in the Pakistani capital, Islamabad, at 7.00 a.m. She was the first woman voter in *Afghanistan's* landmark Presidential election. She is one of 740,000 Afghan refugees in Pakistan who had registered to vote in *Afghanistan's* first democratic elections after a quarter century conflict. She told reporters that she was really happy and could not explain her feelings. "I never have thought I would be able to vote". she said.

Counting for *Afghanistan's* Presidential election got underway on 14-10-04 five days after the landmark polls meant to cement a new era of stability. Officials started the counting process while a panel of foreign experts sifted through several complaints of alleged irregularities from the sixteen candidates including *Hamid Kazai.* None of these complaints appeared serious enough to invalidate the final results. The ballot boxes have flooded in by road, air and even by donkeys from across the rugged impoverished country to the counting centers. Hamid Karzai won the election with thumping majority as was expected by the poll observers.

As the war-ravaged Afghanistan engaged in rebuilding work, India lent a helping hand for the cash-strapped Afghanistan in many ways. The *Ariana* Afghan Airlines flying from Delhi to Kabul carried food trolleys bearing the Air India name, Indian made buses plied on Kabul roads, Bollywood films were shown to packed houses, signifying the omni-presence of India in the war-torn country. Though the Indian Government gifted three airbus aircraft, along with essential spares in 2002, the Air India name still adorns the trolleys. Around 400 Indian-made buses, packed to the capacity, plied on the busy streets of Kabul. These buses were gifted by India to the Afghan Government to boost the public transport system. Of these, most of the buses are operating in Kabul city, 25 in *Kandahar* and 25 in *Herat* provinces. After the 2001 war and fall of the Taliban, Kabul was left with around 50 old and damaged buses, far short of the demand. Buses from India closed that gap substantially. At Bakhtar cinema in down town Kabul, an Indian film was shown to a packed house. Indian films and music cassettes are in great demand and available in every nook and corner in the city. For the cash-strapped Afghan national army, every wheel and every battery matters. And India is helping the new army, whose birth and raising has been one of the biggest concerns of the international community, stand on its own feet, rather move on its own wheels. India also gave the Afghan army forty 2.5 ton troop carriers.

Hamid Karzai was declared the winner of the Afghanistan's first-ever Presidential Election on 03-11-04 after a three week probe into vote fraud found no grounds to invalidate his triumph. The joint U.N. – Afghan electoral board confirmed that the American-backed incumbent had clinched a five-year term as the country's first popularly chosen leader. "His excellency *Hamid Karzai* is the winner of the election," board Chairman *Zakim Shah* said at a ceremony in the capital. *Shah* said *Karzai* won 55.4 percent support in the October 9, 2004 election 30 points clear of his closest challenger and enough to avoid a second round.

It was a strange coincidence that in the first week of November, 2004 President *Bush* was elected for the second term to lead the U.S. for four more years, and American-backed *Hamid Karzai* in the first-ever Presidential election of *Afghanistan* to lead his country for five more years. Afghanistan which was liberated by the U.S. and its allied forces from the oppressed *Taliban* rule owes much to the Americans who wished to set-up a democratic rule in the country which was all along suppressed by different undemocratic regimes.

President *Bush*, therefore, immediately after his re-election for the second term pledged to continue the fight against terrorism "with every resource", An elated *Bush* told his jubilant supporters shortly after his Democratic rival John Kerry conceded defeat in the keenly-contested presidential election stated that "with good allies at our side, we will fight this war on terror with every resource of our national power so that our children can live in freedom and peace."' .We will help the emerging democracies of Iraq and *Afghanistan* so that they can grow in strength and defend their freedom and then our servicemen and women will come home with the honor they have earned". In an explicit appeal to those who voted for *Kerry*, the President said "to make this nation stronger and better, I will need your support and I will work to earn it". He said that a new term to him is a new opportunity to reach out the whole nation.

After obliterating and decimating the *Taliban* rule in *Afghanistan*, *Hamid Karzai* was sworn in on 07-12-04 as Afghanistan's first popularly elected President, as the impoverished country tries to leave its brutal past behind and bolster a young democracy that still faces the twin threats of terrorism and drugs. A smiling *Karzai* wearing a traditional green robe and a black lambskin hat, received a standing ovation on his arrival for the solemn ceremony. The U.S. Vice-President, *Dick Cheney* and *Rumsfled* are two of the most hawkish members of President *Bush's* cabinet and key architects of the Washington-backed war that overthrew the Taliban militia in the wake of the September 11 attacks on the United States were among the 600 guests, including 150 foreign dignitaries. After the Afghan national anthem reverberated around a restored hall of the war-damaged former royal palace, *Karzai* repeated the oath of allegiance read to him by Afghanistan's Chief Justice, *Fazi Hadi Shinwari. Karzai* then sworn in his two Vice-Presidents, *Ahmed Zia Masood* and *Karim Khalili*, members of the country's two largest ethnic minorities.

In his inaugural speech, *Karzai* said that the hopes of ordinary Afghan would drive him during what is likely to be a tough five-year term. He reiterated his main pledges – cracking down on the booming opium trade, disarming militias and lifting living standards. He said he would eradicate terrorism with the co=operation of the international community. Speaking in Pushto and Dari, Afghanistan's two main languages Karzai said that "we have now left a hard and dark past behind us and today we are opening a new chapter in our history in a spirit of friendship with the international community". He said the fight against terrorism was "not yet over" and urged sustained foreign aid and co-operation to defeat the increasing links between extremists and drug-traffickers. He also said that "the same co-operation has led to the rebuilding of the Afghan state and significant progress in restoring peace, stability and security to our country".

Cautions of danger of attacks by the Taliban or the *al-Qaeda* militants on the proceedings, Afghan and international forces launched their biggest security operation since the October 9, 2004 election that gave *Karzai* a massive victory. *Dick Cheney*, the highest-ranking American official to visit Afghanistan since the fall of the *Taliban* in 2001 arrived at the main U.S. base north of Kabul on early 7th December and congratulated some of the 18,000 U.S. troops here for helping give democracy a chance to take root. "For the first time the people of the country are looking confident about the future of freedom and peace," *Cheney* said. "Freedom still has enemies here in *Afghanistan*, and you are here to make those enemies miserable." *Karzai* thanked the United States, his main sponsor, for its help. He said that "without the help, *Afghanistan* would be in the hands of terrorists" and added "terrorism as a force is gone, and as individuals they are all around and we will continue to look for them".

Mohd. Najibullah who became the President of Afghanistan in 1987 was hanged by the *Taliban* after seizing power from him, in 1996. Since 1996 the Afghans lived under the oppressive rule of the *Taliban* that imposed strict religious orders and made them to live in isolation with starvation and poverty always staring at them. The *Taliban* regime imposed a string of social, economic and cultural restrictions. They destroyed all musical instruments in the country labeling them as un-Islamic. Under the puritanical *Taliban* leadership of *Omar* the statue of *Buddha* (*Bamiyan*) was demolished and all the sports and games were banned. In other words, neither *Mohammad Omar* nor *bin Laden* have any aesthetic view and lived with self-satisfaction convictions.

After the fall of the *Taliban* rule *Afghanistan* and after *Hamid Karzai* took over the reigns of *Afghanistan* on 22-12-2002 there was a substantial change in the outlook. Afghan women were again allowed to move out of their houses and work on the fields and in Offices. Men were allowed to participate in the sports and games and artists of Radio Afghanistan returned to their work. Action was also taken to protect the Buddhist statues that had escaped the Taliban destruction in the Central Afghan Province of Bamiyan.

Though, Afghanistan was ruled by different people at different times, and anarchy persisted from 1826 till the end of *Taliban rule.* However it has not lost the glory of works designed to give intellectual pleasure and skillful worship. Thousands of valuable artifacts which they were long feared destroyed or stolen from Afghanistan National Museum survived the last two decades of war hidden away in storage. They are said to be intact and have been packed away since the Russian times. The museum staff together with experts from the National Geographic Society recently completed an inventory of dozens of crates and boxes containing 22,513 items that spent the past 16 years in vaults in the Presidential Palace compound and in the ministry building, through the civil war and the rise of the Taliban movement in the 1990s. *Frederik Hiebert*, an archaeologist and research fellow with the National Geographic Society, said it was widely believed that about 70 per cent of Kabul's museum collection, one of the richest in South and Central Asia, and ranging over 5,000 years of civilization at the heart of the Silk Road, had been stolen, melted down, or otherwise destroyed. But after *Hamid Karzai* came to power it is found that the collection was not only largely intact, but in outstanding condition. Among the rediscovered artifacts is a third century glass vase depicting the lighthouse at Alexandria, one of the Seven Wonders of the World. *Omara Khan Massoudi*, the museum's director, confirmed in an interview that Afghanistan's most famous archaeological finds are safe. These include intricately carved second century ivory panels, known as Bagram ivories from the capital of the Kushan Empire, Buddhist frescos from the caves of the *Bamiyan*, stucco *Buddhist* figures from the site of Hadda in eastern Afghanistan, and thousands of Greek and Bactrian gold and silver coins from *Alexander the Great*.

More than 200 crates and boxes of artifacts were moved from the museum, on the outskirts of Kabul, downtown for storage in the ministry building. The most valuable pieces, including the Bactrian Gold coins a collection of over 20,000 items from 2,000 year-old burial mounds, had already been stored in the palace compound.

After his re-election as the President of Afghanistan, *Hamid Karzai* visited India and has wide range of discussions with Prime Minister *Manmohan Singh* on 24-2-2005. After their extensive talks two memorandum of understanding (MoU) were signed for cooperation in the fields of Civil Aviation and Media and Information. The MoU on co-operation in the field civil aviation was aimed at building capacity and strengthening institutional structure of *Afghanistan's* civil aviation sector.

The MoU on co-operation in the filed of media and information calls for greater interaction between media persons and radio and T.V. Organizations of the two countries.

Democracy as a system of government may indeed be unprecedent in *Afghanistan* after the fall of *Taliban.* Afghans deeply believe Muslim society, yet a country with values that understand and appreciate the democratic practices. That is what had enabled the Afghan people to come forward and participate in the October, 2004 General Elections. The polls, therefore, were as victory for democracy and an emphatic rejection of extremism, which was the legacy of tribulations for the past 25 years. The miseries of Afghans compounded when after the withdrawal of the Soviet Army and the world powers turned a blind eye to the residues of the war. Foreign extremism found a haven in *Afghanistan* where the country was crippled and the society reduced to bankruptcy. The World powers woke up of the gravity of the situation in *Afghanistan* only after the 11/9 attack and the fall of towers in the U.S *Afghanistan,* with the help of the U.S and rest of the international community fought fiercely and won the first part of the battle against terrorism and extremism and striving hard to win a bigger, long term struggle for rebuilding a democratic Afghanistan.

Under the Presidentship of *Hamid Karzai,* the new constitution of *Afghanistan* recognized their culture and heritage and provided their women with at least 27 per cent of seats in Parliament as women are no fewer than men. Of the 8.2 million voters 42 percent were women. It is a great leap as when the *Talibans* were ruling *Afghanistan* women were confined to their houses only and under the grate of "*burqua*".

Geographically, *Afghanistan* is having connection to many countries and once their road network is completed it will be connecting the Central Asia to South Asia and to the Middle East together. *Afghanistan* has also worked on the trans-Afghanistan pipeline project to carry gas from Turkmenistan to Pakistan and further eastward hopefully to India too. Under the democratic set up Afghanistan moved forward and India helped to build road for them. India helped Afghanistan to build a major highway in the west of the country, to construct the Salma hydroelectricity dam near Herat and to build the power transmission line in Kabul from the North of Afghanistan. More notably India helped Afghanistan in the construction of their Parliament building.

President *Hamid Karzai* promised after his election to free *Afghanistan* of opium poppies in five or six years. He added that the elimination of the poppy could be achieved only if Afghan farmers can cultivate other crops as alternative. The President has to mull also over entrenched feudal customs still meant Afghan men often treated women as chattels who could be abused at will without any fear of official retribution. According to the London-based Amnesty International women are raped, murdered and abused with impunity all over *Afghanistan* despite the overthrow of the Taliban rule that was supposed to have ushered in a new era of rights for women. Based on extensive interviews in *Afghanistan* Amnesty said that "throughout the country few women are exempt from violence or safe from the threat of it". Husbands, brothers and fathers remain the main perpetrators of violence in the home but the social control and the power that they exercise is reinforced by both State authorities and informal justice system". The author of Amnesty report *Nazia Hussain*, who traveled all over the country conducting interviews, told "that there was a deep sense of disappointment that matters had not improved since the U.S – led war which ousted the *Taliban* in late 2001. A lot of women told us they had hoped things would change rapidly for the better after the overthrow of the *Taliban* so there is a sense of disappointment". But on education, employment and security there is a feeling that generally things have not improved—— And in some cases have got worse". She cited the case of one woman in an arranged marriage, whose husband beat her from the wedding night onwards and through two pregnancies, who eventually ran away to her parents' home but forced to return because of family pride. She said there were glimmers of hope, with women entering politics and starting to make their voices heard at least in some urban areas. But in the outlying areas there was evidence that if anything matters had got worse. The report said that violence against women was openly tolerated and it was vital that the authorities stepped into protect women, not only from agents of the State but also from private individuals and groups. The report further stated that "reform of the criminal justice system is integral to the protection of all Afghan women and it is the responsibility of the State to provide legal safeguards".

After the fail of the *Taliban* regime India had a big stake in Afghanistan's reconstruction. It is an Islamic country with which India has had very close relations in the past. India has got the privilege to be a partner in the process of economic reconstruction and development. Afghanistan is emerging from the shadow and after-effects of destruction and war for nearly two decades and India's assistance has to reach every part of the country covering crucial areas for development. As a matter of fact, the two countries have to work hand in hand to accelerate the tempo of social and economic development and strengthen the democratic foundation of the polity of Afghanistan. Keeping in view of the above Prime Minister *Manmohan Singh* was the first Indian Prime Minister to visit Kabul in 29 years, the last being Smt. Indira Gandhi in 1976. The Prime Minister who flew to Kabul on 28th August, 2005 offered all possible assistance to *Afghanistan* in dealing with terrorism and rebuilding the war-ravaged country. Afghan President *Hamid Karzai* and Indian Prime Minister *Manmohan Singh* discussed terrorist threat worldwide as also in Afghanistan and in India. They viewed that terrorism poses a threat anywhere and everywhere and had to be dealt together. The Prime Minister stressed the need for joint efforts to tackle the menace of terrorism which posed a serious threat to civilized existence. President *Hamid Karzai* felt that there was a need that India, Pakistan and Afghanistan join hands to fight the global menace of terrorism. Since *Afghanistan* is directly affected by the India-Pakistan peace process, the Afghan President believed that it is the destiny of the people of the region that there is peace and prosperity. He favoured trilateral co-operation between India, Pakistan and *Afghanistan.* The two leaders endorsed the need for greater consultation and co-operation in the project of building a pipeline from Turkmenistan through Afghanistan and Pakistan into India. The Prime Minister announced a $ 50 million package which added up to the $500 million Indian assistance.

India had already committed $25 million for the construction of a new Parliament building for *Afghanistan.* President *Karzai* told the Prime Minister that the above contribution was magnificently meaningful as the parliament is just like what the Taj Mahal is to India. The visit was also an opportunity for India and *Afghanistan* to sign other agreements on co-operation in health and agriculture. etc.

The Parliamentary and provincial elections were the last step of an international plan meant to restore democracy and stability in Afghanistan after 25 years of conflict, nearly four years after the U.S. led forces ousted the Taliban. rule. To woo the voters, candidates seeking the votes offered telephones, televisions and turbans etc., for their elections of 18th September, 2005.. Some residents were given cassette recorders and some had promised cash for putting up a candidate's picture in their car window. About 5,800 candidates contested in Provincial and Parliamentary elections.

For Afghans, 18th September, 2005 elections came after nearly thirty years. It was that long ago, when *Afghanistan* last voted members to its parliament. This was the second time in last two years that the Afghans have voted. In 2004, they turned out to choose their President. On 18th September, it was different affair. Over 2,500 candidates in the fray for 249 seats in the *Wolesi Jirga* (Lower House) and some 3,000 candidates for the 420 provincial council seats in 34 provinces. The mammoth exercise had Afghans mesmerized and to an extent even confused. There was also fear of violence which became true. The Taliban hooligans on the day of polling tried to sabotage the election, but voters still turned out in large numbers. President *Hamid Karzai* called it a defining moment in the struggle to rebuild. The Taliban launched more than a two- dozen attacks across the south and east and two rockets hit a UN compound near election center in Kabul shortly after polls opened, wounding an Afghan UN worker. A French soldier died in a mine blast and two Afghan policemen and three insurgents were killed in a clash near the Pakistani border while a Taliban fighter died before polling started.

It is pertinent to note that in the 249 seat *Wolesi Jirga* National Assembly, 68 seats were reserved for women and election officials said that many women had flocked to vote. Even though, the Taliban fighters tried to sabotage and disrupt the poll 40-42 percent turned out on 18th September to exercise their votes. The polls went off without major incident indicated that Afghans were willing to give this process a chance.

The challenge of *Afghanistan* commenced after the election process was completed. The elections had rekindled national pride. The pressure to emerge from the image of an aid-dependent government to a self-sustaining apparatus had increased. Besides this, Afghanistan remains a big producer of poppy. With 10 of its 30 provinces under opium poppy cultivation, Afghanistan is said to have surpassed Burma as the leading opium producer according to Narcotics Control Bureau (NCB), India. The drug route from Afghanistan to Pakistan and India, and then to Europe posed a big challenge for enforcement agencies. Nigerians remained the major carriers

– though in recent times they have even hired Indians for the task. This precisely what the Memorandum of Understanding (MoU) between the Central Narcotics Agencies of India and Pakistan aimed at checking by putting in place a regular institutional mechanism to intensify mutual co-operation and liaison on drug control matters between both the countries.

After the fall of the *Taliban* regime, Afghans began to take interest in sports and other cultural activities. '*Spring of Hope*' was the first Indo-Afghan co-production film which has as its theme a love story in the strife-torn country. The picture was produced and directed by *Hashmat Khan* and the film depicted renewal of Afghan people's aspirations and their hope to start a new era of peace and harmony. '*Spring of Hope*' was made in bilingual in Afghanistan's dominant language Pushtu and Persian with Indian technicians and Afghan artistes.

Four years after the overthrow of the *Taliban rule*, members of the first Afghan Parliament in decades gathered for its opening session on 19th December '05 with tight security.. Roads around the Parliament building in Western Kabul, refurbished and were blocked by Afghan troops and NATO-led peace-keepers. Snipers were in position on rooftops nearby. The security threat was underlined on 16th December,' 05 when a suicide attacker detonated a car bomb between two NATO vehicles near the Parliament building killing himself and wounding two passersby.

Unidentified gunmen killed the speaker of the northern Afghan provincial legislature on the morning of 1st April,'06 after breaking into his house. *Sayed Sadeq* from Northeastern Takhar province was believed to be the first lawmaker killed since inauguration of the war-torn country's first Parliament and provincial councils in more than thirty years. Takhar province was relatively free of violence linked to a Taliban-led insurgency that experienced nearly daily attacks in southern and eastern Afghanistan.

Afghanistan President *Hamid Karzai* arrived in New Delhi on 9th April' 06 for talks with the Prime Minister of India to root out the *Taliban* and the *al-Qaeda*, insurgents whose resurgence threatened the Afghan political future, or curbing the Kashmir militants operating from Pakistan soil. In the above backdrop of spurt in terrorism in *Afghanistan* both countries had agreed on a collective fight against the menace in which Pakistan could also join. During the talks with President *Karzai* the Indian side raised concern over the security of hundreds of its personnel engaged in reconstruction and other projects in *Afghanistan* and received assurances of their safety from Kabul. As on the date of visit of President *Karzai* on 9th April' 06 the total Indian aid to the war-torn-country was Rs. 2,700 crores while another 50 million dollars as line of credit. President *Karzai* promised to co-operate with any nation that co-operate with *Afghanistan* to fight terrorism.

After concluding his talks with the Prime Minister of India, President *Karzai* visited Hyderabad for two days and watched a presentation at the Tata Tele Services in Hitech-City on 12th April,'06 Impressed by the power-point presentation he said that India has achieved tremendous progress in space technology. *Afghanistan* is a vast country and they were unable to provide teachers, schools, doctors and hospitals in rural areas and wished to extend education and health facilities to the people in rural areas by using technology. He, therefore, urged the Indian IT companies to invest in his country for accomplishment of the tasks of his government.

The Afghan people used to hold small fashion shows in Kabul before the war began in the last 1970s. For the first time in decades in the first week of July,2006 models strode down a catwalk in the Afghan capital Kabul as two designers showed off their clothes behind the guarded walls of a luxury hotel. An audience of expatriates and well-heeled Afghan watched the show in hotel garden, under a clear mid-summer night's sky, to the tunes of traditional Afghan music. All of the models showing the conservatively cut clothes that included designer burqas were expatriate women, to the disappointment of some of the audience. The organizers said that they did not want to court controversy in what was a deeply conservative Muslim country by having Afghan models. Italian designer *Gabriella Ghidoni* who organized the show with an Afghan partner said that they invited a lot of Afghan women to attend the show but not to be models. He expected that the models should have been Afghan but many families did not allow their daughters to do things like models . Members of the audience said that the show organized on 8th July,'06 night was a boost for the city which had seen bloody anti-government and anti-foreign riots and several bomb blasts in the month of June,'06. This was really important for the country, as it was great morale booster for the people. .

A suicide bomber in a car blew himself up in a crowded town market in southern *Afghanisatan* on 3rd August '06 killing 21 civilians. Thirteen people were also injured in the blast at the market in Panjwayi district of *Kandahar* province. The bomber was targeting civilians, because there were no government check points or NATO troops in the area. Some of the victims were children. The attack, one of the deadliest bombings in Afghanistan since the fall of the Taliban rule came just days after NATO forces took charge of security in the volatile South from a U.S-led coalition.

A roadside bomb killed a NATO soldier on 3rd August, 2006 in Afghanistan's South, where the alliance took over security from the U.S forces in the first week of August,'06. Another soldier was wounded when the bomb hit a NATO vehicle in Kandhahar province, a stronghold for Taliban insurgents. Four NATO soldiers, including three Britons, were killed since the 1st week of August,'06 when the group took over security for the south. Six other NATO soldiers were killed as the alliance stepped up its deployment.

Afghan and NATO troops backed by air power killed

94 Taliban rebels in intense battle on 10th September,'06 in southern *Afghanistan*, bringing Operation Medusa's toll to over 450. The insurgents were killed in four engagements in the southern province of Kandhahar. Insurgents also suffered heavy losses when troops launched a separate strike against rebels gathering to counter attack.

It is any body's guess as how long the subversive acts of *al-Qaeda* and *Taliban* insurgents will continue and when complete peace will be restored in Afghanistan and in other parts of the world. In this regard it is not out of place to mention, that on 19th September,'01 President *Musharaff* made a revealing TV address in Urdu, not noticed at the time by many, in which he reassured Pakistanis who sympathized with *al-Qaeda* and the *Taliban* that his decision to line up with the U.S was a temporary expedient. If President *Musharaff* goes by the above assurance it is very difficult to contain the insurgents acts of *al-Qaeda* and *Taliban* in *Afghanistan* or elsewhere and terrorism in Jammu and Kashmir and in other parts of India. *Osama bin Laden* is still alive in the wilderness of hills between Afghanistan and Pakistan and continues to be a threat to peace in the area. Pakistan is still lukewarm in eradicating and controlling the al-qaeda insurgents to keep their politics of gamble alive in Kashmir valley.

20

Gory Acts at Lumbini Park and Gokul Chat Bhandar Hyderabad, Andhra Pradesh

Taking advantage of casual policing despite the fact that Hyderabad is on the radar of the terror net work, dastardly forces struck again – this time with greater precision and to horrific effect For terrorists and fundamentalists, setting up of a base in Hyderabad, particularly in the Old City seems to be a cake walk.

A few years ago, when the police successfully laid their hands on a hardcore Lashkar-e-Toiba (LeT). militant Mohammed Salim Junaid, who was on a mission to Hyderabad to carry out a series of explosion, they were taken aback when the Pakistani national disclosed that he married a local girl from the Old City and managed to obtain a driving license and enroll his name in the voter list. It has rather became a shelter zone for the terrorists from Pakistan, Bangladesh and other parts of our own country.

On 25th ofAugust when the police announced the arrest of the Dubai national, Alkaz Khamis Obaid Khamis Ali from whom fake currency worth Rs.2.36 crore was seized, his was also the same story . Khamis, who operates for the Pakistan's

ISI and traveled to Karachi frequently, too married a girl from the Old City. Since then, he began frequenting the city and managed to set up a network through his friends and relatives in Barkas.

The ISI always insists that if their people have to set up a base in any place in India get married to a local girl which makes them easier to operate. Surprisingly, Hyderabad is one of those destinations where the ISI agents have successfully managed to create a sound network. It is a known fact, that without local support, executing such operations are next to impossible. The person who plants the IEDs could be an outsider, perhaps a Bangladeshi, but the fact remains that the man they are supporting is up to do something terrible.

As a matter of fact, that all terrorist operations are planned over a period of time and with precision. It may take months to plan and execute the operation..The city police seemed to have learnt nothing from the Mecca Masjid blast of 18th May,2007and the people of Hyderabad have suffered heavily. Clearly the terror groups have selected soft targets where security and surveillance were completely missing.

Lumbini Park at Hyderabad, Andhra Pradesh is a magnet for hundreds of families, especially on weekends. Nobody imagined that a crowded place like Lumbini Laserium would become a target for terror The Laserium was inaugurated in January, 2005. This is a place where mostly non-locals enjoy their evenings. Throughout the day, tourists, who after visiting places like nearby Birla (Balaji) Temple, reach the entrance of Lumbini Park to have a glimpse of what was happening. Recently, to celebrate the Onam festival, a group of Malayalis from the Twin Cities had a gala time. The security here has been handed over to a private agency by the Hyderabad Urban Development Authority which manages the park and the security guards apparently confine their functions to collecting tickets at the entrance. No attempt was made to check bags and other belongings of visitors. The fact that Lumbini Park is just a stone's throw from the Andhra Pradesh Secretariat underlines the sheer failure of security arrangements.

The laser show at the Lumbini Laserium started at 7.30 p.m sharp on 25th August,2007. Of the 2000 chairs in the amphitheatre, people generally prefer to take the middle row blue seats for better view of the laser fountain show. Mercifully on this fateful day rain in the evening saw a thin turnout. Normally, weekends see around 1500 to 2000 visit the park. A crowd of around 400 people gathered and were seated in different rows. A few minutes into the show, the explosion caused by an improvised explosive device took place, ripping apart several rows. Three persons died on the spot and six more on the way to hospital. Within seconds, the laserium wore the look of a battlefield with blood all over the place with pieces of flesh and a deep crater at the explosion site. Blue coloured chairs were uprooted from the middle of the amphitheater. Footwear, packets of eatables and mobile phones were found all around while pieces of cloth was found around the blast site " Not many persons were seen carrying luggage. Normally, we make it a point to check the packets being carried by the visitors. But how the man managed to carry an IED inside is surprising" recalled a shocked security in-charge at the amphitheatre. The terrorists apparently placed the bags loaded with IEDs under the seats in the amphitheatre just before the laser show, slipped out minutes after the show began and triggered the explosives through a remote control.

On the evening of 25th Saturday, the rain notwithstanding, promised a pleasant outing. But the showers which halted for a while brought tears instead of cheers. Within a matter of minutes, the happy faces at the Gokul Chat Bhandar at Koti, Hyderabad gave way to inconsolable sorrow. Around 7.30 p,m.on the 25th of August, the cheerful bustle of Koti gave way to spine-chilling shrieks as the blast ripped through the Chat Bhadar. Shock waves shattered window pans and almost cracked the walls of nearby buildings. Thirty-two people died on the spot and scores of others were injured, Such was the intensity of the explosion that many bodies were blown to bits. While others were mangled beyond recognition.

Meanwhile, the police located an IED packed in a plastic cover under a Foot Overbridge in busy Dilsukhnagar. The bomb, which was timed to go off at 10.35 p.m. on 25th August was defused by experts. The police had also seized two IEDs from cinemas in Narayanaguda and Dilsukhnagar, Hyderabad.

The twin explosions came close on the heels of the deadly blast in Mecca Masjid on 18th May, 2007 in which 10 persons were killed and 48 injured. 25th August,2007 was the 100th day of Mecca Masjid blast and Shahid *alias* Bilal the mastermind behind the Masjid blast

Harkat-ul-Jehad-al Islami (HUJI) a militant outfit of Bangladesh suspected to be behind the twin blasts at Lumbini Park and Gokul Chat Bhadar which claimed the lives 41 persons and 100 others injured, some of them seriously. Various agencies, including the top officials of the internal security wing of the Home Department, City Police, counter-intelligence, Intelligence Bureau Central Bureau of Investigation and forensic experts after rummaging through the blast sites and numerous records suspected that it was the handiwork of HUJI and the man behind the blasts was international terrorist and local man Shahid. However, they are pursuing the matter simultaneously to apprehend the culprits.

Approximately two kg of Ammonium Nitrate-based explosive were used in the bomb at the Lumbini Park. Many ball bearings and other materials like glass pieces were packed into the device which was attached to a timer – a Quartz watch. This was the deadly combination that wrecked havoc at the laser show. The device that went off at Gokul Chat suspected to have contained a couple more kgs of the same chemical. Ammonium Nitrate when mixed with kerosene or petrol becomes highly sensitive. It requires a small spark to explode.

The same chemical was used in the October,2005 suicide bomb attack in the Task Force Office, Hyderasbad.

The bomb was probably planted in the ninth row (from the top) in the Lumbini Park. The man was carrying a black bag in which there was a container made of wood. The bag was placed on the empty seat. Subsequently he must have left. Even in the Gokul Chat Bhandar blast and the IEDs which were recovered, a black bag was used with the same components. The moment the IED went off, three chairs from as many rows were flung into the air and landed a good distance away. Had it been a closed auditorium, the impact would have been devastating.

Whoever prepared the Improvised Explosive Devices (IEDs) used on 25th August, 2007 was in deadly earnest about inflicting the maximum damage in terms of the human toll. In many explosions earlier, terror groups have used quartz clocks in which, once the time is up, the IED explodes. But in regard to 25th August blasts, the alarm in the quartz clock was set. The moment it went off, so did the IED. This is the first time that such a mechanism has been used in the State. Another interesting aspect was the use of wooden hemispherical containers in which the chemical was stuffed – again found for the first time in the State. It was deliberately given the shape of a boat to align the IED in such a way that once the IED went off, the splinters were channelised in one direction. Obviously, the IEDs were so placed as to affect the largest cluster of people. The use of a large number of metal balls indicated that the maker wanted maximum damage.

It is no surprise that India is the second worst sufferer of terrorist atrocities in the world in the past three years – after Iraq. This in itself should be a reminder that for all our chest-thumbing about 9 per cent growth, when it comes to terrorism and the inability to prevent such atrocities, we share space with some of the most dysfunctional and damaged societies in the world. The main reason for such a sad state of affair is vote bank politics of the political parties. Most of the political parties are in India are involved in vote bank politics and not ready to take any tough decisions that would contain the terrorists. The case of Afzal Guru who attacked the Indian Parliament House while it was in session is the best example of vote bank politics of the political parties. It is not known how long the politicians play politics on the dead and wounded bodies of innocent people and how many Hyderabads do we need to contain and wipe out terrorism from our country. In the name of privileges our Ms.L.A and Ms.P are wasting precious time in Assemblies and Parliament by involving in war of words over non-issues. The Andhra Pradesh Government is spending Rs.8,000/- per minute for conducting the Assembly Sessions and the sacred building became a battle ground for the political parties to pay off their old scores rather than discussing on the development of the State. It is fascinating to bring forth the fact that right in front of the Assembly building in a spacious lawns there is a big statue of our Father of Nation, Mahatma Gandhi in a sitting meditating posture. It was installed with a great pomp and ostentation with a vow to pursue his policies and preaching It is not an exhibition piece but installed, at the expense of exchequer to draw inspiration to follow his foot steps. Oblivious, to the principles of ,the Apostle of Peace, some members are entering the Assembly building with a resolute mind to indulge in mud-slinging and making mockery of our democracy. After the terrorists attack on Task Force Office and blasts in Mecca Masjid no political party seems to have seriously thought over to contain the crisis or otherwise the gruesome acts at Gokul Chat Bhandar and Lumbini Park would not have been repeated.

It is not enough for India to develop rocket science and chest-thumbing about nine per cent growth. Need of the hour is to part with the archaic procedures, vested-interest and vote bank politics and modernize the military and the police forces with latest training and equipments to strike the terrorists before they strike. It is a known fact, that the bulk of participants in terrorist incidents receive support from across the border. To root out the terrorism, India should contain cross-border pursuits, destroy militant training camps by covert means and assassinate all key figures in the terrorists hierarchy. The minds and hearts of the terrorists are made of mud and they are brazenly, unmindful of the peaceful preaching and psalms. After so many gruesome and grisly attacks perpetrated by the terrorists India should declare a war on terrorism and bullet for bullet should be our policy against terrorists.

Index